THE
LITERARY
VOICES OF
WINNIFRED
EATON

THE LITERARY VOICES OF WINNIFRED EATON

Redefining Ethnicity and Authenticity

JEAN LEE COLE

Rutgers University Press

New Brunswick, New Jersey, and London

Library of Congress Cataloging-in-Publication Data

Cole, Jean Lee.
    The literary voices of Winnifred Eaton : redefining ethnicity and authenticity / Jean Lee Cole.
        p.cm
    Include bibliographical references (p.) and index.
    ISBN 0-8135-3086-5 (cloth : alk. paper) — ISBN 0-8135-3087-3 (pbk.: alk. paper)
    1. Eaton, Winnifred, 1879–1954—Criticism and Interpretation. 2. Women and literature—Canada—History—20th century. 3. Authenticity (Philosophy) in literature. 4. Racially mixed people in literature. 5. Alberta—In literature. 6. Ethnicity in literature. 7. Japan—In literature. I. Title

PR9199.3.W3689 Z64 2002
813'.52—dc21

                            2002024702

British Cataloging-in-Publication information is available from the British Library.

Manufactured in the United States of America

For my P

Contents

Illustrations

Acknowledgments

MANY PEOPLE HAVE helped me realize this project. First, I must thank all the "Winnyers," as Diana Birchall calls us. The living descendents of Winnifred Eaton have been enthusiastic cheerleaders: Diana, fellow grandchild Tim Rooney, his wife, Mary, their daughter, Elizabeth, and Diana's son, Paul Birchall, faithfully attended academic conferences and graciously answered the most seemingly obtuse queries in addition to infusing the driest academic settings with warm familial camaraderie. Elizabeth, a librarian by profession, has generously shared the numerous previously unknown texts she has discovered. Diana deserves thanks above and beyond my expression: she sent me reams of materials from her own collection, tipped me off to the work of others, and transcribed archival materials at my rushed request. Most importantly, she has brought together an entire community of Winnifred Eaton scholars who are distinguished by their generosity and enthusiasm. Through the course of writing our respective books, she has become a close colleague and confidante. Diana introduced me to Dominika Ferens, who has also become a dear friend; I shudder to think what would I have done without her sensitivity and her astuteness, not to mention her insistence that she be allowed to read everything I have ever written. Diana also introduced me to Maureen Honey, who has been interested in Eaton perhaps longer than any of us; she has been wonderful to work with on our reprint edition of Eaton's *A Japanese Nightingale* and John Luther Long's *Madame Butterfly* and has provided valuable professional guidance in other ways.

This project depends heavily on archival materials, much of which would have been inaccessible without the help of librarians and their staff. Thanks to Rachel Howarth, formerly the head of the reading room at the Harry Ransom Humanities Research Center, University of Texas–Austin, for staying on the lookout for interesting materials and for "greasing the wheel" when necessary; to Cathy Henderson of the HRHRC for her encouragement in using the rare books and manuscript collections; to Paul Gehl at the Newberry Library for rooting through the Rand, McNally archives for me; to Scott Curtis at the Academy of Motion Picture Arts and Sciences for finding the telegram that definitively linked Eaton's 1930 scripts for *Barbary Coast* to the 1935 film; and to Kevin Lavender, head of the rare books room at the University of North Texas, for locating a number of illustrations used in this book. Special thanks to Jean Tener, former archivist at the University of Calgary Library, for painstakingly and meticulously organizing the business correspondence in the Winnifred Eaton Reeve Fonds and transcribing letters she thought would be of special use to me. And above all, thanks to Apollonia Steele at the University of Calgary Library, for her willingness to photocopy archival materials at the drop of a hat, her prompt responses to my queries, and for all the other things that demonstrated her enthusiastic support of this project.

Thanks to Janet Staiger, Evan Carton, and Jenneken Van Keppel for reading and commenting on early drafts of this manuscript. Hiroko Sato of Tokyo Woman's University made insightful suggestions regarding the connections between Eaton and Willa Cather in response to an earlier version of chapter 4 that was presented at the 1999 American Studies Association Conference, and Brian Bremen and Rosa Eberly made many helpful comments at my dissertation defense and during the course of manuscript revision. Thanks to Michael Winship, my committee chair, for his support as both a teacher and a friend and for his consistent encouragement to write well rather than quickly (but to finish sooner rather than later). The anonymous reader for Rutgers University Press provided a useful perspective on the original manuscript that greatly aided in the revision process; many thanks go to Leslie Mitchner, Amy Rashap, Marilyn Campbell, and the rest of the staff at Rutgers University Press for their enthusiasm and congeniality.

This project would never have seen the light of day if it hadn't been for nonacademics. My colleagues at the University of Texas Press and St. Stephen's Episcopal School in Austin encouraged me to finish this project when I thought I'd rather not. I would especially like to thank David Cavazos and Teresa Wingfield at UT Press for always placing a higher priority on my dissertation than on my design projects. Thanks to Frank Minogue, erstwhile production assistant at UT Press, for his photographic expertise, and Kelly Kessler for her help in obtaining the screen shots of *Barbary Coast*. Thanks to Allison Faust for the astrological advice and long lunches, not to mention all the laughs. Speaking of laughs, I would be in a much darker place without the friendship of Jennifer Huth, Brett and Michele Holloway-Reeves, Jenneken Van Keppel, and Laura Tillotson, my brothers, Keith and Kevin, my brothers-in-law, David and Andrew, and sister-in-law, Ann. Thanks to my parents for their unwavering faith that I would, indeed, complete this project, and to my parents-in-law, David and Susan Cole and Pamela and Alan Everson, for their constant support. And thanks to Palmer Emerson for being the kind of grandmother I never thought I would ever have. I have to thank the monkeys, of course—even though none of them knows how to read—for making all that time in front of the computer less lonesome. And Matt, thank you for your love, your wit and critical acumen, your understanding and willing acceptance of my limitations, and for never deeming it necessary to establish a "Winnifred Eaton Free Zone."

THE
LITERARY
VOICES OF
WINNIFRED
EATON

Through me many long dumb voices,
Voices of the interminable generations of prisoners and slaves,
Voices of the diseas'd and despairing and of thieves and dwarfs,
. . . .
Through me forbidden voices,
Voices of sexes and lusts, voices veil'd and I remove the veil,
Voices indecent by me clarified and transfigur'd.
—Walt Whitman, "Song of Myself"

Introduction

GUIDED BY VOICES

The voice simply is the mind and is the heart. It
can't go wrong in interpretation, because it has
in it the thing that makes all interpretation.
—Thea Kronberg, in Willa Cather's
The Song of the Lark

WINNIFRED EATON REEVE, known best under her pseudonym,
Onoto Watanna, was a half-English, half-Chinese writer born in
French-speaking Canada and active in the United States and
western Canada during the first half of the twentieth century.
Her romances with Japanese and Eurasian heroines sold well,
garnering favorable reviews from William Dean Howells, among
others. But her reputation failed to outlive her. By her death in
1954, few people knew who she was, and most of her books
were out of print. Only in the 1980s did Asian American literary
scholars rediscover her work, along with that of her sister, Edith
Eaton (Sui Sin Far).[1] Currently, she is enjoying a sort of critical
renaissance: her novels are being reprinted, and scholars are
publishing articles and writing dissertations about her work.[2]

Perhaps the most surprising thing about Eaton is her sheer
productivity. Between the late 1890s and the late 1920s, she
published over a dozen novels and hundreds of short stories
and magazine articles; as a scenario editor in Hollywood during
the 1920s, she also wrote dozens, if not hundreds, of scenarios

and screenplays. Perhaps because of her unusual background as a mixed-race English speaker born and raised in French Canada, Eaton had an uncanny affinity for human speech. In the pages of her work we witness an almost overwhelming variety of voices: the pidgin English of Japanese geishas and half-breed Indians and the lilting brogues of Irish maids, the slang of Chicago working girls and Canadian cattle ranchers. Despite the amazing variety of voices Eaton adopted throughout her career, however, her decision to remain silent about her Chinese identity, her adoption of a Japanesque pseudonym, Onoto Watanna, and her public pose as the descendent of Japanese and English nobility have struck many disappointed recent scholars as an embarrassed denial of her true heritage.[3] The fact that her sister, Edith, embraced her "Chinese side," took a Chinese pseudonym, Sui Sin Far, and used her writing to advocate for the rights and humanity of Chinese immigrants in the United States and Canada only emphasized the extent of Winnifred's apparent betrayal. Although Winnifred was far better known during her lifetime than Edith, and far more prolific, the fact that she apparently relished her pose as an exotic authoress of popular, conventional romance novels made her a less than appealing "mother figure" of Asian American literature.[4]

Since the 1970s, scholarship on the Eaton sisters has contrasted Edith's "authentic," politicized voice with Winnifred's "shallow" desire for commercial success. S. E. Solberg, one of the first to write about the two sisters, contrasted Edith's "integrity" to Winnifred's "willing capitulation to market forces" (27);[5] Amy Ling, too, notes that Winnifred's "personal integrity did not measure up to Edith's" (*Between Worlds* 49). The editors of *The Big Aiiieeeee!*, in a more polemic vein, claimed that in her era, Edith alone wrote "from reality instead of prejudice" (iii), neglecting to mention that Edith even had a sister, much less one who wrote. The conscious and complete omission of Winnifred from the pages of *The Big Aiiieeeee!* testifies to the editors' understanding of her place among the "real and the fake."[6] Recent critics have followed in these footsteps, producing a significant body of work on Edith and largely ignoring Winnifred.[7] Eve Oishi, in her introduction to the 1999 reprint of Eaton's first novel, *Miss Numè of Japan* (1899), attributes this imbalance to the fact that most scholars "simply do not know what to do with a Eurasian writer of Chinese and Anglo descent who assumed a Japanese identity and a Japanese sounding pseudonym—Onoto Watanna—in order to write romance novels about Japanese and Eurasian women" (xi).

Eaton is especially troubling for scholars of Asian American literature because she appeared simply to parrot conventional stereotypes about Asians, and Asian women in particular. Her Japanese and Eurasian heroines are shy, delicate, tantalizingly inscrutable objects of white male fantasies, the apparent embodiment of the type of the giggling, sexualized Japanese maiden that had been popularized by John Luther Long's novella *Madame Butterfly* (1898), songs such as "The Mousmee; or, His Sweetheart in Japan" (1893), and light operas from Gilbert and Sullivan (*The Mikado,* 1885) and Sidney Jones (*The Geisha,* 1896).[8] Onoto Watanna's name appeared alongside Long's as well as those of Lafcadio Hearn, William Elliott Griffis, and other aficionados of Orientalia; because of the irrefutable similarities between her work and theirs, Oishi writes that one cannot ignore "the rather disturbing fact . . . that Winnifred Eaton was not merely capitalizing on the western stereotypes of Asia and Asian women, she was instrumental in creating them" (xxii).

Yet it has been impossible for Asian American literary scholars to reject Eaton altogether. She was, after all, the first writer of Asian descent to publish a novel in the United States. And she remains the most prolific: in contrast to Eaton's fifteen known novels, Maxine Hong Kingston, the only Asian American writer to surpass Eaton in popularity before 1980, has published only three to date.[9] Because of Eaton's importance to Asian American literary history, Ling and others have attempted to characterize her use of stereotypical representations of Asians and her reticence regarding her ethnic identity as acts of subversion, depicting her as a "trickster" figure who undermined racist and patriarchal ideologies even as she appeared to embrace them.[10] Ling, for example, argues that "we may read the novels of Onoto Watanna as the brain children of Asian America's first trickster hero" because she uses her perceived "faults—chicanery, cheating, and lying" and "clever deviousness and deception" in order to achieve "victory or a balance of the scales" ("Creating One's Self" 312–313). Yuko Matsukawa expands on this idea, claiming that "when we view her self-construction not simply as an example of the inauthentic, we find that her tricksterlike self-fashioning is inextricably linked to her experiments in redefining conventional frontiers of ethnicity and authenticity through the contingencies of her life" (123).

The rejection of "authenticity" as a standard for judging Eaton's work has enabled analysis that moves beyond the "good sister, bad sister" assessments of the 1980s and early 1990s.[11] As the quote from Matsukawa implies, however, scholars are still largely preoccupied by her "self-construction," "self-fashioning," and the "contingencies of her life"—as an Asian American. As a result, scholarly attention has remained almost completely restricted to works that appear to explicitly address Eaton's Asian identity—that is, the texts that have Asian characters and address Asian themes, and her semiautobiographical novels, *Me: A Book of Remembrance* (1915) and *Marion: The Story of an Artist's Model* (1916), which by their very autobiographical nature promise self-disclosure. Works about "Irish maids, cowboys, illegitimate sons, and others," as Dominika Ferens has put it, in contrast, have been almost completely passed over, even though they provide the strongest evidence for Eaton's redefinition of "conventional frontiers of ethnicity and authenticity."[12] In novels such as *The Diary of Delia* (1907) and *Cattle* (1924), stories like "Margot" (1901), and her film scripts, we hear diverse voices: Irish maids, a Scottish doctor, an androgynous (and misanthropic) British spinster, naïve Norwegian farm girls, Canadian ranchers, Chinese cooks, "half-breed" Indians, and headstrong saloon-keepers' daughters. If we agree with Willa Cather's opera singer Thea Kronberg that the voice "has in it the thing that makes all interpretation," it seems essential to listen closely to those voices.

Exploring the notion of voice itself can tell us much about why these "other" texts of Eaton's have been avoided—or simply unheard—by present-day scholars. All too often voice is simply equated with the identity of a particular group—the "Chicano voice," the "woman's voice," the "Asian American voice." The editors of *Aiiieeeee! An Anthology of Asian-American Writers,* for example, claim that "more than a whine, shout or scream," this anthology constitutes "fifty years of our whole voice." For many minority groups, this "whole," collective voice represents power and agency—an expression of cultural nationalism—that speaks in opposition to the subjugated state of silence imposed on them by an oppressive white-dominated society. What defines this voice is a new way of speaking, a new language that "talks back" to the "standard" language of the dominant culture: in defining the voice of the collective, critics emphasize their different accents, slang words (*ofay, bokgwai, gringo*), and verbal practices (for example, signifying, talk-story).[13] This voice and the language it speaks come to stand for nothing less than the group identity. In *Borderlands/ La Frontera: The New Mestiza,* for example, Gloria Anzaldúa writes, "if you really want to hurt me, talk badly about my language. Ethnic identity is twin skin to linguistic identity—I am my language. Until I can take pride in my language, I cannot take pride in myself. . . . I will no longer be made to feel ashamed of existing. I will have my voice" (59).[14]

In recent years, with the introduction of postmodern, postidentity, and postnational theories, ethnic studies scholars have taken pains to acknowledge that the "ethnic voice" is itself characterized by diversity. Anzaldúa, for example, claims not just one voice, but many. "I will have my serpent's tongue—my woman's voice, my sexual voice, my poet's voice" (59). And Lisa Lowe insists on the "discontinuous, heterogeneous range of Asian American alternative narratives" (51). Nevertheless, by virtue of the simple fact of their ethnic difference, ethnic voices are still assumed to be united in speaking out against an oppressive, mainstream, white culture. Lowe, for example, describes Asian American literature as an "oppositional practice" and an "alternative cultural site" whose role is to "displace the fiction of reconciliation, disrupt the myth of national identity by revealing its gaps and fissures, and intervene in the narrative of national development," which posits a universalized (white), homogeneous citizenry (ix–x, 5–9).[15]

It is only natural that critics whose understanding of voice conflates it with identity and further equates the ethnic voice with oppositional politics have responded negatively to Eaton, who spoke from a multiplicity of apparently mutually exclusive perspectives: Canadian, American, Japanese, Chinese, Irish, "mongrel," "white." It is difficult for these critics to read her work as anything but a failure, since she did not voice her "true" identity as half-Chinese, nor did she speak out against an oppressive dominant culture. Yet contemporary readers—and, I would argue, Eaton herself—had a much different understanding of voice. If we think of voice today as a marker of one's core identity, one's authenticity, in the early twentieth century vocal production could be described instead as opportunities for ventriloquism. In the literature of the day, it seemed that everyone was speaking out of the mouth of another. White men took on the voices of black ex-slaves (Joel Chandler Harris, Mark Twain), German immigrants (William Dean Howells), Irishmen (Finley Peter Dunne), and Creoles (George Washington Cable); northern blacks spoke in the tones of educated white northerners and ex-slaves (Charles Chesnutt and Paul Laurence Dunbar); society women adopted the voices of the working girl and illiterate rural folk (Marie Van Vorst, Mary Murfree).

This preoccupation with voices was brought to a head in the late nineteenth century by the emergence of an increasingly insistent diversity of speakers. With the influx of immigrants from eastern and southern Europe and Asia, New York had become a "New Babel," whose inhabitants spoke a "New Yorkese" that was almost unintelligible to outsiders (Jones 135).

The voices of laborers, suffragettes, and educated blacks appeared in the same newspapers and magazines; vaudeville performers appeared in blackface, yellowface, or without any "face" applied, speaking in Irish, German, Chinese, and plantation dialects one after another, or all at once;[16] the "new journalism" spoke on behalf of "the other half," while practitioners of the new field of anthropology introduced voices of "primitive" cultures to American shores.[17]

Of course, the influx of all of these strange accents and new languages was perceived by many as what James Clifford has described as a "predicament of culture," a threat to what they believed was a unified, Anglo-Saxon–based American society. Amy Kaplan writes that in response to this threat, "journalists, reformers, and pulp novelists depicted the city as a new frontier or foreign territory to settle and explore and regarded its inhabitants—usually immigrants—as natives to civilize and control" (*Social Construction* 45). The representation of "alien" languages in dialect fiction, in newspapers, and on the vaudeville stage were thus attempts at containment: by speaking in the voice of the other, one could somehow control what was said.[18] At the same time, the widespread use of dialect and the interest—even if it was of a patronizing or even prurient kind—in other cultures provided a venue for those very minorities and immigrants to speak to a broad, "mainstream" audience. In *Strange Talk: The Politics of Dialect Literature in Gilded Age America,* Gavin Jones writes: "Dialect writing was not always a proof of hegemonic command. It could also register an anxious, constantly collapsing attempt to control the fragmentation and change that characterize any national tongue. And dialect could encode the possibility of resistance, not just by undermining the integrity of a dominant standard, but by recording the subversive voices in which alternative versions of reality were engendered" (11). Thus dialect did not "belong" either to a particular ethnic, racial, or regional group or to a dominant, elite society. Instead, it constituted a field where meanings were debated, hashed over, brought into conflict, and resolved.[19]

Yet even though dialect enabled ethnic minorities to enter the literary field, the form restricted them to certain ways of speaking. In an odd sense, they practiced a form of double ventriloquism, speaking in ethnic, alien voices that had been already shaped by white writers who often had very different motivations for speaking in the voices of others. Patricia Wald has shown how writers attempting to tell "untold stories" must often use familiar forms and conventional language to express their unfamiliar ideas. "Social unacceptability and political censorship, personal prohibitions and cultural conventions, the literary market and language itself all contribute to the shaping of stories," she argues; writers "must choose between conforming to cultural prescriptions and refusing comprehensibility" altogether (1–2). As we shall see, Eaton conformed to cultural prescriptions throughout her career.

Eaton's ethnic characters, however, did not simply mouth the words of generic convention. As Ferens writes of her Japanese romances, she "reproduced Orientalism with a difference" (1). Her characters, in a sense, spoke with a slightly different inflection, a different accent, demonstrating Eaton's own differences as a mixed-race woman writer in an age that still adhered to the idea of the "gentleman author" as the only legitimate purveyor of culture. Although her geisha heroines laugh and sing, they are also willfully defiant; her Irish maids are ideal servants but demand that their labor be acknowledged and even respected. When she wrote her own life story (in a highly fictionalized form) in *Me,* she fulfilled the stereotype of the uneducated but eager-to-learn, naïve yet worldly working-class heroine, but she also used that character to voice criticisms of a society that instilled dreams of upward mobility and artistic possibility in those who could never attain success due to their race, class, or gender.

I have focused here on dialect fiction because it was within this genre that Eaton achieved her initial success as a writer, and also because it highlights, in a particularly useful way, the cultural and historical nuances of the "ethnic voice." Yet Eaton also responded to other cultural developments that changed ideas of voice. In her later fiction, we can see manifestations of the individual, idiosyncratic voice that achieved its literary apotheosis in high modernism (see chapters 3 and 4); at the same time, in her screenwriting we can how the advent of sound technology in film resulted in the reassertion of typed, generic voices rather than encouraging vocal diversification.[20] By examining the different contexts that shaped Eaton's work, we can begin to understand how Eaton participated in specific cultural conversations that have gone unheard by present-day scholars. Although my main purpose in taking this approach is to establish a coherent sense of Eaton as a writer, I also offer these readings as examples of a methodology that may help balance the presentist slant of ethnic literary criticism. Jinqi Ling has noted that the tendency to judge literary works according to present-day "cultural or political needs" is particularly pronounced in the case of Asian American literary criticism, which often "equates the articulation of individual Asian American writers at given historical moments . . . with the actual presence of fully realized Asian American agency" (9).[21] Likewise, Ferens notes that "when applying a broadly defined criterion of subversiveness to literature, we are obliged to pass over or oversimplify texts that are perhaps ideologically dated and therefore less useful to us today, but without which we cannot begin to reconstruct the intellectual climate of their day" (2).

Ling maintains that by forgetting that the idea of an "Asian American identity" did not even exist prior to the 1960s, critics either read early texts with "ahistorical expectations of thorough treatments of a full range of important social issues (race, gender, class, sexuality, postcolonialism, imperialism)" or make "reductive assessments of writings unable to live up to those expectations" (10). (It probably goes without noting that critics have responded to Eaton's work in precisely these ways.) Instead, Ling calls on Asian American critics "to be more responsive to the complexities of individual Asian American writers' voices, more alert to the dangers of subsuming or silencing their historical specificity in terms of presentist theoretical agendas" (viii).[22]

Eaton herself acknowledged the complexity of her own voice; in 1906 she declared that she was "Irish more than English, Chinese as well as Japanese." This study is an attempt to make sense of this statement in light of her career as a professional writer. Eaton's writing was, in fact, "guided by voices"—voices that were produced by fictional genres (dialect fiction, melodrama, romance), cultural and political movements (feminism, naturalism, political and cultural nationalism), and concerns of the time (immigration, miscegenation, the servant problem, American and Japanese imperialism, film censorship). Each chapter examines how these voices operate in a given text or group of texts—as historically specific participants in what Steven Mailloux has described as "cultural conversations," as constitutive and constituted elements of Foucauldian discourse, as physical manifestations of rhetorical practices and strategies. By using the term "voice," I thus draw on a variety of theoretical positions without locking into their tendency to generalize meaning over entire groups of speakers or conflating varied and conflicting articulations into distinct, coherent ideologies. At the same time, locating the physicality of utterance in the voice rather than in the body of the speaker can help us begin to escape what Tomo Hattori has described as "the prison of the endless performance of the yellowness of our bodies" (244).[23]

This study is obviously motivated by a historicist impulse. However, rather than using literary texts as portals to gain access to broader historical and cultural themes, I have tried to use historical and cultural phenomena as portals into the texts. My intention is not to reconstruct the entire sociocultural-historical canvas in which Eaton's texts operated (as if that were possible) but to select salient details that help gain purchase on the often hidden complexities of Eaton's work. One of the most striking aspects of Eaton's writing, and one of the most bewildering, is the sheer range of subject matter she addressed, even within the formulas of popular fiction. As a result, her texts are both infuriatingly simple and frustratingly opaque. I have found that a pragmatically historicist approach can help complicate the formulas Eaton employed while rendering visible some of the more baffling elements of her texts. In one of the first articles she wrote about Eaton, Amy Ling described her as a writer who had her "finger squarely on the pulse of the time" (*Between Worlds* 55), and in many ways I have taken that as my cue: what was that pulse?

Chapter 1 focuses on Eaton's Japanese romances, in which Japanese and mixed-race heroines negotiate love relationships with white, primarily American, men sojourning in Japan. I show how these novels participated in a conversation regarding the increasingly conflicted relationship between Japan and the United States. Other Orientalist texts from the period, especially those by Lafcadio Hearn and John Luther Long, the author of the story that Giacomo Puccini immortalized in his opera *Madama Butterfly,* represented Japan as unknowable, and therefore desirable, either through the collection of Japanese objects or by possessing its women. At the same time, anti-Japanese sentiment was expressed through physical violence against Japanese immigrants as well as by textual means.

Eaton's early works capitalized on this fad for "things Japanese" at the same time that they explored its ideological contradictions. In *A Japanese Nightingale* (1901), she takes on the voice of a mixed-race girl who is the logical outcome of the sexual unions with Japanese women that Hearn and Long idealized in their texts. Despite her broken, pidgin English, Eaton's "mongrel" heroine, Yuki, charmed hundreds of thousands of readers. Because her author placed her in a distant, romanticized context, Yuki is not repugnant or pitiable, as real mixed-race children were viewed at the time, but an attractive and humanized object of Orientalist fantasies. William Dean Howells himself indulged these fantasies, as we see in his glowing review of her novel. In the same review, however, he also criticized another novel that addressed the effects of miscegenation: Charles Chesnutt's *The Marrow of Tradition*. Howells's assessment

of Chesnutt's novel as far too "bitter" to be believable is a revealing contrast to his unstinting praise of Eaton's novel for "its
directness, and sincerity, and its felicity." Yet his failure to recognize Yuki as biracial indicates the ways in which Eaton's
contributions to the cultural conversation surrounding miscegenation failed to be fully understood. Although the form of
Japanese romance allowed Eaton to speak about alienation,
voicing and language, and racial indeterminacy in a way that
also made her accessible to a large American audience, the
genre still limited her in ways that prevented her from being
fully comprehended.

Chapter 2 focuses on several texts that constitute Eaton's
"return home"—in a figurative and literal sense. Amid rapidly
changing conceptions of American womanhood and escalating
hostility between the United States and Japan, Eaton created in
A Japanese Blossom (1906) a utopian vision of domesticity that
places American domestic nationalism in a seemingly alien Japanese setting. Speaking in the voice of an idealized American
woman, Eaton's white heroine, Ellen Kurukawa, is able, by virtue of her embodiment of domestic values, to naturalize and
feminize the values of Japanese militarism. *The Diary of Delia*
(1907), in contrast, brings Eaton to an American setting; speaking in the brogue of an Irish immigrant, she reveals the contradictions inherent in the seemingly progressive aspects of
domestic science and new womanhood. By recasting domestic
ideology from the perspective of an immigrant domestic, she
reveals the deeply racialized nature of the American home. In
both cases, Eaton uses the domestic space—and the debates
surrounding it—as a site for cultural and ideological exchange;
in these texts, she connects the seemingly "separate spheres" of
domesticity, nationalism, and nativism in ways that may only
have been apparent to a woman who stood, as a mixed-race
suburban wife, mother, and professional writer, at their points
of intersection.

Chapter 3 argues that Eaton's autobiographical novel, *Me*
(1915), participated in the contemporary debate surrounding

female creativity embodied by the hypothetical "woman of genius." In this novel, Eaton spoke from the perspective of a female artist who achieves success in the often hostile, male-dominated world of art yet is able to preserve the feminine qualities that many believed were anathema to artistic creation. Combining the Romantic individualism of the *Kunstlerroman* exemplified by Joyce's *Portrait of the Artist* (1915) and Theodore Dreiser's *The "Genius"* (1915) with the more traditional courtship plots that featured female protagonists, Eaton, along with Mary Austin (*A Woman of Genius,* 1912) and Willa Cather (*The Song of the Lark,* 1915), attempted to defuse the potentially threatening aspects of feminine artistry. Eaton's representation of her heroine as an immigrant of mixed race gives her novel yet another twist: she represents the possibility of not only a female artist but an ethnic one. Like James Weldon Johnson's *Autobiography of an Ex-Colored Man* (1912), *Me* presents the ethnic artist with ambivalence: both Johnson's unnamed protagonist and Eaton's Nora Ascough feel that they have "sold their birthright for a mess of pottage." Yet Johnson's satirical treatment of the biblical story of Esau indicates differences between Johnson's and Eaton's understanding of the relationship between success, artistry, and race that explain why Johnson, unlike Eaton, has been embraced by later scholars.

Chapter 4 examines the new literary terrain Eaton traversed after moving to Canada in 1917. Alberta provided a geographical and literary frontier for Eaton, which she explored in her novels *Cattle* (1924) and *His Royal Nibs* (1925). New voices—especially those of Angella Loring, an androgynous woman rancher, Jake, a mentally deficient but sympathetic Métis Indian, and Hilda McPherson, a racially ambiguous "child of nature," demonstrate, perhaps for the first time in her fiction, Eaton's understanding of cultural difference and the oxymoronic aspects of multiculturalism.

Chapter 5 assesses Eaton's experiences in the film industry, where she worked, primarily for Universal Pictures, between 1925 and 1930. During this tumultuous period of film history, the introduction of sound resulted in a variety of responses, ranging from amplified protests against immorality in film to the silencing of ethnic voices. Tracing the revision process of one of Eaton's projects, *Barbary Coast,* we see how the multicultural, matriarchal voices she developed in *Cattle* and *His Royal Nibs* were gradually transformed into the bland, conventional speech of Hollywood melodrama. Far from creating a multivoiced community, the collaborative nature of film work reinforced a unified, white- and male-centered view of the world that became the hallmark of the "Hollywood Style" and, many would argue, American mass culture in general.

Although the chapters are arranged roughly chronologically, I have resisted the urge to make sense of Eaton's "development" as a writer. Her literary practice was governed less by her sense of her developing art than by practical exigencies, and she often took stances and made statements that appeared to contradict earlier convictions. I have found it more productive to examine these texts according to specific themes, or discourses, that were of particular salience during their cultural moment. Thus I examine *A Japanese Nightingale* in terms of the national obsession with Japanese culture and Japanese goods; *A Japanese Blossom* and *The Diary of Delia* in relation to debates regarding the role of domesticity in the formation of American citizens; *Me* in light of discussions surrounding the concept of "genius" and its application to women; *Cattle* and *His Royal Nibs* as examples of an imaginary, multiethnic "frontier" that was both idealized and seen as a source of anxiety; and the script for *Barbary Coast* as it was affected by the changes in film content wrought by sound technology.

Although none of the themes I address, except perhaps that of the relationship between the United States and Japan, explicitly relates to issues of ethnicity and race, I have tried to show how these issues do in fact play a crucial part in the development of a "national culture." Like José David Saldívar, I believe it is crucial to "unify the history of the Americas" by demonstrating the common concerns of the various forms of

American literature (*Dialectics* 5). Saldívar, Amy Kaplan, Lisa Lowe, Eric Sundquist, and others both from ethnic studies and from the "New Americanist" group of American literary critics have demonstrated how "national" and "mainstream" cultures have not just constituted but have been constituted by their relationships with and against immigrants, aliens, and ethnic and racial (and gendered) minorities. At the same time, it is perhaps worth reminding ourselves that at certain points, the "citizen" and the "alien," the "mainstream" and the "minority," the self and the other, necessarily merge—as we can see in figures like Winnifred Eaton. The nature of the merger calls for closer scrutiny.

ONE

Hiding behind Shoji

WINNIFRED EATON AS

ONOTO WATANNA

> At home again, I slide open once more my
> little paper window, and look out upon the
> night. . . . I see the broad shoji of dwellings
> beyond the river suffused with the soft yellow
> radiance of invisible lamps; and upon those
> lighted spaces I can discern slender moving
> shadows, silhouettes of graceful women.
> Devoutly do I pray that glass may never
> become universally adopted in Japan,—
> there would be no more delicious shadows.
> —Lafcadio Hearn, *Glimpses of Unfamiliar Japan*

> But as she glides past him, beautiful, laughing
> softly behind her fan, don't we who are men sigh
> with hope? We, who are not handsome, nor
> brave, nor powerful, yet somehow
> believe . . . that we deserve a Butterfly.
> —Gallimard, in David Henry Hwang's
> *M. Butterfly*

AT THE BEGINNING of *A Japanese Nightingale* (1901), in the "seraphic light" of the full moon, we find ourselves in a picturesque Japanese teahouse, waiting in anticipation, like the Japanese and American men within, of an evening's entertainment. After the food, and the sake, and the toasts to the moon, the lights dim; then, out of the darkness emerges a "wild, vivid figure clad in scintillating robes" (5). To the music of the koto and samisen, the figure begins to dance. Her costume is colorful and her movements evocative, but we see just one glimpse of her face, as the music winds down: "underneath the rainbow of the gown, a girl's face, of exquisite beauty, smiled and drooped. Then the extinction of light—and she was gone" (6).

But after the tumultuous applause tapers off, she unexpectedly begins to sing from the darkness: "All the notes were minors, piercing, sweet, melancholy—terribly beautiful. She was singing music unheard in any land save the Orient, and now for the first time, perhaps, appreciated by the foreigners, because of that voice—a voice meant for just such a medley of melody. And when she had ceased, the last note had not died out, did not fall, but remained raised, unfinished, giving to the Occidental ears a sense of incompleteness. Her audience leaned forward, peering into the darkness, waiting for the end" (8–9).

But the song, as incomplete as it seems, has ended, and the girl disappears into the night. It is only at the end of the first chapter that we are told by the proprietor of the teahouse that this mysterious, beautiful figure is really just "a cheap girl of Tokyo, with the blue-glass eyes of the barbarian, the yellow skin of the lower Japanese, the hair of mixed color, black and red, the form of a Japanese courtesan, and the heart and nature of those honorably unreliable creatures, alien at this country, alien at your honorable country, augustly despicable—a half-caste!"(15).

"Augustly despicable" as she might be, Yuki, the heroine of Winnifred Eaton's second novel, still enchanted hundreds of thousands of readers. The book went into multiple editions and was translated into at least four different languages, made into a Broadway play (1903), and eventually adapted for the screen (1918). This novel also established Eaton's career. For several years Eaton, writing under the pseudonym of Onoto Watanna, had been placing stories and articles in magazines such as *Frank Leslie's Popular Monthly* and *Ladies' Home Journal*. Her first novel, *Miss Numè of Japan*, had been published in 1899 to largely favorable reviews.[1]

But it was in *A Japanese Nightingale* that Eaton found a formula that enabled her to develop a marketable voice. In telling the story of a half-Japanese, half-American girl who becomes the love object of an American man, Eaton was able to connect her own experience to her writing in a way that appealed to a mainstream audience. Through heroines like Yuki, Eaton could address issues such as interracial romance, biraciality, and ethnic difference; at the same time, by setting the novel in faraway Japan and taking on the quaint, charming voice of the geisha, Eaton capitalized on an audience that seemingly could not get enough of "things Japanese." Indeed, *A Japanese Nightingale* is, in many ways, a simple recasting of John Luther Long's novella *Madame Butterfly,* which appeared in the *Century Magazine* three years before Eaton's novel. In plot and characterization, the stories are of a piece; the only obvious difference between the two is that *A Japanese Nightingale* ends in marital bliss.

Through various retellings, most notably Giacomo Puccini's operatic version (composed in 1904), the figure of Butterfly has evolved into what playwright David Henry Hwang has recently called a "cultural stereotype."[2] In his afterword to his "deconstructivist" version of the story, *M. Butterfly,* he explains that he based his play on the story even though he had never seen or read any of the different versions: "I didn't even know the plot of the opera! . . . Yet, I felt convinced that the libretto would include yet another lotus blossom pining away for a cruel Caucasian man, and dying for her love. Such a story has become too much of a cliché not to be included in the archetypal East-West romance that started it all" (95).

In their surface similarity to stories like Long's, *A Japanese Nightingale* and subsequent novels such as *The Heart of Hyacinth* (1903), *The Love of Azalea* (1904), *Tama* (1910), and *Sunny-San* (1922), may very well have contributed to building the "archetype" of the East-West romance that Hwang lambasts in his 1986 play. Scholars have dismissed them as a result; Amy Ling, for example, writes that in Winnifred Eaton we have "not a challenger or protester, not a word-warrior, but a woman with her finger squarely on the pulse of her time" (*Between Worlds* 55). Certainly, the fact that many of Eaton's stories end in happy marriages is not sufficient to mark her work as a significant departure from the stories of Long and others, who sincerely believed that Asian women were oversexed, subhuman playthings who could be "treated like pets and discarded as easily on leaving" (Wilkinson 115). Yet a close examination of Eaton's novel exposes differences in style and characterization that indicate that Eaton was not just aping generic conventions established by Long and other writers of Japanese romance. Rather, she used these conventions as screens to soften the outlines of potentially offensive ideas regarding interracial couplings and persons of mixed race. In doing so, she used the genre as an opportunity to voice a story that until then had gone unheard in American literature.

Eaton's "real" story, had she tried to tell it—as she eventually did in a distinctly *un*believable way, in her autobiography, *Me*[3]—would have been difficult for most Americans to swallow. She was of Asian descent but had never been to Asia; her father was British but she had never been to England; she was living in the United States but was a Canadian by birth. She was, in a sense, an alien in several different contexts, and her story would certainly have sounded just as fantastic to readers of the time—even more fantastic, perhaps—than the story she concocted for Onoto Watanna, who was purportedly descended from an English nobleman and a samurai's daughter. By taking on an exotic pseudonym and writing within the romance genre, Eaton thus gave comprehensible form to a voice that, like Yuki's, was as yet "unheard in any land"—the Orient *or* the West. However, although Yuki gave comprehensible form to Eaton's ideas, Yuki proves to be ultimately inadequate in expressing them completely; like her song, she remains incomplete, unfinished, an alien presence in the story despite her centrality in the plot.

As we discover, Yuki is not really a geisha, but—like Onoto Watanna—descended from an English nobleman and a samurai's daughter. However, Eaton submerges Yuki's story under several layers of narrative obfuscation, which allow the reader to indulge in the exotic and the fantastic without having to confront the brute fact of her mixed-race, "mongrelized" identity. Perhaps most importantly, the narrative remains centered on the point of view of Jack, the American she marries, rather than Yuki's. We see through Jack's eyes and are party to his ruminations about the mysterious geisha girl he has fallen in love with and married. At the beginning of the novel, Eaton writes, "But why had she come to him asking him to marry her? He shook his head at that; he didn't quite like it. But—oh, well, you know, these Japs have no end of queer customs. This incident just illustrated one of them. She was clearly a superior kind of a girl. . . . He had seen enough of the geishas at tea-houses to know that she was of a different kind" (41). As he tries and fails to understand her, he becomes increasingly frustrated, so that he finally realizes that "he had never been able to bridge that strange distance which lay like a pall between them, the feeling always that she was not wholly his own, that she had been but . . . a tiny wild bird that he had caught in some strange way and caged" (118).

Although Yuki is portrayed sympathetically, the reader actually learns very little about her through the course of the novel. The dialect Eaton uses in rendering Yuki's speech distances her from the outset. Her speeches largely consist of conventional "Japanese" phrase—"your augustness," "sayonara," "excellency," "whichever." At other times, she resorts to mimicry—of Jack, of the animals, of the birds. "She mimicked everything and everyone," Eaton writes (60–61). One evening, Jack hears a "long, thrilling note of sheer ecstasy and bliss, that quivered and quavered a moment, and then floated away into the maddest peals of melody, ending in a sob that was excruciating in its intense humanness." Thinking it is Yuki's pet nightingale, he goes into the garden and finds that the song has come from Yuki herself.

"Tha's jus' me," she says, "I jus' a liddle echo!" (134–135).

When she does say something of substance, the dialect is so tortured that it makes most modern readers cringe: at one point, she apologizes, "I very sawry. I din know you caring very much for poor liddle me" (90). The primary effect of Yuki's speech is one of alienation and difference, just as the effect of her song at the teahouse is one of strangeness and incompleteness. When Jack hears her speak, "the queer quality of her voice thrilled him strangely" (26); throughout the novel he thinks of her speech as queer, odd, strange; a "fairy language" (222). For example, this is how she tells him her life story:

> My people? Who they are? My august ancestors came from the moon. My one hundled grade-grandfathers fight and fight and fight like the lion, and conquer one-half of all Japan—fight the shogun, fight the kazoku, fight each other. They were great Samourai. . . . So much bloodshed displeased the gods. They punishing all my ancestors, bringin' them down to thad same poverty of those honorable peebles killed by them. Then much distress an' sadness come forever ad our house. All pride, all haughty boasting daed forever. Aeverybody goin' 'bout weepin' like ad a funeral. Nobody habby. What they goin' do git bag thad power an' reeches ag'in? Also one ancestor have grade big family to keep from starving, an' one daughter beautiful as the moon of her ancestors. He . . . weep an' weep till he go blind like an owl ad day-time. Then the gods begin feel sawry. One of them mos' sawry of all. He also is descendent of the Sun. Well, thad sun-god he comin' down ad Japan, make big raddle an' noise, an' marrying with thad same beautifullest daughter of thad ole blind ancestor. Thad sun-god my fadder. Me? I am the half-moon-half-sun offspring. (112–113)

Jack simply interprets this history as nothing more than yet another one of her "rambling . . . fairy tales of nonsense" (112). He fails to see that Yuki has related her life story in allegorical form: the moon-people, her samurai ancestors, have fallen on hard times, only to be rescued by the sun-people from the West, one of whom marries her mother. To him, her story remained "nonsense," pure and simple—an evasion, a lie.

The troubling facts of Yuki's existence—forced, after being ostracized from the rest of Japanese society, to become a teahouse entertainer in order to make money, compelled to marry a "foreign devil" because she had no prospect of marriage with a Japanese, living a life without friends and with a dishonored family—merely constitute a backdrop of events that enable the coincidences and recognition scenes that lead to the traditional romantic ending: amid a shower of cherry blossoms, Yuki and Jack vow that "the broken threads" of their lives will "never be broken" again (225). If the "half-caste" inhabits "one of the most pitiful and undesirable positions in society," as Eaton wrote in an earlier magazine article,[4] her readers hardly noticed it in this novel.

What they saw instead was a "prettily decorated," "daintily illustrated" book, a "fragrant flower" of a story (Henderson 66–67). Reviewers noted the attractiveness of the book just as often as the story contained within it. Harper and Brothers, in their advertising for the novel, stressed the book's aesthetic appeal: in one advertisement for their "Christmas List," *A Japanese Nightingale* was touted as one of "Four Artistic Gifts," juxtaposed with the "Four Great Novels" described underneath (figure 1). Clearly, the artistic gift books, which included a new illustrated edition of *Alice in Wonderland,* Howells's *Heroines of Fiction,* and a short story illustrated by Charles Gibson, were valued just as much for their presence on a parlor table as for the entertainment they provided. *Alice in Wonderland* is "not only a beautiful book—it is a work of art. It is THE great gift for Christmas"; *A Japanese Nightingale* is "one of the daintiest books from any press this season." In contrast to the stories of "intense human and dramatic power," "true pathos and real humor," provided by the great novels advertised in the bottom half of the advertisement, *A Japanese Nightingale* is merely "a love story of Japan."

1. *Harper and Brothers advertisement for* A Japanese Nightingale. (Publisher s Weekly *[December 7, 1901]: 1418.*)

The marketing of Eaton's novel as a charming Christmas gift contributed to the perception that it, like Yuki's story, was nothing more substantial than a "fairy tale of nonsense." Although the novel was ostensibly written by a mixed-race, part-Asian woman, a person who would have been condemned by the majority of the American populace as a "mongrel," a "yellow Jap"—indeed, a despicable half-caste—her readers did not care; in fact, they found it a source of appeal. The reason they could do so lay in the distinction Americans drew between Japanese art and the Japanese race. The former was fashionable, collectible, and readily assimilable to American culture; the latter was not.

The craze for "things Japanese" was inspired in Europe in the mid-nineteenth century, following Commodore Matthew Perry's visit there in 1848. Although Perry's visit opened the country to American trade, *Japonisme* did not flower on American shores for several decades, due to the turmoil of the Civil War and Reconstruction (Weisberg 16). Sparked by the Japanese exhibits at the Philadelphia Centennial Exhibition of 1876, it achieved its apotheosis in 1893 with the installation of the popular Japanese pavilion at the World Exposition in Chicago.[5] During the 1880s and 1890s, scholars including William Elliott Griffis, Ernest Fenollosa, and Lafcadio Hearn, the writer Henry Adams, and the artist John LaFarge went to Japan and were overwhelmed by the quantity and quality of Japanese decorative arts. From the tone of their writings, collecting screens, prints, paintings, silks, and even toys, became no less than an obsession. Adams wrote in 1885 to John Hay: "Every day new bales of rubbish come up from Tokyo or elsewhere, mounds of books, tons of bad bronze, holocausts of lacquer. I buy literally everything that is merely possible. . . . A man at Osaka has sent up some 250 dollars' worth of lacquers, sword-hilts, inlaid work and such stuff. As he has the best shop in Japan, we took the whole lot and have sent for more" (quoted in Dulles, 236–237).

Even Fenollosa admitted that though he wanted to respect the wishes of the Japanese, who wanted his extensive collection of art to remain in Japan, he "bought a number of the very greatest treasures secretly. The Japanese as yet don't know that I have them" (quoted in Chisholm 65). Perhaps as an attempt at penance, Fenollosa used his collection as the basis for the Boston Museum of Fine Arts collection of Japanese art and later curated numerous exhibitions that exposed Americans to the aesthetic principles of Japanese art and design. But he was the exception rather than the rule. Lafcadio Hearn perhaps more honestly summarized the motivation behind most visitors' desire to accumulate Japanese objects. In his characteristically intimate style, he wrote, "Every time you dare to look, something obliges you to buy it . . . the resources of irresistible artistic cheapness are inexhaustible. The largest steamer that crosses the Pacific could not contain what you wish to purchase. For, although you may not, perhaps, confess the fact to yourself, what you really want to buy is not the contents of a shop; you want the shop and the shopkeeper, and streets of shops with their draperies and their habitants, the whole city and the bay and the mountains begirdling it, and Fujiyama's white witchery overhanging it in the speckless sky, all Japan, in very truth" (8–9).

The closest most Americans could get to "buying Japan" was to indulge in the numerous magazines and books treating Japanese subjects published in the 1880s and 1890s. Most popular were works by William Elliott Griffis (*The Mikado's Empire,* 1880), Basil Hall Chamberlain (*Things Japanese,* 1890), Lafcadio Hearn (*Glimpses of Unfamiliar Japan,* 1894, among many others), and John Luther Long. The proliferation of writing about Japan was such that Chamberlain quipped in 1905, "it may be inferred that *not* to have written a book about Japan is fast becoming a title to distinction" (*Things Japanese* 64).

Eaton's romantic novels sat nicely on this shelf of "Japonica." Her books, like the porcelain and lacquers that became more and more common in American homes by the turn of the century, were highly decorative: floral designs were stamped with colorful foils on the covers, the edges of the pages were gilded, even the interior pages were specially printed with scenes reminiscent of Japanese screens. Reviewers clearly conflated the

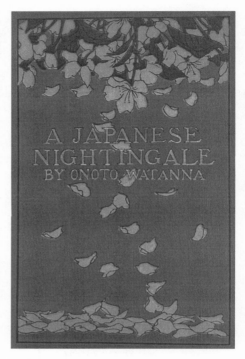

2. Cover of A Japanese Nightingale *with elaborate stamping and gilt lettering.*

physical form of the book with its contents; the "fragrant flower" of a story described in one review of *A Japanese Nightingale* mirrors the pink cherry blossoms that cascade down its front cover (figure 2).

More significantly, readers conflated not only form and content but book and author. In his assessment of another of Eaton's Japanese romances, *The Love of Azalea* (1904), the *Philadelphia Record* reviewer wrote that "this half-Oriental, half-Occidental author weaves a peculiar garment of such graceful texture that the reader finds only charm and fascination; his critical instincts are lulled completely and he sees the almost child-like little Jap at his, or her, very prettiest."[6] For this reviewer, the book functions only as a "peculiar garment" that, when purchased and read, reveals the buyer to be in posses-

3. A study in contrasts: Winnifred Eaton "à la japonaise" (left) and in Western dress (right). (Left: photo accompanying the article "Notes of a Bookman," Harper's Weekly [December 21, 1901]: 2348; right: Harper's Weekly Supplement [December 5, 1903]: 1959. Courtesy of University of North Texas.)

sion of the "little Jap" herself—fulfilling the desire expressed by Hearn to buy "all Japan, in very truth."

Moreover, unlike a Japanese tea set or a samurai's sword, Onoto Watanna's books allowed their collectors—particularly male ones—to indulge in erotic fantasies of possessing a geisha of their very own. Eaton encouraged this fantasy in publicity photos of herself: dressing in kimonos, wearing her hair in the Japanese style, and posing in front of Japanese screens, gazing demurely at the camera or shyly into the pages of a book (figure 3). These photos, which appeared as the frontispieces of her books, in the magazines that serialized her novels, and in reviews, reinforced the idea that when readers purchased her books, they were also, in a sense, purchasing *her*.

Eaton's performance of Watanna as geisha encouraged readers to believe that she was actually Japanese, even though she made clear in biographical statements at this time that Onoto Watanna was of Japanese and English descent and had in fact lived in Canada and the United States for most of her life. Those who met the "Japanese authoress" emphasized Watanna's Japanese qualities. One wrote that "in her simplicity of speech . . . she resembles the fascinating characters of her own stories"; another made a point of noting that she spoke "with just the suggestion of an accent"—whether this was an affectation on her part or the willing misperception of the interviewer is unknown.[7] A reviewer of *A Japanese Nightingale* commented on Watanna's "daintiness of touch, . . . delicacy of treatment, . . . fineness" and believed her "sudden flashes of passion and pathos" were obvious markers of "those of her race who possess the artistic instinct" (Henderson 67).

This misunderstanding of Watanna's heritage further obscured the story of the half-caste that Eaton tried to tell in *A Japanese Nightingale*. Nearly all reviewers referred to the novel's "Japanese" heroine; William Dean Howells himself wrote that despite her "half-caste origin," Yuki is "justly Japanese in what makes her loveliest" (881). Eaton's failure to convince her readers of the significance of Yuki's biracial makeup, as Carol Vivian Spaulding and others have pointed out, came at least partly as a result of the "one-drop" view of race, which by 1901 had attained the status of ideological truth. But it also resulted from the fact that most Americans could only imagine Yuki as Japanese, another Madame Chrysanthème or Cho-Cho-San—even though Eaton endowed her with the distinctly un-Japanese traits of blue eyes and curly red hair.

Only a few of Eaton's more perceptive critics appreciated the difference that Onoto Watanna's background made in her writing. Some pointed out her ability to understand American culture: one reviewer remarked that Watanna's "American characters are pictured with the accuracy of a photograph"; another noted that she regarded "American life with remarkably clear vision."[8] Others went a step further and attributed the very success of her fiction to her understanding of both cultures, since she was descended from both of them and thus could mediate between them. A 1904 review of *The Love of Azalea* claimed that "Onoto Watanna's stories of Japanese life have in them just that touch of Western civilization necessary to make them thoroughly comprehensible to Western readers, but not so much as to spoil that delicious fragrance of the spirit of old Japan that pervades them."[9]

A reviewer for the Charleston, South Carolina *News* expressed the idea most fully:

> This story [*Miss Numè of Japan*] is something of a novelty in American fiction, for it is written by an Americanized Japanese. . . . The author . . . possesses a rare endowment of genius and sympathy, giving her the true artist's touch with all human life. Very wonderful are the insight and facility with which she depicts the life and throb of affection, aspiration, and passion in the forms in which they have been wrought by the venerable institutions and traditions of the Orient, working upon the people with cumulative results through a hundred generations. This, however, is not so remarkable when we consider her advantages of heredity as that she should be able to take on by sympathy, and portray with equal fidelity and power the play of the human heart as it is in the newer world and life of the West.[10]

Howells, too, found that despite the fact that Yuki is "Japanese in what makes her loveliest," the novel was able to access human emotions and feelings in a way that distinguished the book from others in the romance genre. In his essay "A Psychological Counter-Current in Recent Fiction" (1901), he writes: "all is very strange under that remote sky; but what is true to humanity anywhere is true everywhere, and the story of Yuki and Bigelow, as the Japanese author tells it in very choice English, is of as palpitant actuality as any which should treat of lovers next door. If I have ever read any record of young married love that was so frank, so sweet, so pure, I do not remember it" (880–881). He praises Watanna for restricting her use of melodramatic incident to that which "is characterized and does not characterize" and for focusing her readers' attention on "the supreme interest" of Yuki's "personality." He continues, "such a lesson in the art of imitating nature . . . has not come under my hand for a long while. It has its little defects, but its directness, and sincerity, and its felicity through the sparing touch make me unwilling to note them. In fact, I have forgotten them" (881).

Howells's glowing assessment of the book as a realistic novel may be difficult to comprehend today. In fact, it demonstrates an aspect of Howellsian realism that is often overlooked: that the "art of imitating nature" did not simply involve the pursuit of verisimilitude but the achievement of psychological empathy. Howells believed that by depicting real people in real situations, writers could demonstrate the profundity of human emotion as it is experienced in daily life. Fiction could thus play a vital role in healing the growing rifts he perceived in American society—between people of different regions, classes, races, and nations. By adopting what he called an "aesthetic of the common" that focused on "common people" and their "commonplace" lives, novels could demonstrate their "common humanity." They could show, as he put it, that "men are more like than unlike one another."[11]

Although Howells was certainly motivated by democratic ideals in his championing of the common, Amy Kaplan has pointed out that his goal was not to "jar readers with the shock of otherness," but to "create 'solidarity,' to pave a common ground between diverse social groups through the recognition of the essential likeness of individuals in all social classes" (*Social Construction* 22–23). Paradoxically, because readers—Howells included—could achieve solidarity only with perspectives that they recognized, writers needed to depict those perspectives in recognizable, "common" terms to appeal to what Kaplan described as a "communal consensus about the way all things are." Eaton's reliance on stereotypical representations of Yuki—and herself—as geisha thus resonated with Howells as being realistic precisely by virtue of its conventionality.

According to Gina Marchetti, the popularity of *Madame Butterfly* and other romances between Asian women and American men appealed to readers during this post-Victorian age because in them, "romantic involvements and sexual liaisons unacceptable in mainstream Anglo-American society become possible. Erotic fantasies can be indulged, sexual taboos broken" (*Romance* 1). Far from jolting her readers with the shock of otherness, Eaton thus gave them, especially men, yet another opportunity to engage in the semierotic fantasies about Asian women that they had indulged in reading these earlier works. Howells, "pious old maid" that some thought him,[12] enthusiastically succumbed to this fantasy. He declared, "Nothing but the irresistible charm of the American girl could, I should think, keep the young men who read Mrs. Watana's [sic] book from going out and marrying Japanese girls."

To give Howells some credit, Eaton's depiction of the geisha did differ in significant ways from that of other practitioners of the genre. Most of the time, Japanese women were characterized in distinctly inhuman terms. John Luther Long's Miss Cherry-Blossom, for example, is described as a "sociological fact," "the most delightful of *fin de siècle* products" (*Blossom* 32); Cho-Cho-San is described by her American husband, B. F. Pinkerton, as "an American refinement of a Japanese product, an American improvement on a Japanese invention" (*Butterfly* 13). In both stories, the Japanese woman is merely a plaything, a bauble, for the superior white man; Pinkerton sees Cho-Cho-San as "dainty, vivid, eager, formless material" that can be "mold[ed] . . . to his most wantonly whimsical wish" (59).

Cho-Cho-San, like Miss Cherry-Blossom, is also easily discarded by her American lover—so easily discarded she removes herself. Perhaps the most disturbing aspect of *Madame Butterfly* is not the sacrifice of Cho-Cho-San for the sake of Pinkerton per se, but the way in which her attempted suicide is described.[13] Long writes, "She could not help a little gasp at the first incision. But presently she could feel the blood finding its way down her neck. It divided on her shoulder, the larger stream going down her bosom. In a moment she could see it making its way daintily between her breasts. It began to congeal there. She pressed on the sword, and a fresh stream swiftly overran the other—redder, she thought" (83–84). The wound Cho-Cho-

San inflicts on herself is almost painless—both for us and for her. In fact, as she gazes at herself in the mirror, she almost seems to enjoy watching the blood "making its way daintily between her breasts." She realizes for the first time that it is "sad to die," not because life is worth living after all, but because without Pinkerton, she is left with "nothing—nothing but this" (84–85). Pinkerton, on the other hand, is not even left with the guilt that her body, or even traces of blood, would have summoned; Cho-Cho-San's maid cleans up the mess and removes the corpse, so that when Pinkerton and his new wife arrive the next day, the house is "quite empty" (86).

Even those writers who were sympathetic to the Japanese fell short of humanizing them. Frances Little's *The Lady of the Decoration* (1906), which made the *Bookman*'s top ten best-selling list in 1907, referred to the Japanese as "queer, small people who run about smiling, and bowing and saying pretty things to each other" (25). The students at the kindergarten established by the heroine remain an undifferentiated mass: "a hundred blessed babies in gay little kimonas [sic], who look like big bunches of flowers" (216). And Lafcadio Hearn, who married a Japanese and was adopted by a Japanese family, still emphasized the homogeneity of the Japanese "race-soul," writing that the Japanese "are equally characterized by a singular placidity,—expressing neither love nor hate nor anything save perfect repose and gentleness,—like the dreamy placidity of Buddhist images . . . with growing acquaintance each face will become more and more individualized for you by characteristics before imperceptible. But the recollection of that first impression will remain with you; and the time will come when you will . . . recognize in the memory of that first impression one glimpse of the race-soul, with its impersonal lovableness and its impersonal weaknesses" (*Glimpses* 477).

Long's Cho-Cho-San is the epitome of Hearn's impersonal loveableness and weakness; she never attains the status of an actual character but merely functions as a foil for the roué Pinkerton. Pinkerton, for example, takes pleasure in the fact

that Cho-Cho-San's "little, unused, frivolous mind" (75) is unable to follow his "witty" repartee. When Cho-Cho-San asks
him why she cannot bring her relatives to their house, he says,

> "I shall have to serve in the capacity of ancestors, let us say
> ancestor-at-large,—and the real ones will have to go—or rather
> not come."
>
> Again he had the joke to himself; his wife had gone away to
> cry. (6)

Pinkerton—and the reader, we assume—have many such chuckles
at Cho-Cho-San's expense.

Yuki, however, is not to be trifled with. Far from having a
"little, unused, frivolous mind," she is resourceful and hard-
headed; she originally sees her marriage to Jack as a simple
business transaction that will help her pay for her brother's
education and bring him home. When she realizes that Jack has
actually fallen in love with her, she leaves him because "it was
bedder so" (130); but rather than deciding to kill herself for the
sake of Jack's future happiness, as Cho-Cho-San does, she joins
an American theatrical troupe to seek her fortunes elsewhere.
Details such as these humanize Yuki, distinguishing *A Japanese
Nightingale* from other stories in the genre. Yet it is important
to note that though Eaton was able to establish her readers'
sympathy for Yuki, she never asked or expected them to transfer that sympathy to Eurasians (or Asians) as a whole. The limitation of her vision to the particular has been criticized.[14]

Yet it seems singularly unproductive (and unfair) to judge a
writer's work based on our present understanding of identity
politics and issues of oppression and empowerment. It seems
more useful, rather, to take the works of writers like Eaton at
face value: to see what they do say and to examine how they
participate in their literary and historical context. In *Modernism
and the Harlem Renaissance,* for example, Houston Baker Jr.
makes a useful distinction between two kinds of African American literary responses to mainstream white culture. Those who

engaged mainstream literature through a "mastery of form"—
his examples are Booker T. Washington and Charles Chesnutt—
played to white expectations so completely that they were able
to transform their audiences' understanding of slavery and the
meaning of minstrelsy. Chesnutt's conjure stories, Baker writes,
so aptly exploited the tropes and conventions of minstrelsy that
his "white audience thought they were hearing merely entertaining syllables of a lovable darky," when in fact they are being "put . . . through changes" (46–47). He contrasts the mastery
of form exemplified by Chesnutt to the "deformation of form"
that constitutes W.E.B. DuBois's *Souls of Black Folk* (1903),
which, in its melding of black spirituals, sociological inquiry,
and autobiography, becomes the "singing book" of a distinctly
African American culture (68). Although Baker clearly sees the
"master of form" as one step toward the evolution of a more
productive "deformation of mastery," he exhorts us to recognize that the evolution itself is necessary and valuable.

Eaton had much in common with that master of form, Charles
Chesnutt: both wrote within distinct and popular forms (Chesnutt's wrote within the tradition of Joel Chandler Harris's Uncle
Remus stories and Thomas Nelson Page's *In Ole Virginia*); both
used dialect writing to express cultural differences. Chesnutt,
too, was one of the first writers of color to achieve success
within the mainstream American literary establishment. However, he never achieved the height or duration of success that
Eaton did. After the successful publication of his Uncle Julius
tales, in *The Conjure Woman and Other Stories* (1899), he left
the dialect form to write a novel about the 1898 race riots in
Wilmington, North Carolina. In this novel, *The Marrow of Tradition* (1901), Chesnutt issued a bleak assessment of the lasting
value of Reconstruction and also implicitly condemned
northerners' willingness to ignore atrocities committed against
blacks after Reconstruction in their efforts to reunite the nation.
Howells reviewed Chesnutt's novel in the same essay that praised
A Japanese Nightingale for its "freshness," its "directness, and
sincerity, and its felicity"; a comparison of his reaction to *The*

Marrow of Tradition reveals much about the kinds of limitations imposed on writers of color at the turn of the century.

"I wish I could at all times praise as much the literature of an author who speaks for another colored race, not so far from us as the Japanese, but of as much claim upon our conscience, if not our interest," Howells begins. "Mr. Chesnutt, it seems to me, has lost literary quality in acquiring literary quantity" (881–882). Although he praises Chesnutt as "an artist whom his stepbrother Americans may well be proud of," he also writes that as a black writer, his first responsibility is "to get rid of the cakewalk . . . it is not for him to pick up the cheap graces and poses of the jouster" (882). To accuse the author of a serious, and ultimately tragic, work of literature of exploiting the cakewalk, of playing the jouster, is odd indeed, especially when the book is viewed in contrast to his earlier conjure tales, which relied heavily on minstrelsy for their humor. The key for Howells, however, is that Chesnutt is "too clearly of a judgment that is made up": he has been too heavy-handed in conveying his message. "The book is, in fact, bitter, bitter," he writes; "There is no reason in history why it should not be so . . . yet it would be better if it was not so bitter" (882). In *The Marrow of Tradition,* Chesnutt exceeded the bounds of comprehensible storytelling. Even Howells, who was sympathetic to the racial issues presented in Chesnutt's novel, could not accept the book in the terms in which they were presented. He recognizes that *The Marrow of Tradition* and the conjure stories are both about race relations; his qualms have to do with the different way Chesnutt wrote about them in his novel.

After the commercial and critical failure of *The Marrow of Tradition,* Chesnutt abandoned the idea of becoming a professional writer and returned to his career as a stenographer. He published several more collections of stories and novels, but they received little notice. Eaton, in contrast, continued to be successful. The novels she published on an almost yearly basis between 1899 and 1912 sold well enough for her to be able to support herself, her intermittently employed first husband, and four children.[15] She became enough of a celebrity to elicit feature articles in magazines and newspapers of the "author at home" variety, and reviews of her books often knowingly referred to her as "the Japanese authoress"—indeed, as early as 1903, *Harper's Weekly* proclaimed that "the name of Onoto Watanna . . . is known everywhere" (figure 4).[16] The key to her success, as one reviewer put it, was that she was able to give "the reader the Japanese point of view, almost without his becoming aware of it."[17] Yet she became weary of doing so. In an unpublished autobiographical piece, she wrote, "I was 'labeled' Japanese. . . . I dreamed of the day when I could escape from the treadmill of a subject I did not love."[18] She eventually did so, but early in her career financial considerations led her to stick with the formula she established in her second novel.

Eaton did depart from this formula, especially in her magazine writings, and it is interesting to see how she carries some of the same themes from the Japanese romances to non-Japanese settings. In her short story "Margot," for example, which was probably written at about the same time as *A Japanese Nightingale,* her heroine, a country girl with a talent for music, is described as "a caged nightingale" (204). Though she is unable to express her feelings through her rude country speech, she is able to communicate through her violin, just as Yuki is able to communicate through her song and dance. Eaton writes, "Out upon the silence of the dingy hall a long plaintive note stole, so weirdly strange" that her listener "held his breath in an agony of feeling" (207). In both this story and her novel, Eaton expresses her sympathy for "the outcast" and shows her concern with recognizing the different ways ideas and emotions are expressed.

Perhaps more revealing, however, is another earlier version of her half-caste story that was more directly critical of the prevailing tradition and her own later work. In 1898, she published the story "A Half-Caste" in *Frank Leslie's Popular Monthly,* a story that directly confronted the prejudices against half-castes and the limitations of the Japanese romance genre. This story, like *A Japanese Nightingale,* begins with the dance of a geisha

4. *Winnifred Eaton in her library, 1903.* (Harper's Weekly Supplement [December 5, 1903]: 1960. *Courtesy of University of North Texas.*)

girl who, like Yuki, is half Japanese. But Kiku refuses to dance for "the foreign devil" who specifically requests the teahouse proprietor to engage her for him. Hilton "could not understand her . . . they generally were so willing and eager to please" (491–492). It is only when the angry teahouse proprietor threatens to dismiss her that Kiku finally serves Hilton his sake. He asks her if she is, as a result, "only pretending to smile." "Yes," she says: "Tha's worg' for geisha girl. Whad you thing we goin' to git paid for? Account we frown? Or account we laugh? . . . Thad is my worg. You nod onderstand? *You* worg, *I* worg, *aeverybody* worg. All different ways. Geisha girl *mus'* be always gay—always dance, laugh, sing; laugh mos' of all— to mek you laugh, too, so that you pay the money, mek us reech. I nod lig vaery much

thees work, but whad kin I do? Thad I nod worgin' I goin' to
starve. Tha's bedder I worg foraever" (492).

Hilton is highly amused by this little speech; "you are a phi-
losopher," he says. Enchanted, he continues to pursue her. Much
to his surprise, Kiku becomes "the one woman in the world he
had loved during all his long, checkered career"; she reminds
him of his first wife, a "little Japanese woman who had once
really loved him for himself" (490). Kiku, meanwhile, has discovered that Hilton is, in fact, her father; another geisha has
recognized him and identified him as the man who had married her mother and then abandoned her after a "dreamy sleepy
summer" (494) before she was born, just as Pinkerton aban-
dons Cho-Cho-San in *Madame Butterfly*. She decides to encourage Hilton's interest, and then reject him, in order to revenge
her mother, to "mek [him] suffer lig her" (496). When Hilton
professes his love for her, she rebuffs him coldly. Then she tells
him her story: "you nod understand. . . . I bin mos' vaery onhappy
long time now, because aeverybody hate me. Account I loog
lig American. You nod onderstand? No? My fadder . . . he leave
my modder. We vaery onhappy . . . w'en she die I worg, worg
hard at the factory, an' here. Nobody lig me account my fadder
American, an' I thing account thad I goin' hate all Americans
foraever" (495–496).

When Hilton hears this, he is overcome by "pain and horror"; he "could not think of Kiku-san as his own child—his very
own blood—he would not!" But Kiku will not let Hilton remain
in ignorance. She asks him insistently, "You nod understand?
You nod understand?" At the end of the story, she finally resorts to displaying the physical evidence of her heritage—something Hilton finally comprehends. Eaton writes,

> She suddenly loosened her hair, and it fell down around her in
> thick, shining brown curls.
>   "Thad lig Japanese girl?—thad?—thad?—thad? Thad?"
>   She pushed back the sleeves and showed him the white pu-
> rity of her arms.

Then she turned and left him, with the same still look of despair on his face and the pitiless sun beating on the golden fields. (496)

"A Half-Caste" explicitly tells the story of miscegenation that Eaton later casts as Yuki's fairy tale in *A Japanese Nightingale*. Eaton writes that Kiku "said things that no American girl would say, and that few Japanese girls would understand" (494), and in this story she allows her to express them. She exacts revenge for her father's conquest of her mother and the life of pain and work that followed his desertion of them.

In this story Eaton enacts a fantasy of what she would do if she, like Kiku, could ever confront the person responsible for the prejudice she and her siblings suffered due to their mixed race. She later wrote that growing up, she "felt ashamed and humiliated" to hear the townsfolk discuss her father and his "leetle foreign wife" (*Marion* 1). Yet "A Half-Caste" is the only story that addresses this issue so directly. One must ask, of course, why Eaton chose to obscure this message in her later stories and novels. Many of the answers are necessarily speculative. She may have received negative responses from readers of *Frank Leslie's Popular Monthly,* where "A Half-Caste" appeared. She may have been discouraged from following that particular line of storytelling by her editors. Or she may have chosen to abandon it on her own.

No evidence exists to support any one of these hypotheses. But it was certain that at this time, printing stories that spoke about interracial couplings at all, let alone sympathetically, was a risky proposition. John Luther Long, for example, proposed to R. W. Gilder of the *Century Magazine* a sequel to *Madame Butterfly* that treated a happy marriage between a Japanese woman and an American man. Long wrote, "I would have written it long ago had I not had doubts of its finding a publisher" and admitted that the plot "seems daring, of course. But if the Eastern atmosphere is sufficiently retained, so that the reader will be in Japan, and not in America while he reads, and if the story is told with delicacy and refinement as it can be, it ought not to be offensive." Gilder rejected the story despite Long's protestations. "I am sorry," he wrote succinctly: "it is questionable whether Jap. [sic] ideas can be instilled into American minds."[19]

Editorial concerns aside, from the point of view of a popular novelist, it would have been difficult to continue in the vein of "A Half-Caste." As Janice Radway and others have pointed out, the continued salability of popular authors depended on a "standard reliance on a recipe that dictates the essential ingredients to be included in each new version of the form" (29). Kiku's story, unlike Yuki's, cannot be readily duplicated. Kiku leaves her readers in "still despair" after laying bare the "white purity" of her half-caste condition, denying any possibility of future happiness or even of further understanding. Yuki and Jack's story, in contrast, follows the conventional lines of romance—boy meets girl, boy gets girl, boy loses girl, boy gets girl in the end—that readers to this day have found repeatedly appealing. In her variation on the form, Eaton's "worg" was like the geisha's: to cater continually to her audience's curiosity and to create herself in their image—to sing the haunting melodies that mystified and thus titillated them. Eaton, as Onoto Watanna, continued to "dance, laugh, sing . . . so that you pay the money, mek us reech."

Eaton did become rich at points in her life, but her decisions about what and how to write would always be heavily influenced by her finances. The decisions and sacrifices she made in order to sell her books were not experienced by her alone; they are, perhaps, experienced by all writers. But it is a fact of the writer's existence that has, until recently, gone largely unexamined. Certainly in studies of ethnic literature, commercial considerations have been condemned as a sign of ethnic backsliding, of "selling out."[20] But to assess the work of a writer without considering his or her financial constraints and needs is to ignore the influence of economics not only on literature but on minority populations in the United States. Eaton wrote the way she did because she needed to make money; if it was a "cheap and popular device," as she described her Japanese guise in her autobiography (154), it nevertheless provided for her and her family.

Granted, Eaton's novels did cater to "commonly held (often racist) values of American society" (Shea 19). Gina Marchetti has rightly described the various forms of Asian romance, and the Madame Butterfly story in particular, as a way for Americans to displace their very real anxieties regarding race and gender simply by shipping it overseas (*Romance* 6). In a characteristic reversal, however, Eaton redirected the ultimately reactionary thrust of the Madame Butterfly narrative. As a popular novelist, Eaton could not demand the repentant acknowledgment from her audience that Kiku demands of Hilton in "A Half-Caste." However, by enjoying and purchasing novels like *A Japanese Nightingale,* readers implicitly recognized the existence and humanity of Pinkerton's daughters. In her Eurasian romances, she succeeded in describing a potentially threatening, multiracial society of which both she and her audience were already a part.

TWO

Not Quite at Home

EXPLORING THE DOMESTIC SPACE

Such is the patriot's boast, where'er we roam,
His first, best country ever is, at home.
—Oliver Goldsmith, *The Traveller*

WITH THE successful publication of *A Japanese Nightingale,* Eaton embarked on her career as a full-time professional writer. She also took on another career—that of wife and mother. In the next decade, she published half a dozen novels and dozens of short stories and essays and gave birth to four children. She remarked during this prolific period that she was producing at a rate of "a book and a baby a year." The shift away from the concerns of a single woman—specifically, the search for a husband—to the domestic pursuits of a mother and wife duly reflected itself in Eaton's writing. Although Eaton continued to write romances in the vein of *A Japanese Nightingale,* she also branched out into other areas: her fiction became peopled by mothers, children, and household servants in addition to young single women, and her stories concerned family dynamics and household management as well as young love.

These novels, as well as the domestically oriented nonfiction pieces she published in popular magazines such as *Harper's Weekly* and *Good Housekeeping,* participated in a wide-ranging conversation about American womanhood and the American home that included other novelists, domestic scientists, and social reformers. But like her Japanese heroines, Eaton spoke with a voice accented by racial difference, a difference that, perhaps without Eaton even realizing it, denaturalized accepted notions of femininity and domesticity and opened a space for largely forgotten or intentionally excluded voices from below—the woman of color, the foreigner, the immigrant. In *A Japanese Blossom* (1906), for example, she places the familiar scene of American domesticity within a Japanese setting and shows how a true embodiment of womanly values enables an American woman not only to appreciate but to assimilate to Japanese culture. In *The Diary of Delia* (1907) and "A Neighbor's Garden, My Own, and a Dream One" (1908), she describes American domesticity in the voices of immigrant outsiders, revealing the labor, usually performed by immigrants and racial minorities, that contemporary writings on domestic reform often rendered invisible. These works question the boundary between the foreign and the domestic—and I mean "domestic" in both senses of the word; they show the inseparability of the domestic, public, and international spheres.[1]

Competing images of American womanhood proliferated at the turn of the century. No longer simply the "angel in the house," American women like Hull House founder Jane Addams, writer Charlotte Perkins Gilman, and suffragist Carrie Chapman Catt strode boldly into the public sphere. More and more women were attending college, and many of these New Women not only remained single after graduation but pursued lifelong careers as teachers, journalists, doctors, and lawyers.[2] Yet most American women did not wholly reject the ideal of True Womanhood and still desired a quiet married life with children. Even the most militant suffragettes desired to be described as True Women. Historian Martha Banta, for example, describes a 1912 *Good Housekeeping* article titled "The Feminine Charms of the Woman Militant: The Personal Attractiveness and Housewifely Attainments of the Leaders of the Equal Suffrage Movement," wherein the author "declares that the most famous suffragists were all accomplished in the women's sphere. Elizabeth Cady

Stanton was the 'head of a beautifully ordered home.' . . . Susan B. Anthony was 'an adept with her needle' and 'did the most exquisite darning when she was thinking of her speeches.' Carrie Chapman Catt still 'goes into the kitchen to make pumpkin pies . . . [from] real pumpkins, not base tinned imitations . . . [for her] famous Thanksgiving dinners'" (65).

As this article shows, women's magazines like *Good Housekeeping,* where Eaton's gardening essay, "A Neighbor's Garden, My Own, and a Dream One," appeared, were a test kitchen of ideas regarding femininity, domesticity, and womanly duty to home and nation. Although most of these magazines were established in the 1880s and 1890s by men (such as Edward Bok of *Ladies' Home Journal*), in the first decades of the twentieth century they became dominated by women's voices, particularly from the new field of domestic science. According to historian Laura Shapiro, the domestic scientists taught their readers that "if the home were made a more businesslike place, if husbands were fed and children raised according to scientific principles, if purity and fresh air reached every corner of the house—then, at least, the nation's homes would be adequate to nurture its greatness" (4). To that end, writers such as Fannie Farmer, Ellen Richards, and Christine Frederick instructed their readers not only in home decoration and the latest fashions but in household management, technological innovations, sanitation, and nutrition. Shapiro writes, "The new domestic heaven they were promoting was a household that ran as quietly and productively as a machine, under the guidance of a benevolent technician" (41).

More drastic measures were suggested by feminists and social reformers like Charlotte Perkins Gilman and Jane Addams, who advocated the socialization of housework, community housekeeping, and day care for children of working mothers. Addams's Hull House was based on a communitarian model, where all residents shared household duties and participated together in household activities such as meals and evening entertainments. Gilman, in her utopian novel *Herland* (1912), went so far as to imagine a community of self-sufficient, self-reproducing women who have created a society where men are wholly unnecessary. Without them, they have created a nurturing, peaceful and, above all, efficient society that is a wonder to the group of American male adventurers who stumble upon them. Vandyck Jennings, the most perceptive of the group and the novel's narrator, describes their differences this way:

> When we say *men, man, manly, manhood,* and all the other masculine derivatives, we have in the background of our minds a huge vague crowded picture of the world and all its activities. To grow up and "be a man," to "act like a man"—the meaning and connotation is wide indeed. . . .
>
> And when we say *Women,* we think *Female*—the sex.
>
> But to these women . . . the word *woman* called up all that big background . . . and the word *man* meant to them only *male*—the sex. (135)

The women are initially hungry for knowledge about the world outside, but they soon become disgusted by the pride the men display in keeping women to what they see as a demeaning, degraded position.

Writers of domestic fiction, though less militant about the need to transform domestic ideology, were no less concerned with it than Gilman. Frank Luther Mott notes that the turn of the century witnessed a "great outpouring" of domestic fiction in the American literary marketplace that rivaled its initial efflorescence half a century earlier (216). The heroines of this fiction, like their real-life counterparts, struggled with their conflicting desires to be both True and New Women. Margaret Paget, the twenty-something heroine of Kathleen Norris's best-selling novel *Mother* (1911), pities her mother for being "condemned" to a life of respectable poverty making ends meet for her husband and brood of eight children. Margaret is determined not to follow in her mother's footsteps: she decides to stay unmarried, leave the dreary, stultifying town of Weston where she has

lived her entire life, and make her own way in the world of the
rich, famous, and cultured as a New York society woman's
personal secretary. Yet she comes to realize that success in the
public sphere cannot compete with the most fulfilling occupation of true womanhood: nurturing and caring for one's family.
At the end of the novel, she suddenly comes to understand that
her mother, simply by embracing her maternal role, has contributed to society more than most women could ever hope of
doing:

> All her old castles in the air seemed cheap and tinselled to-
> night, beside these tender dreams that had their roots in the real
> truths of life. Travel and position, gowns and motor-cars, yachts
> and country houses, these things were to be bought in all their
> perfection by the highest bidder, and always would be. But love
> and character and service, home and the wonderful charge
> of little lives—the "pure religion breathing household laws"
> that guided and perfected the whole—these were not to be
> bought, they were only to be prayed for, worked for, bravely
> won. (192–193)

Mother, in fact, is nothing short of a polemic on the need for
educated, independent women to marry and have children.
Margaret's fiancé, college professor John Tenison, admires Mrs.
Paget precisely for this accomplishment. "In these days," he
tells Margaret, "when women just serenely ignore the question
of children, or at most, as a special concession, bring up one or
two—just the one or two whose expenses can be comfortably
met!—there's something magnificent in a woman like your
mother, who begins eight destinies instead of one! She doesn't
strain and chafe to express herself through the medium of poetry or music or the stage, but she puts her whole splendid
philosophy into her nursery—launches sound little bodies and
minds" (179–180). In *Mother*, Norris echoed the prevalent view
that women, as primary caregivers, were responsible not only
for the welfare of their individual home and family but for the

creation of good Americans—and many of them. As the muck-raker Ida M. Tarbell put it, "Learning, business careers, political and industrial activities—none of these things is more than incidental in the national task of woman. Her great task is to prepare the citizen" (81).

This "national task" became an increasingly urgent one with the perceived encroachment of undesirable immigrant and minority populations on "American" society. The 1890 census revealed that minorities and immigrants from eastern and southern Europe were reproducing at a much higher rate than "old stock" populations, raising the specter of what President Theodore Roosevelt came to call "race suicide." Roosevelt saw the decreasing birthrate among white (and well-to-do) women as nothing less than a national emergency. In his 1906 State of the Union address, he attacked women whom he perceived were engaged in "willful sterility—the one sin for which the penalty is national death." Equally disturbing to many Americans, men and women alike, was the flight of native- and English-born women from domestic service to better-paying and less restrictive secretarial and shop work and their replacement by immigrant women, especially the Irish, who were untrained in American manners, cookery, or—many assumed—morality. The American way of life was threatened as a result of this "servant problem"; the very existence of "Bridget" in American households foretold the corruption of American family values and, ultimately, American society. "As Bridget rules the roast in the kitchen, so she rules the toast at the table, and gives tone to conversation in the parlor" (16), wrote Harriet Prescott Spofford; "Bridget and Nora . . . are not merely the queens of the kitchen, but, to all intents and purposes, they are the heads of the household too" (30).

Responses to race suicide and the servant problem took various forms. Nativist politicians attempted to curb immigration through legislation that restricted the numbers of new immigrants or made permanent residence in the United States difficult or unappealing through taxes and land ownership restrictions. Reform societies and women's clubs, in contrast, focused on those who had already landed on American shores. They invited lecturers to teach working women about democratic philosophy and American history. They also offered classes in proper food preparation and housekeeping for the general purpose of Americanizing immigrant girls and women and, more specifically, to train them as domestic servants, which many of them would inevitably become.[3] One group even established cooking schools on Indian reservations in order to provide the Indian woman with the "refinements of a cultured home" and to expose her to "civilization and a taste of cleanly comfort" that would enable her to become a productive American citizen (Shapiro 147). These programs met with varying degrees of success. In all cases, however, it was assumed that immigrants and minorities needed either to assimilate to or be excluded from American life.

Chinese immigrants, as Asian American historians have noted, were perceived to be particularly unassimilable. In *Strangers from a Different Shore,* Ronald Takaki writes that during the first decade of the twentieth century, these prejudices were "inherited" by the newly emerging Japanese American population, who were not immediately distinguishable from the Chinese in most American eyes and whose numbers had not yet been "contained" by exclusion laws (181). In California especially, Japanese Americans endured verbal and physical abuse, were prevented from residing in "white" neighborhoods, and were relegated to the least desirable occupations—truck farming and domestic service. Moreover, the Japanese conquest of China and Russia in the recent Sino-Japanese and Russo-Japanese wars reawakened fears of a Japanese yellow peril, culminating in the various pieces of legislation enacted in the 1900s and the 1910s that restricted Japanese immigration and prevented the permanent residence of those who had already arrived. President Roosevelt himself supported these measures because he believed that the "culminating points of two such lines of divergent cultural development would be fraught with peril" (202).

Justification for exclusion, as the quote from Roosevelt implies, focused largely on the "unnatural" domestic life of Asian immigrants. Many Japanese workers did not even have homes to speak of: migrant farm workers slept in the fields in which they worked, and railroad workers packed themselves into boxcars fitted with makeshift bunks. The lifestyle of these early Japanese Americans did indeed fly in the face of what was considered "respectable" or even acceptable living—by either Americans or Japanese. Takaki explains that their behavior exhibited a "sojourner" mentality: "Thinking they would be here only temporarily, Issei [first-generation Japanese immigrants] did not seem to care about their shabby living conditions and their indiscreet behavior, which included drinking, gambling, and carousing with prostitutes" (195).

Some argued that the use of Chinese and Japanese immigrant labor was inherently unfair to American workers because the immigrants ate less and more cheaply and therefore could be paid less than American workers. One senator remarked on the evolutionary implications of this fact in his arguments for Asian exclusion, arguing, "You can not work a man who must have beef and bread, and would prefer beef, alongside of a man who can live on rice. In all such conflicts, and in all such struggles, the result is not to bring up the man who lives on rice to the beef-and-bread standard, but is to bring down the beef-and-bread man to the rice standard" (quoted in Levenstein 24). Thus the issue was not only that Asians could not assimilate to American culture but that American culture itself would regress—devolve—through contact with them.

Eaton had begun her career as Onoto Watanna writing articles for women's magazines about Japan and had staked her fortune on the American fascination with Japanese culture. The environment of intensifying anti-Japanese sentiment thus threatened her very livelihood. But rather than retreat from her Japanese identity as it became a liability, she defended it; in particular, she insisted on the refinement of Japanese culture and the wholesome quality of Japanese home life. At the beginning of

"Every-day Life in Japan" (1904), for example, she declares that "no nation is uncivilized which in the actual every-day living practices the little niceties and politenesses of convention" and takes great pains in the ensuing article to show exactly how "niceties and politenesses" permeate Japanese daily life—in ways, she implies, often absent from American households. The servants, rushing about from the crack of dawn, "do all the housework for the day" in the very "hours when the average Western servant is sleeping." The conversation at the breakfast table assiduously avoids argument and conflict; "How sad to begin the day with harsh words!" she writes. She describes the role that Japanese mothers play in their children's education, not only in manners and polite speech but, most importantly, in "the first principles of patriotism and loyalty" (501). In the afternoons, Japanese women, like their American counterparts, might partake of a little shopping or call on their friends. Most often, however, they spend time with their children, working embroidery in the garden while their children play. "Here, their hands employed sewing, their eyes and senses delighted by their surroundings, watching the children playing, is it any wonder that the Japanese woman is the calm of soul?" (502).

Like Kathleen Norris's Mrs. Paget, the Japanese *okusama* in "Every-day Life in Japan" instills in her children, and her household in general, a sense of love, duty, and consideration that many believed should be the goal of all women. In *A Japanese Blossom* (1906), Eaton takes this logic one step further, suggesting that the American domestic ideal was compatible not only with Japanese domesticity but with an aspect of Japanese culture that seemed antithetical to womanly virtue: Japanese militarism. The novel's American heroine, Ellen Kurukawa, is the model of American motherhood: she is kind, educated, and wise, the mother of three children who adore her; yet, as her name indicates, she is the wife not of a New England preacher or Midwestern farmer, as were many of the matriarchs depicted in domestic fiction, but of a Japanese businessman, Kiyo Kurukawa, who has brought Ellen, her two children from a previous marriage (from which she was respectably widowed), and their newborn mixed-race infant to Japan to live with the three children from his previous marriage.

National, domestic, and filial responsibility clash from the very beginning of the novel. When Kiyo and Ellen Kurukawa arrive in Japan, they discover that Kiyo's eldest son, Gozo, has decided to enter the military, preferring to serve the emperor rather than betray his country by accepting a "barbarian woman" into the family. Kiyo deems this act "unfilial" and "rebellious," a sign of Gozo's need for "the guiding hand of a father" that has been absent during the years Kiyo spent as a businessman in the United States (50–51). Yet Kiyo has his own conflicts to resolve. Because he is descended from samurai, "patriotism was as natural and deep-rooted as life itself" (107). But at the very moment when he feels most compelled to serve his emperor, he also feels a responsibility for the happiness of his American wife, who he assumes "believed that the men of his age did their duty best by remaining at home, the protectors of the weak. So she had told him many times" (107). He believes that Ellen will never understand the Japanese point of view—in particular, the point of view of a proper Japanese wife, who would be "the first to urge" her husband to enlist and would even "command him to leave her" (107). Indeed, Ellen is initially oblivious to the shame Kiyo experiences at town gatherings and celebrations when he finds himself one of very few able-bodied men who has yet to enlist. At one of these celebrations, Kiyo is asked by his son to tell the family a story "about war." He agrees; but the story he tells is not about fighting or manly heroism, as his son Taro and Ellen's son Billy expect, but about a woman—the epitome of Japanese womanhood—or, at least, Eaton's version of it.

"The Widow of Sanyo" is a preternaturally beautiful young woman who, because of her gender, is barred from the active combat that she wishes she could undertake in service to her country. "What could she do, a helpless maiden? All the employment left to women she scorned. She wanted to do something more than a mere woman could accomplish," Kiyo relates (94). Yet, unlike Fa Mulan, the Chinese "woman warrior" made totemic by Maxine Hong Kingston, she does not prove herself as a soldier but, rather, uses her very femininity to patriotic ends. She asks the local matchmaker to find her a man "so depraved of mind that they prefer not to go to war." She immediately marries the "man-worm" the matchmaker finds for her, but demands that before they can consummate their marriage, he must first enlist and serve his country. As expected, her new husband, cowardly as he is, makes a less than ideal soldier and is killed in short order. She immediately returns to the matchmaker and sends her next husband to the same fate. After she is married and widowed seven times, she decides that because seven is a lucky number, "If I marry another I will have no more luck. He will live, and I have already given seven men already to the Emperor. What woman of Japan has done more?" (102).

The family's reaction to Kiyo's story illustrates the gap between American and Japanese attitudes toward both war and women's place within it. Thirteen-year-old Plum Blossom finds the Widow of Sanyo "beautiful"; Ellen's teenaged daughter, Marion, in contrast, finds her "horrid" (102). Ellen finds the story utterly fantastic, and the widow's actions less than laudable. "What a story to tell children!" she exclaims (100). Kiyo himself admits that the story may have been "foolish"; it nevertheless illustrates his view of true womanly heroism, one that the Americans, Ellen and Marion, obviously neither condone nor understand. Initially, Ellen's attitude toward the Japanese embodies what Vicente Rafael has described as the "touristic sublime"—the willful elevation of the "colonial picturesque" (639, 649). She can see Japanese women only as quaint, pretty, dainty—"playthings," as John Luther Long's Pinkerton and his American wife, Adele, describe Cho-Cho-San—not as brutal, man-killing viragos.

Yet Ellen comes to understand her husband's absolute loyalty to his country, and his desire to defend it, when she discovers that he has been avidly but secretly following the news of the war, reading the newspapers late at night after she has retired. "I understand—everything!" she cries when she discovers the truth at last. "Why did you not tell me before?" Kiyo tries to explain that he has kept it from her because she is an American and therefore would never understand Japanese ways—to which Ellen responds, "It ought to make no difference what I am. I am your wife. Do not treat me as an alien—a stranger" (110). Kiyo is eventually convinced of Ellen's resolve. He declares, "you are my own true wife—not foreign to me, but as my wife should be" (112–113).

From that moment on, Ellen is determined to behave in the proper Japanese fashion. She realizes now that when she has seen Japanese women give up their husbands to war without tears or protest, "It is not because they do not love their husbands. . . . It *is* brave to give up loved ones freely, willingly" (114). From that moment, she forgoes tears and instead turns her attentions to preparing the rest of the family for their father's departure. The Japanese children, of course, are only too happy at their father's "glorious news" that he has decided to enlist. Marion, however, is distraught. Eaton writes,

> She cried out her thoughts in her mother's arms.
>
> "Oh mamma, mamma, hear them singing! Oh!—and papa may be killed, and they are *glad—glad*!"
>
> She had expected her mother at least to understand, and to weep with her, but to her astonishment her mother put her gently from her arms.
>
> "Listen, Marion! Listen, darling, to what they are singing! Don't you know what it is? It is the national hymn, Marion. Oh, my little girl, be brave, too, with them. There is nothing to cry about—nothing—nothing!" (117–118)

After Kiyo leaves, Ellen learns that her support for the war effort involves more than her willingness to "give up her husband." She joins a women's aid society and discovers that "no

Western women's club or society ever worked harder than did these little Japanese women" during the war. She finds the work "a wonderful comfort" (141) because it occupies her time but also because it is a way for her, like the Widow of Sanyo, to contribute to the war by means available to her.

She later carries this mentality over into her own household with the help of her new Japanese family and friends. One day she is told by her mother-in-law, Madame Sano, that other war wives have dismissed their servants, sending them either to help the poor and widowed in this difficult time or to enlist themselves. When she is asked if they too will not dismiss their numerous servants, Ellen initially sees it simply as a matter of economy. "But why?" she asks. "We can afford to keep them, can we not?" She eventually discovers from one of her aid society friends, however, that in the Japanese view, servants, new clothes, and fancy foods must be sacrificed during times of war because "their husbands, sons, fathers, and brothers were suffering hardship and peril. It would be unseemly . . . to live in luxury" (142–143). When she understands this, she immediately dismisses all but the most necessary servants and assigns tasks to the various family members. And she discovers that the children are not only willing but work "cheerfully and happily" (144). Eaton writes, "They who had never known what it was to wash their own bright faces, now joyfully did all such services for themselves and for one another. They were always so busy that they found no time for sadness" (145).

As the novel and the war progress, we witness these and other domestic adjustments made by the various members of the Kurukawa family. Marion eventually becomes nearly as patriotic as her Japanese stepsiblings, while her brother Billy comes to understand that war is not simply about conquest and killings but about a deeper commitment to nation and family. Meanwhile, the Japanese children, who initially see their new mother as an "alien" and a "stranger," come to accept and greatly respect her. These domestic developments, significantly, are described in detailed particulars, whereas the war remains far in the background.[4] News from Kiyo comes in one single, long-awaited letter, and the absence of news finally drives Ellen to Tokyo to find out if he has been killed. After two months of fruitless searching, she receives letters from all of her children urging her to return home. Plum Blossom writes to her, "Earnestly I endeavor to follow your honorable counsel. . . . I praying until you *please* come home with us. Tha's very sad that our father die and go way, but tha's sadder that we lose our mother also" (218).

The sight of her children when she returns makes her exclaim suddenly, "as if she had only just realized it, 'what a lot there is to live for!'" (219). She has the same epiphany experienced by Margaret Paget—that motherhood, more than anything else, gives purpose to a woman's life. Although Ellen has gathered no concrete information regarding Kiyo's safety in Tokyo, she maintains hope that he is still alive. Conjugal, familial, and national love combine in Ellen, so that she becomes, as the novel's title has foreshadowed, "like a flower opening to the sunshine and spring rain. . . . She moved like a new person" (220–221). Buoyed by the love of her family and her faith that Kiyo will return, she in turn transforms the house; "Gloom slipped out of the door and sunshine ventured in with summer," Eaton writes. "And this is as it should be in the house of children" (221).

Kiyo is finally found alive, though wounded; news of his heroism comes by way of his long-lost son Gozo, who has seen the error of his ways and has returned home to his new mother and family. Together, he and Ellen travel to the military hospital where Kiyo is recovering. The changes in Ellen are immediately apparent to her husband. "What a *mother* you are," declares Kiyo when they are reunited. Ellen replies, "Yes . . . that's my strongest trait—maternity. I love all children. There's nothing sweeter in the world than baby arms about one's neck, baby voices, baby kisses, baby touches. Oh, they are the most precious things in life!" And, she adds, "husbands are the biggest babies of all!" (233).

Meanwhile, the family remaining at home prepares the house for Kiyo's homecoming. As Ellen's mother-in-law, Madame Sano, walks through the house, she notes: "From the top to the bottom of the house work was in progress" (240). The entire chapter consists of a room-by-room description of all the furnishings and embellishments and their appropriateness and cleanliness, seen through Madame Sano's eyes. In the course of her observations, Madame Sano notes that even Ellen's "long, white, foreign bed seemed not at all out of place" in the bedroom. The children all pitch in, and the servants too are filled with joyful anticipation; one of the cook's assistants, at the very end of the chapter, breaks into a song "of war, furious, glorious war!" as she prepares the homecoming meal (245). When the dishes are submitted for Madame Sano's approval in the absence of Ellen, she declares that "the okusama would be honorably pleased, indeed" (244). Whereas Madame Sano had to instruct Ellen in the appropriate behavior of a Japanese wife earlier in the novel, here she judges and approves of Ellen's housekeeping—a testament to Ellen's successful "blossoming" into a full womanhood that takes the best from the American and the Japanese. As Kiyo walks through the door, he declares that the house is "the most beautiful place on earth" (250). The novel ends in domestic bliss, the reunited family in their beautiful home, living in perfect harmony.

According to Dominika Ferens, this novel "condemns war and brutality" even as "the Russo-Japanese war provides the narrative with a glamorous, titillating backdrop" (165). I would argue instead that *A Japanese Blossom* attempts to naturalize Japanese militarism and, by extension, the Japanese in general, by describing it in terms of American domestic nationalism. Eaton's choice to pair an American woman with a Japanese man enables her to show that Kiyo, not only in spite of but because of his samurai heritage, is the quintessential family man: kind, respectful of his wife, adoring yet not overindulgent with his children. Far from an embodiment of the yellow peril—inscrutable, mysterious, malevolent, a potential enslaver of white women—he is "ebullient with humor and good nature" (30). He is loved by his whole family, including his "little Yankee girl," Marion (192), who cries more than anyone else at her stepfather's parting. His desire to fight in the war results not from blood lust but from national love—a "greater, deeper emotion" even than fatherhood (106).

If stereotypes about Japanese men are challenged in this novel, so too are ideas regarding ideal American womanhood. Ellen Kurukawa is the quintessential American woman who nevertheless easily adapts to Japanese life. She dresses in "the national kimono" (85), as does her daughter, Marion, who realizes the "dear old loose thing" is simply *"comfy"* in comparison to the stiff starched frocks to which she had been previously accustomed (61). She eats Japanese foods with "relish" (133). She quickly learns to speak Japanese "with more than usual fluency," and within the first weeks of arriving in Japan "her husband's friends in the town were hers" (172, 141). In fact, those very qualities that make her a good wife and mother in America—self-sacrifice, loyalty, devotion—not only enable but require her easy assimilation of Japanese ways. "I did not require that *you* should become like my people," she tells Kiyo. "*I,* as your wife, was willing to become one of you" (113).

In *Herland,* Charlotte Perkins Gilman also reversed the presumed assimilation of one's husband's nationality. Yet whereas Eaton's reversal makes her white heroine adopt her Asian husband's nationality (rather than the customary story of an Asian woman adopting American ways, as Cho-Cho-San did when she married Pinkerton), Gilman's American male adventurers are expected to adopt the national customs of the Herlanders—an expectation that none of the men are prepared to meet. Vandyck Jennings described their frustrations in this way:

> You see, in any other imaginable marriage among the peoples of the earth, whether the woman were black, red, yellow, brown, or white; whether she were ignorant or educated, submissive or rebellious, she would have behind her the marriage tradition of

our general history. This tradition relates the woman to the man. He goes on with his business, and she adapts herself to him and to it. Even in citizenship, by some strange hocus-pocus, that fact of birth and geography was waved aside, and the woman automatically acquired the nationality of her husband. (120–121)

In both cases, Eaton and Gilman expose the logical contradictions between nationalistic and gender ideology that seemed so natural to their American readers and, in both cases, few were ready to change their views. A reviewer snidely remarked, "American wives have devoted their husbands to a country before, but it was not to Japan."[5] To be sure, Eaton's complete lack of irony in presenting American readers with a family most of them would find "monstrous," to use Madison Grant's description of mixed-race unions, was naïve. Many of Eaton's readers believed that the Japanese were an inferior race, found lynching a just punishment for a black man who was seen consorting with (or simply looking at) a white woman, and suspected that mixed-race children were mentally and morally deficient. If anything, the Kurukawas would be a threat—yet another example of race suicide rather than part of its solution.

Even those who were the strongest advocates of the Japanese would have found *A Japanese Blossom* difficult to accept. Like Ellen Kurukawa, Mary (Mrs. Hugh) Fraser, the wife of a British ambassador to Japan, was thrust into Japanese society at a time of national turmoil—the years immediately preceding the 1894–1895 war between Japan and China. She published her recollection of her years spent in Japan in the widely read *Letters to Japan: A Record of Modern Life in the Island Empire* (1899). Despite the pressing international interests that have brought her husband to the "land of the samurai," she intends to focus on the domestic side—the Japanese way of life—during her sojourn. She writes,

I would rather not have a host of first impressions of the ordinary kind, which, as it seems to me, satisfy meagre minds, and prevent their ever really understanding new places and races. I have talked to people who had brought nothing away from Japan but the recollection of a waiting-maid and a tea-house, or one brain photograph of a short dark man dressed in unbecoming clothes. Others have seen a procession, or a dinner with chopsticks, or a missionary school, and keep all their lives one silly memory of the strangest country in the world. . . . I should like to understand a little, to love or hate, to praise discerningly or condemn dispassionately—to make a friend, in fine. (1:1–2)

During her stay in Japan, she probably gets to know the country and people better than any Western woman before her. She lauds the "innate refinement" of the Japanese girls and women she meets, both from the noble and working classes (1:304); she starts a reading group for her Japanese friends (2:190–195); she and her husband decide to build a Japanese-style house in the country. The warmth of her feelings for Japan and the Japanese people are evident on practically every page.

Yet she never attains the same accord with the Japanese that Ellen Kurukawa achieves in *A Japanese Blossom*. Though sympathetic to the utmost degree, Fraser also makes clear that she still sees them as a fundamentally different race. She never for a moment considers abandoning her Victorian-style dress, despite the fact that it is both "uncongenial" (1:29) and a constant source of wonderment to the natives (1:118). Finding "rice and pickles" less than tempting (1:99), she takes as evidence of refinement her Japanese friends' decision to replace traditional foods with French haute cuisine. (She herself, it turns out, prefers "American cookery" [1:104].) Although she comes into close contact with various Japanese noblewomen, including the empress of Japan herself, most of her experiences of everyday Japanese life—the aspect of Japan she initially intends to study— come from distant observation: from her room at the British Legation, from her hotel window, from official ceremonies and festivals. It would obviously be unladylike to get any closer. At one point she encounters a fellow Englishman, "a tall, smart-looking man, sitting in native cotton dress . . . laughing and chattering in fluent Japanese with a swarm of Atami girls." She is curious to meet him; she thinks his face is "a familiar one" and admires his "clear brown eyes and strong happy face." However, she ends up keeping her distance because "his dress was poor and common in the extreme." She decides he "was probably one of those harmless maniacs who travel every-where . . . and try to see the country from the Japanese side of life" (2:118). From Fraser's elevated and only partially open window (both literally and metaphorically), the "Japanese side of life" remains largely on the level of caricature—and in the end, the common folk are simply "vulgar and profane" (1:143), even if they are amusing.

It is difficult to imagine that Fraser would have wanted to emulate Ellen Kurukawa. Those who were sympathetic to the Japanese could not identify with the character, while those who were wholly unsympathetic, such as the reviewer quoted above, found her altogether distasteful. Eaton's misjudgment of her audience was reflected in *A Japanese Blossom*'s low sales, un-usual for Eaton's books, especially considering the success of her two previous novels, *The Love of Azalea* and *The Daughters of Nijo,* both from 1904.

Ironically, Eaton seemed to foreshadow the inability of her readers to truly sympathize with the Japanese in the depiction of Ellen Kurukawa's Irish servant, Norah. Norah never accli-mates to life in Japan; from the beginning, when Ellen and the rest of her family are introduced to Kiyo's Japanese children, it is Norah's face that "frightened them most" (30). Given charge of the baby, she takes his carriage outside of the Kurukawas' garden because she finds the garden too small for a good stroll and also because she is homesick. Outside the walls, she be-lieves, she might find another Irish person, in the form of a policeman if nothing else. What she wouldn't do, she sighs, for "the soight of the face of a foine cop!" (63).

As she wheels the baby's carriage down the street, she finds herself surrounded by "a fine lot of haythens" who have gath-ered in wonderment of this "most extraordinary looking foreign devil, a giant in size, pushing an outlandish jinrikisha" in front of her (64–65). "Off wid you all, or Oi'll make short worruk of the boonch of yez," she threatens; when they fail to disperse, she lays to, "spanking a little boy on her right, pushing along by the ear another, and cuffing a giggling maiden of fifteen" (66). At this, the crowd of "haythens" becomes "aggressive" and surrounds her even more closely. Her cries of "Murdher! Hilp!" do succeed in bringing one of Tokyo's finest to the scene, but to poor Norah's increasing consternation, he not only isn't Irish, he arrests her for disturbing the peace.

"Oh, wirrah, wirrah, wirrah!" is her constant lament. "And why did I iver lave the ould country? And why did I iver come to this haythen land of savages?" she cries (68). When Ellen goes in search of Kiyo, Norah offers her resignation. She writes that although "I like you very much, mam, and I love the precious lambs . . . I must go back to the old country, for I cannot bear so much trouble. . . . Will you buy my ticket, please mam?" (218). The trials and tribulations of poor Norah, expressed through her overwrought dialect, are largely intended as comic relief. Yet her response to Japan, as stereotyped as it is, is still somehow easier to swallow than Ellen's bottomless well of understanding and wisdom.

In fact, Norah may have provided a way for Eaton to abandon (if temporarily) the Japanese genre that had become problematic with the changing times. Her next novel, *The Diary of Delia* (1907), is told from the first-person perspective of the live-in Irish domestic employed by a New York family. As with Norah in *A Japanese Blossom,* much of the humor in *The Diary of Delia* comes from Eaton's exploitation of national stereotypes. Delia's "diary" is rendered in the same kind of dialect as Norah's speech in *A Japanese Blossom,* and her observations reveal her lower-class immigrant background. Accompanying the Wolley family to the country house they are renting for the summer, she writes, "It's a wild wilderniss of a place is this and its hard indade for a pure loansum innercent female to bare the silence of the atmustfear. Whin Miss Claire a spoke of the country

I had thort of Asbry Park or Coney Island and such like sinsible places, but indade theres no boardwalk here at all at all and the only kinds of bands and orkistrys is in the trees. Wirra, wirra, wirra!" (39). At the same time, however, Eaton juxtaposes Delia's humorous misunderstandings with the equally laughable foibles of the family she serves. The Wolleys are a typical "modern" family of New York City's upper middle class. The daughter, Claire, pictured in the novel's illustrations as a Gibsonesque beauty, is a plucky yet easily flummoxed "New Woman"; her older brother, John, is a bookish editor of an unnamed New York magazine; her younger brother James is a muckraking newspaper journalist. Mrs. Wolley is obsessively concerned with keeping up proper appearances for the other families on "the Point"; Mr. Wolley, "the auld gintleman," rises at ten and appears to do little but rail dyspeptically at the crumbling state of civilization.

The book is loosely structured around a triple romance: Claire marries the son of her father's sworn enemy, John marries the sensible young widow across the street, and Delia herself is won over by the Irish servant next door. Each character marries someone of similar ethnic background within his or her class, thus providing a marked contrast to the Japanese romances, whose heroines moved freely between and among groups. Yet, as Ferens has pointed out, Eaton's decision to tell the story in Delia's voice has the "unexpected result of leveling all the characters, whatever their class" (176). The class leveling of Delia's narration is not the result of any conscious criticism or attack on Delia's part; on the contrary, she is steadfastly loyal to her employers and seemingly oblivious to their faults. But her unwittingly insightful observations and unintentionally appropriate malapropisms cleverly forward Eaton's lampoon. John, for example, who usually has a more than healthy appetite, refuses one day to eat breakfast. Rattling his newspaper "the way he has of doing when provoked," he requests only a cup of hot water. Delia asks him why. "'I'm dying Delia' ses he," she writes. "'Dying!' ses I, shocked so that I drapped and broke the china in me hands" (4–5). John clarifies that he is "Dy-et-ing," not "dying," but it is all the same to her—that eating could be a luxury, something to be denied on a whim, makes no sense to someone in Delia's circumstances.

Eaton reserves most of her barbs, however, for the new-fangled ideas about housekeeping that young Claire imposes on the family and, in turn, the family's only halfhearted commitment to progressive ideas. When Delia, at the encouragement of her hard-nosed friend and fellow domestic Minnie, quits her position to look for a better-paying one, Claire proudly declares that they "can get on famissly widout her" (17). A week later, however, she appears at the employment agency where Delia has been seeking a new position and reveals that her attempt at housekeeping has been an abject failure. She initially took on the cooking herself, to the howling protests of the other family members, and afterwards hired and dismissed eleven other servants. As Delia relates in her diary, Claire sobs, "I did thry to do my best, but its like attempting to pleese a family of porkypines since you left" (34). Moreover, since they have decided to take a house in the country for the summer, they "*must* have a girl. It's dredful to think of being widout one" (35).

Delia agrees to return, mostly out of pity for the family, of whom she is truly fond. But she demands a reduction of responsibilities. "I'm for uther wark than gineral housework," she tells Claire (36). In acquiescence to her wishes, Claire takes on the role of housekeeper herself and assigns household tasks to the other members of the family—just as Ellen Kurukawa did in *A Japanese Blossom.* "Iverybody . . . has got to do his indivijool share of work," Delia reports that Claire says. "The lons must be cut. A garden must be planted. Frish vegitables are absolootly nicissiry" (48). Thus she assigns the mowing of the lawns to James; John is tasked with livery duty; Mr. Wolley is to go to town to pick up the mail; Mrs. Wolley is given the care of the chickens; and, as for Claire herself, she says, "as my cheef and spechul jooty outside of the hivvy housekaping wid the constant tack and diplomassy it intales to kape our unsertin Delia, I will undertake to—er—rayse sweet *flowers* for the beutifying of our lons and house" (54). Delia, of course, is still left with the primary tasks of cooking and "light housekeeping"—sweeping, dusting, and washing.

Despite their supposedly enlightened perspectives, the family members are reluctant to accept their duties. James, the bohemian journalist, cries "in thoondering toans, 'I cut lons! Why me deer sister its aginst me most artistick instink. . . . Do you mane to assert that the fat broaker who kapes his lons and drives clane as a well swipt parlor has the same artistick sinse as the chap who lets his grarss grow gracefully aloft?" (45–46). John claims never to have "handled a horse in me life," and draws "the line at stable work" (52). Mr. Wolley agrees to go for the mail only if they keep a horse—at the local livery stable, since John will not take on the responsibility himself. Mrs. Wolley, after wholeheartedly agreeing with Claire's assignments for James and John, balks at the idea of tending the coop. "Aren't there such things as—er—lice—connected with chickens?" (54). "You're all just horrid," Claire cries. But thanks to a combination of parental fiat and the family's real inability to pay for an adequate staff, they undertake their respective duties: James, despite his "artistick instink," is to cut the grass once a week; John (winning his point about the livery stable) is to raise "addicut vigitables for the table"; Mr. Wolley will ride for the mail; Mrs. Wolley will feed the chickens (it is assumed that Delia will keep the coop lice-free); and Claire and Delia will do the cooking and housework. Even six-year-old Billy, the youngest child, is assigned the task "of carrying water to the hungry thoorsty wans what toyle" (65).

This attempt at "collective housekeeping" gets off to a promising, if rocky, start. Delia is amazed to find Claire, "slaves" rolled up and apron on, digging a bed for her "flouring hidge" (60). Her pockets "boolging out" with gardening books, she declares that her "gardin will be one glow of luvliness from spring till frorst" (60). Meanwhile, the family wakes to find the "lons" freshly cut by James, who "sonters in" to breakfast at eight "frish from his after cutting lon bath" (67). Mr. Wolley appears to relish going for the mail, despite the "infernul evil smelling noysy cursed cars" that have overtaken the roadways of late (71). The widow who lives across the street stumbles upon them as they are "all ingaged at our respictuf toyle," as Claire describes it, and declares, "What fun! . . . How perfeckly deliteful. It mus be just like playing, isn't it" (92–93).

Within a week, however, the scheme has become a shambles. John decides he has grown "tired of this gardin bisiness," and imposes on Delia to plant the seeds, even though she tells him that she is "oop to me ears" in work (77). He gives her the seed packets along with a book with "fool instruckshuns" on seed planting. He buys her silence with a dollar and warns her only to "do it whenever the feeld is cleer." Mr. Wolley discovers that James has overcome both his "artistick instink" and his reform-ist scruples and has hired an Italian—a "dago," as Delia refers to him—to mow the lawns every morning before the family is awake. Even Claire fails to hold up her end of the bargain. After finishing her "floury hidge," she commences on the beds but asks Delia to "do the digging for me like an angel" (80). The end result, as Delia writes to her friend Minnie, is that "wid the wark of a family of six to do, besides helping Mr. James to cut the lons, Mr. John to plant the gardin, whitewashing of the chicken coop for Mrs. Wolley, I'm clane doon up whin nite cums" (101).

According to family lore, Eaton's send-up may have been based on the experiences of a real family that lived nearby the small suburban estate she and her first husband Bertrand Babcock purchased in Westchester in 1905. Regardless of its basis in fact, however, Eaton's story drew on characters and situations that would have been familiar to any reader of con-temporary magazines. Historian Daniel Sutherland noted that pieces discussing and debating the "servant problem"—a criti-cal shortage of domestic labor and the perceived deterioration of domestic service—dominated the popular press into the 1920s

(169), appearing side by side with domestic scientists' and social reformers' suggestions for reorganizing household labor
along the lines that Miss Claire attempts to follow in the novel.[6]
"Americans devoured any and all information concerning management of households and servants," he continues (171). Yet
despite the democratic impulse that lay beyond many of the
new schemes and the willingness with which American housekeepers embraced them, very few of the reforms actually took
hold. Even Lucy Salmon, whose monograph *Domestic Service*
(1901) became a sort of bible to domestic reformers, failed to
implement her own methods. Sutherland writes that she was
"plagued by an endless history of servant problems. She treated
her domestics . . . in accordance with all of her carefully formu-
lated principles. Yet something always went awry. Whether
because her methods were unsatisfactory or because her servants were unreceptive, nothing could halt the procession of
workers parading through her kitchen" (176).

Some writers on the subject recognized that the greatest impediment to solving the servant problem was the practically
ineradicable social stigma of housework. Harriet Prescott
Spofford wrote, "It is not the circumstance that servants are
called servants which makes the trouble. It is that we do not
think highly enough of them as a class; that we are apt to
regard their work as degrading and themselves as automata;
that too frequently we feel about them as if they were as different a race from ourselves as though they were chimpanzees"
(13). In one of the very few instances where a servant's point of
view was actually put into print, one woman corroborated
Spofford's assessment. She wrote, "Leaving the question of thir-
teen, fourteen, or fifteen hours a day of hard drudgery out, I
cannot see why any one of pride and spirit would choose that
kind of work. . . . The negroes in the South have as much chance
of social recognition as have those who do domestic service in
the North."[7]

The analogy that both Spofford and the unnamed servant
above drew between class and race was not wholly accidental.

Spofford, whose tract on the servant question was first published in 1881, recognized the effect that the influx of immigrant labor in the domestic sphere had on "degrading" the occupation as a whole. "It is not upon nationality nor upon religion that the trouble hinges altogether," she wrote, but she stressed that "these things have very much to do with it. You may think, for instance, that nothing could be worse than your Irish girl, till you get an African one; the Swede who takes the latter's place is only good while she is fresh . . . the sprightliness of the French maid is as aggravating in its own way, and the stolidity of the German makes you long for the blarneying tongue of Bridget once more" (17). Or as Salmon put it, "the class line which was only faintly drawn in the early part of the [nineteenth] century between employer and 'help' has been changed into a caste line. . . . The native born American fears to lose social position by entering into competition with foreign labor" (65).[8]

The problem of class and "caste," as Salmon described it, touched Eaton especially. It dominated her 1907 essay "The Japanese in America," which was a refutation of a *New York Times* article supporting the San Francisco school board's recent decision to segregate Asians in separate schools. The primary point in the *Times* article to which she objects is the writer's claim that segregation is justified because the Japanese are racially inferior, only fit to be servants to white Americans—a "servile race." Eaton acknowledges the fact that the only Japanese immigrants with which most Americans have had contact are indeed domestic servants. But, she writes, "the fact that California knows the individual Japanese as a domestic servant does not make of the Japanese a servile race" (103). She continues, "We are all servants—of various sorts. I serve you, for whom I write. You serve your customers, or your clients. Shall each one of us kick at the one below us?" (104).

Eaton was not the first to point out the relativistic state of servitude; Spofford, for example, wrote, "In more or less degree we all serve each other; one serves with service, another serves with money; the public pays its servants with money and with honors, its servants strive for its situations, and glory in the name" (12). But the reformers sought to break down the social barrier between domestic service and other occupations for different reasons than Eaton's. Most of those who suggested ways to eradicate the social stigma of domestic labor did so not to "elevate" the immigrants who performed it but rather to make it a more acceptable occupation for more desirable native-born girls and women. One writer, after recommending that employers of live-in maids reduce working hours, allow callers, and encourage their servants' participation in family activities, wrote, "Oh, my gentle reader, I can see your eyebrows lifting and your lips curling, but a maid so treated . . . stays with you as long as you let her." She continued, "I like a well bred American maid in my kitchen, probably you do the same; but they are scarce. . . . If your work wears down the constitution of the hearty foreign girl how could an American endure it? And yet you fret about ignorant foreigners and sigh for trained American help" (Godman 2464). Salmon takes great pains to show the historical factors at the root of "the unwillingness of American women to engage in work stigmatized by an offensive term applied to no other class of laborers," and directs her reforms to making domestic service more attractive (72). Spofford goes so far as to argue that unless domestic service be made a more socially acceptable occupation, housekeepers will need to turn to their "last resort"—the labor of Chinese men. Tempted by rumors of the efficiency of "John Chinaman," the low wages and inferior food he is willing to accept as payment, she warns her readers of the housewife who

> dreads a little, to be sure, the innovation of the cued and trowsered man where she has been wont to see only the woman of flounced petticoats and frizzled hair; she would prefer to have things . . . as they were in her grandmother's day, but knows that is already past question and past cure; and although the strangers upset her habits of thought . . . visions of a spotless

and faultless pantry and scullery, the work of their hands, dance before her eyes. . . . if the Irish girl will still give her no rest, and the American girl refuse her succor, she will find out some honorable way to bring John Chinaman to her rescue! (180–181)

Clearly, "John Chinaman" is a solution to be avoided at all costs.

Eaton, in contrast, defends domestic service as an occupation precisely for the sake of the "yellow Jap," "John Chinaman," "Bridget," and "Nora." In "The Japanese in America," she writes, "The 'social ostracism' of certain races is a sad thing, indeed; but when it strikes at a proud and noble people it is not only sad—it is foolhardy" (103). She defends the Japanese servant as "a self-respecting, clean, decent person, who in his very character has elevated the station of the servant. . . . He comes of a race which deems no employment degrading" (103–104). Employers' "contempt" of their servants, she warns, will leave them not only without the native-born servants who are already so scarce but without servants altogether, for even "the meanest Japanese has pride" (104). Eaton goes on to extend her understanding of the plight of the Japanese servant to servants of other races and nations, proclaiming, "I am not Oriental or Occidental either, but Eurasian. I must bleed for both my nations. I am Irish more than English—Chinese as well as Japanese. Both my fatherland and my motherland have been the victims of injustice and oppression" (104). Scholars have noted that this was one of the only times she ever directly acknowledged her actual Chinese background. It was also one of the few times she acknowledged her Irish heritage (her father was half Irish), which was equally notable since it aligned her with the predominant, and most objectionable, ethnic groups performing domestic service on both coasts.

Eaton clearly felt as much an outsider in the affluent world of the New York suburbs as her Irish servant Delia, for whom the "country" meant nothing more rural than Coney Island. In "A Neighbor's Garden, My Own, and a Dream One," published in *Good Housekeeping* in 1908, she describes, in the voice of

5. *An early-twentieth-century "do-it-yourself" suburban garden. (Bailey, plate X.)*

Onoto Watanna, her own experiences setting out a garden on the "frowsy acre" surrounding their country house in Westchester. Brought up knowing only the "ugly hotel window ledge, or the roof of some city house" on which her mother carefully nurtured the "seeds and slips" of plants she had brought with her from Japan (347), she is initially mystified and intimidated by the spectacular gardens of her neighbors, who live in "sumptuous . . . mansions set amid grounds kept as perfect and smooth as a well-swept parlor" (348; figure 5). She finds her "unshorn lawns and overgrown carriage drives . . . a reproach to an otherwise immaculate community" and believes her neighbors must be "convinced I am an eccentric" (348). Despite her desire, Onoto is daunted by her lack of a hired gardener and the exorbitant cost—the previous owner of her house, an actress, boasted that she spent five hundred dollars yearly on plantings.

It is her nursemaid, Norah, who shows her a means of entering this forbidding yet enticing world: by crawling under the fence. She appears one day with "a great bunch of lilies-of-the-valley in her hand, and a mass of buttercups in her apron"

(349). In her glee, Onoto demands to be shown the source of these lovely flowers, and is taken by Norah to a corner of their yard. She initially sees nothing, at which point Norah "kneeled down and put her hand under the fence. Lilies! I turned pale, kneeled also and looked" (350). Having discovered a source of flowers under the fence, she convinces Norah to help her look over it, which she does with some trepidation, giving "a cautious look at the rather frowning looking" house on the other side. Here she finds exactly the kind of garden she has been dreaming of for her own: "filled with old-fashioned and odorous flowers," including honeysuckle and hyacinths as well as lilies of the valley (350). She decides to search out the owner of this garden and to find others like it. "There must be gardens somewhere," she tells Norah. "If the people don't call on me, I'll call on them, or rather on their gardens, and if they snub me, Norah, I'll send you over to *steal* their flowers. You do get your hand so beautifully under fences" (350).

Though Norah is suitably scandalized by her mistress' plan, she remains a steadfast ally in Onoto's quest to create a garden to rival those of her neighbors. With her experience as a servant, Norah in fact is more familiar with the expectations and mannerisms of these suburbanites than Onoto is. When several of them come to call, Norah demands that Onoto change out of her "decent skirt and waist, the latter with sleeves rolled comfortably to the elbows," and into more appropriate dress for entertaining visitors. "There's three grand ladies in yer parlor!" she cries. "Hurry!"

The relationship that Eaton depicts in this piece is less of one between mistress and maid than one of conspirators in class transgression; like Norah, Onoto figuratively creeps under the fences of her neighbors and steals their secrets for her own.[9] Though she initially feels "very ignorant and awed" in the presence of her gardening neighbors, she is inspired to follow their example. Mrs. C, the neighbor whose beautiful garden Onoto has coveted, boasts to her that the informal garden behind the house contains "not a flower . . . that I did not plant or raise myself." Onoto takes this statement at face value and is inspired by it. "If a woman of the age of my neighbor (she was about fifty-five) could with her own hands set out an plant a garden, why could not I, young, healthy and ambitious, do likewise?" (484). She takes the roots and seeds her neighbors give her and sets to work digging; "How I dug! And dug! It was hard, hard work, but I kept at it till my back ached and I was as grimy as a hired man" (484).

After her initial consultation with her neighbors, Onoto is determined to make good on her own, armed with nothing more than gardening books, seed catalogs, and her uninformed common sense. Her beds, like Claire's "floury hidge," turn out disastrously—she plants four-foot-tall flowers in her window boxes and mistakes her seedlings for weeds. Onoto is ashamed to tell anyone about it, especially since Mrs. C suffers under the delusion that Onoto, like "all of [her] countrywomen," is "a natural gardener." But she finally reveals the truth about her garden. After seeing Mrs. C's garden in full summer bloom, she cries, "And you planted it all yourself? What an utter little failure I must appear to you!" (489). Mrs. C then makes her own surprising revelation. "It was then she made to me a queer confession," Eaton writes. "The garden was her own personal handiwork, she could truthfully say. But she had hired men (strong-armed men, who are good for so much in this world) to do the digging—*and* the weeding!" (489). With this, Onoto realizes that she is, in fact, less than a failure.

> The digging! Why, that was what had discouraged me from the first. At the outset to be fronted with the heavy labor of a man.
>
> And the weeding! How could *I* tell a weed from a flower in its infancy? But the practiced eye of a regular gardener could at the outset have discerned the difference.
>
> "Next year," say I, "I, too, will have a man." (489)

Mrs. C's confession, in effect, allows Onoto (and Eaton) entrance into this alien, suburban world—she now has the knowledge to join them in their gardening successes. Eaton's essay, in turn, reveals the hired (and often immigrant) labor that lay behind the seemingly practical, do-it-yourself atmosphere of the gardening advice books and columns that had become so popular at the turn of the century. These books, predominantly written by "commuters' wives," as historian Beverly Seaton describes them, emphasized "the theme of the woman doing the garden work" ("Gardening Books" 44). Even if the hired gardener actually appeared in the photographs that illustrated various methods of bed preparation, planting, and weeding—as he did in several illustrations from Ida D. Bennett's popular *Flower Garden: A Handbook of Practical Garden Lore* (1903)—he usually remained "a nameless character in the garden drama. . . . The role of the male in the woman's flower garden was that of the animated shovel, or as Sophia Johnson called him in the nineteenth century, 'Mr. O'Shovelem'" ("Gardening Books" 45).[10]

In "A Neighbor's Garden," "The Japanese in America," and above all, *The Diary of Delia,* Eaton directs attention to the silent (and silenced) workers who made the domestic ideal possible for most well-to-do American women. Although the popular press raged with ideas about managing this labor, few made any real effort to see the situation from their perspective. Most viewed the immigrant laborer in the same way that Lily Bart, the heroine of Edith Wharton's *The House of Mirth,* did: an utterly debased yet vaguely threatening presence. The charwoman who sells Lawrence Selden's letters to Lily symbolizes "the kind of vileness of which people whispered, but which she had never thought of as touching her own life" (82; figure 6).

Even those who truly were sympathetic to immigrant women workers felt more pity for them than a sense of communion with them. "'Protection' is the key word, not 'equality,'" writes historian Doris Weatherford (xvi). The exposés written by numerous women journalists and sociologists who posed for a few days or weeks as women laborers focused not so much on the women they were impersonating but the terrible working

6. *Lily Bart and the charwoman. (Illustration from the serial publication of* The House of Mirth, *by Edith Wharton, published in* Scribner's *[1905].)*

conditions they suffered. Moreover, they overwhelmingly stressed the need for upper-class, educated women to provide working women with a gentrifying influence, an object of aspiration. Laura Hapke writes that these writers "preach[ed] about a female underclass so prone to workplace temptations, mili-

tance, and vulgar conduct that uplifting rescue is for the few";
yet at the same time, they "could not shed the ideology of
uplift" (66–67).

The helplessness of these women in the face of oppressive
conditions was almost universally assumed. The German immigrant mother of Theodore Dreiser's *Jennie Gerhardt* (1911),
for example, is described as "helpless," "timid," "hopeless," "over-
awed," "nervous," and "abashed"—all in the first chapter alone.
The senator who takes notice of her and her beautiful, naïve
daughter (with whom he eventually has an affair) remarks to
himself that "there's something very pathetic about those people"
(15) and later, that there is something "exceedingly pathetic"
about Jennie in particular (22). The pathos in Jennie's character
comes from her vague and passive yearning for upward mobility. "Isn't it fine to be rich?" she asks her mother (9). "It must be
nice to be famous" (16). Her aspirations mirror her literary pre-
decessor Carrie Meeber's vague desire for fame and fortune,
which she fulfills, though through no clear agency of her own.
Dreiser writes that Carrie "was created with that passivity of
soul which is always the mirror of the active world" (150).

The passivity of working-class women, especially domestics, and their reluctance or inability to express their views on
the servant problem and on their lives in general is reflected in
the scarcity of their writings. Daniel Sutherland notes that although the "majority of servants could both read and write,"
they remained "part of history's inarticulate mass." He specu-
lates that aside from being too busy and exhausted from their
labors, they may have remained silent because "they had no
incentive to write—no one to write to and no desire to write
even if they had a correspondent" (202). This reluctance to put
their experience in words comes through in the few texts that
do exist. One writer, telling the story of her maid, describes her
as "very taciturn," despite the clear indication that she was "quite
a superior girl" (Angstman 91). Another piece, "The Story of an
Irish Cook," which appeared in the *Independent* in 1905, began,
"I don't know why anybody wants to hear my history" (715).

The servants' problems with the "servant problem" thus remained contained within a supposedly private, domestic sphere.

Reticence, however, is completely foreign to Delia's character. She is nothing if not vocal. When she relents to Claire's pleading to return to her post, her first order of business is to write a "warning" to the family, "in plane litters and langwidge," which she posts "artiskully upon the dining-room door—facing all eyes" (figure 7). Later, unexpected guests arrive for lunch, and she is forced to make do with one can of potted ham and leftover mashed potatoes. When family members snidely refer to her creation as "patty de 4 grass a la Delia" and "snow hash," Delia goes on a rampage. She reveals to the assembled family and guests that she has fed them all using one can of potted ham. "Shure the potted stuff is good enuff for you," she cries.

> Wid that I wint into the pantry and got the can and tuk it into the dining-room and showed it to the silent family.
>
> "Is it misdoubting me word ye are" ses I. "Then see for yersilves." And I showed them the can wid its pretty ligind: "Guvvymint inspeckshun."
>
> Mr. James got up and left the room. Mr. Wolley, groonting, followed.
>
> "Excuse me!" ses I and walked out also. (82)

Written entirely from Delia's perspective, her voice dominates the text. Her "plane litters" boldly "face all eyes." Although the voice of Eaton's actual Irish servant is obviously filtered through Eaton's authorial consciousness, it is a consciousness that does not pity her, as Dreiser clearly pities Jennie Gerhardt and other girls like her, but rather joins her in her demand for common human courtesy and consideration. This, in the end, is worth far more to Delia than social advancement. But if *The Diary of Delia* is not the novel of class mobility that readers today might find more palatable, neither is it a novel of class containment. The strength of Delia's character and the stridency of her voice overwhelm all the others—even the "thoondering

7. *Delia's "artistick creation."* (Diary of Delia 44.)

toans" of the muckraker, James. She subjects them all—and their misguided, if progressive, ideas and attitudes—to her own "langwidge."

In *A Japanese Blossom,* Eaton used the voice of American domestic ideology to naturalize the seemingly alien aspects of Japanese culture. Doing so, in turn, made strange the familiar terms of that very ideology. *The Diary of Delia,* in contrast, used the accent of the foreigner to cast a gently satiric light on the seemingly progressive perspectives of the modern American upper class. In both cases, Eaton focused on the domestic space as a site for cultural and ideological exchange rather than simply one of conflict and oppression. Her ability to speak from both sides—as an American suburban wife *and* as a foreigner, an "alien"—enabled her to show the way these two seemingly distant worlds were mutually constitutive.

T H R E E

Me: A Book of Remembrance and the *"Woman of Genius"*

The dear woman had written a hundred stories,
but none so curious as her own.
—Henry James, "Greville Fane"

"A Man of Genius, you said?"
"Yes, he failed in art and actually admitted it—
then went into business and succeeded."
—*New York Times,* 1904

WINNIFRED EATON may inspire as much curiosity among her readers today as she did at the height of her popularity a century ago. Scholars have rooted among crumbling magazines, newspapers on microfilm, and archival collections in their attempt to gain a sense of who she was—who she *really* was—and how she was perceived by her contemporaries.[1] Most of all, they have turned to her purported autobiography, *Me: A Book of Remembrance* (1915) for her life story. Because here Eaton was speaking in what scholars assumed was her own voice, they have hoped that this text could fill an early gap in Asian American literary history. But though Eaton promises in the opening chapter that "this story is frankly of myself" (4), scholars have been frustrated by how little Eaton actually reveals about herself in the text and, especially, how little she says about her ethnicity. Aside from a few glancing references to her "foreign" looks and her mother's exotic ancestry as a "tightrope dancer" from a "faraway land," the novel primarily concerns a young woman's struggles in the worlds of work, writing, and romance in turn-of-the-century Chicago. Annette White-Parks is clearly disgusted with Eaton's presumed reticence regarding her ethnicity when she describes *Me* as a "denial of racism" (34). Others have attributed Eaton's fabrications and dissimulations— her decision to publish her autobiography anonymously, her decision to give her heroine a distinctly "white" name, Nora Ascough, and her refusal to pinpoint Nora's identity as half Chinese—as moves of necessity, since if she had revealed the truth about herself, she would have undermined the validity of a biography that she had taken great pains to create and on which she based her literary success.[2]

Therefore, critics have largely looked to Eaton's next novel, *Marion: The Story of an Artist's Model* (1916), for Eaton's "ethnic autobiography."[3] Although this story did not center on Eaton but her sister Sara (named "Marion" in both *Me* and *Marion*), Eaton did describe in detail how she and her siblings were treated by their Montreal neighbors and how the Eaton children's Chinese ancestry becomes a factor in their relationships with each other, their parents, and potential romantic partners. This text, in contrast to *Me,* gave literary scholars what they were looking for: anguished depictions of cultural difference, incidents of both accommodation and resistance, and experiences of discrimination. Early in the novel, Marion overhears gossip at the corner store, and thinks: "I felt ashamed and humiliated to hear our family thus discussed. Why should we always be pointed out in this way and made to feel conspicuous and freaky? It was horrid that the size of our family and my mother's nationality should be told to everyone" (1–2). *Me* never even approaches this level of frankness. Linda Trinh Moser, in her afterword to the 1998 reprint of *Me,* notes that the "textual silence regarding Eaton's Chinese ancestry makes it difficult to read *Me* as an autobiography, let alone an ethnic one" but main-

tains that "it is not impossible" to do so (358). In making her
argument, she relies on what she claims "has long been described as an 'interlocking' synthesis of race, class, and gender
oppression in the lives of women of color" (364). Reading race
into incidents involving class and gender, she somewhat vaguely
concludes that the novel reveals the general "internalized oppression experienced by racial 'others'" (372).

To a large extent, the frustration experienced by present-day
critics and scholars when confronted with Eaton's autobiographical text comes by way of comparison. Edith, writing under the
Chinese-derived pseudonym Sui Sin Far, published an autobiographical essay several years before the publication of *Me* that
focuses on exactly those aspects of life that receive the slightest
treatment in Winnifred's text: her mixed-race identity and her
treatment at the hands of a largely indifferent and sometimes
outright racist white American society. In "Leaves from the Mental
Portfolio of an Eurasian" (1909), Edith writes, "I look back over
the years and see myself so keenly alive to every shade of
sorrow and suffering that it is almost a pain to live. The question of nationality perplexes my little brain. Why are we what
we are? I and my brothers and sisters. Why did God make us to
be hooted and stared at? . . . Why? Why?" (115).

Edith's autobiography, far more than Winnifred's, fulfills the
expectations we have of autobiography as a genre and women's
and Asian American autobiography in particular. We have become accustomed to texts that bare the souls of their authors in
order to lay bare the oppressive structures of patriarchy and
racism. From *The Bell Jar* to *I Know Why the Caged Bird Sings,*
The Bluest Eye to *The Color Purple, Fifth Chinese Daughter* to
The Woman Warrior, in the twentieth century we have been
immersed in an autobiographical literature that describes life
experiences as a form of protest.[4] One could argue that texts by
feminists and minorities "entered into the house of literature
through the door of autobiography";[5] as Frank Chin has angrily
pointed out time and time again, women's autobiographies criti-
cizing American racism and patriarchal oppression at the hands

of both white and Asian men have predominated in the Asian American literary canon.[6] Thus, whereas Edith's "Leaves" is held up proudly as an early example of Asian American autobiography and literature, *Me* is discussed hesitantly—when it is discussed at all.[7]

If we read *Me* alongside more representative contemporaneous texts, however, it appears in a far different and more revealing light. In telling her life story, Eaton drew far more heavily on the popular conventions of the working-girl romance than on ethnic autobiography. Her work was in fact mistaken for that of Dorothy Richardson, whose commercially successful novel *The Long Day* (1905) exposed the sexual danger and demoralizing working conditions experienced by young working women.[8] The working-girl novel, along with the closely allied form of tenement fiction, exposed American readers for the first time to the experiences of immigrant women in the workplace.[9] Eaton's depiction of her alter ego, Nora Ascough, as a naïve, badly dressed, penniless Canadian desperately searching for work in Chicago echoed the works of Theodore Dreiser (*Sister Carrie*) and Marie Van Vorst (*The Woman Who Toils*) as well as Richardson's *The Long Day*.

Yet there is more to Nora's story than her experiences as a worker. Above all, she desires to be a writer. In this, *Me* would have resonated with a spate of novels from the period that also told the story of a young person with artistic ambitions. These texts include Mary Austin's *A Woman of Genius* (1912), Willa Cather's *The Song of the Lark* (1915), Theodore Dreiser's *The "Genius"* (1915), and thematically, if not stylistically, James Joyce's generically eponymous *Portrait of the Artist as a Young Man* (1915).[10] The preponderance of the words "genius" and "artist" in the titles of these works (*The Song of the Lark's* original title, *Artist's Youth,* was changed at the request of her publisher) testify to the societal fascination with the concept of "genius"—the "godlike capacity for breathing on the dust and making it a living creature."[11]

The idea of genius itself, of course, was nothing new. Since

8. *Some "men" of genius, c. 1890. Top to bottom, left to right: Oliver Gold-smith, George Eliot, Joseph Addison, Robert Burns, Charles Lamb, Edward Gibbon, Thomas Carlyle, Elizabeth Barrett-Browning, Wolfgang Amadeus Mozart. (Royse 47.)*

the age of Plato scholars and philosophers have wondered what enables certain individuals to achieve greatness rather than others. Through the centuries genius was determined to result from a divine gift, environmental factors, hard work, or mental abnormalities, the last theory gaining prominence with the introduction of psychology as a field of scientific study, the introduction of Darwinian theories of evolution, and the vogue of eugenics in the mid- to late nineteenth century. During this period, Cesare Lombroso's *The Man of Genius* (1891), the second edition of Francis Galton's *Hereditary Genius* (1892), and William Hirsch's *Genius and Degeneration: A Psychological Study* (1897) became major texts in the field and were widely discussed.[12] As the title of Lombroso's work implies, these studies of genius were almost completely restricted to men—although most of the experts included some women, most notably George Eliot—in the ranks of literary geniuses (figure 8). N. K. Royse wondered in 1890 if it were "a freak of masculine unfairness, a prophetic intuition, or a mere verbal preference, that caused the Roman to restrict the birth-presiding *genius* to the male sex?" In answer to his own question he decided: "Whatever be the explanation, certain it is that the history of mankind, both ante and post Roman, has vindicated the sagacity of the ancient limitation, by discovering almost every instance of genuine genius among the males of the human family" (18).

Clearly, although certain *women* were accepted as geniuses, *woman* as a gender was excluded from consideration. Appealing to naïve evolutionism, Royse speculated that "the latest utterances of modern science would have us regard the female as the conservative factor in reproduction, and all new variations as caused by the influence of the male" (18–19). Those individual women who were included in the ranks of geniuses were overwhelmingly characterized as aberrations: their physical or psychic abnormalities somehow manifested themselves in genius of one form or another. The degenerative theories of genius and the connection between genius and insanity—William James, for example, included "genius" with hysteria, another woman-oriented disorder, as an "exceptional mental state"—thus enabled women to enter the hallowed halls of genius but limited their position there as "freaks": of womankind, of human nature generally, and of the evolutionary process.[13] The most commonly noted aberration of women of genius was their lack of traditionally feminine traits. One male critic scoffed at the end of the nineteenth century that "there are no women geniuses. The only women geniuses are men" (quoted in Boumelha 166). George Eliot's masculine appearance was ridiculed in the popular media (and continues to be to this day); of her unloved but brilliant author Margaret Aubyn, Edith Wharton wrote, "Genius is of small use to a woman who does not know how to do her hair" (*Touchstone* 270).

For women writers, the Hawthornian legacy of "scribbling women" added yet another dimension to their claims of artistic greatness. Elizabeth Ammons notes that until the late nineteenth century, women writers "decided against being artists. They stayed within women's realm producing writing—but not 'art'— while they simultaneously raised families and ministered to husbands. Or so the popular picture of the respectable white midcentury woman maintained" (10). The very popularity of women's writing testified against artistic achievement; Henry James's fictitious authoress Greville Fane, for example, was "not a woman of genius" (436) despite or, more accurately, because of her overwhelming popularity. As fictional characters, women writers flirted with the idea of art before succumbing to marriage, wasted their talent because of pressing financial needs, or gave up their art in deference to their "more deserving" brothers, fathers, or husbands (*The Beth Book,* 1897; George Gissing's *New Grub Street,* 1891; Ella Hepworth Dixon's *The Story of a Modern Woman,* 1894). Those who succeeded, like the unnamed narrator in Sarah Orne Jewett's *The Country of Pointed Firs* (1896) or Wharton's Margaret Aubyn, remain solitary, lonely figures; Mrs. Aubyn, in fact, is not even allowed a life within Wharton's narrative, which begins some years after her death.

One way that women writers avoided the limiting ideologies surrounding female authorship was to place their artistic consciousnesses in female artists from other fields. Austin's Olivia Lattimore, for example, is an actress, and Cather's Thea Kronberg an opera singer. In other examples, Virginia Woolf portrays her female artist in *The Voyage Out* (1915) as a pianist, and Kate Chopin's Edna Pontellier is a painter (*The Awakening,* 1899). In all of these cases, regardless of their specific métier, these women struggle to transcend the disapproval of their communities and their own self-doubt to find success and even happiness in their art. Ammons writes that women writers such as Cather and Austin "found themselves, often in deep, subtle ways, emotionally stranded between worlds. They floated between a past they wished to leave . . . and a future they had not yet gained" (10). Likewise, throughout *Me,* Nora repeatedly negotiates the conflicts between her desires as a woman and her desires as an artist; she wonders whether she truly has the "divine sparks of genius" or simply "a mediocre talent" (153). Yet her conclusion at the end of the novel to leave romance behind—because "God had planted in *me* the fairy germs; that I knew" (350)— Eaton creates what Linda Huf in 1983 called a "missing character in fiction"—the nonwhite woman writer (14).[14]

Eaton begins her novel as Nora leaves Quebec for Jamaica, where she has landed a position as a journalist for an English-language newspaper. On the very first page, Nora addresses the unusual nature of her parentage: her father is of "English-Irish" descent and met and married her mother on his travels in China and Japan. She reveals these details, she writes, "in the possibility of their proving of some psychological interest later" (3–4). She describes herself as "not beautiful to look at . . . a little thing, and, like my mother, foreign-looking"; however, she mitigates these defects with her "bright, eager face, black and shining eyes" and claims to have "the most, acute, inquiring, and eager mind of any girl of my age in the world" (6). On the boat, Nora tells her seasick bunkmate "all about the glorious plans and schemes I had made for my famous future" as a writer. She reads, out loud, all of the poems and stories she has brought with her, oblivious to the poor girl's acute distress. Her new friend finally goes "on strike," but only after four entire days of listening to this "voluble stream" (12–13). Time and again we witness Nora's complete absorption in her writing; she will read her poems and stories to anyone who will listen. Her cynical, worldly roommate Lolly, her friend Robert Bennet, and especially her mentor and infatuation, Roger Avery Hamilton—they all listen, listen, listen.

We also witness Nora's absolute commitment to her art. After working as a stenographer in a stockyard office every day, she returns to her room at the YWCA, where, she says, "if I came in early enough, and if I were not too desperately tired, I would write things. Odds and ends—what did I not write?" (125). If she is too exhausted to write, she dreams of her future success: "I would lie wide awake. . . . Visions would then come to me—the wavering quaint persons and plots of the stories I would write. Dreams, too, came of the days when I would be famous and rich. . . . My poems would be on every one's tongue, my books in every home" (153). Looking back on these "clean, inspiring days" (263), she wryly comments on "the extravagant dreams of the youthful writer! What is there he is not going to accomplish in the world? What heights he will scale!" But despite the futility of those dreams, she maintains that there is "comfort" and "sublime compensation for all the miserable realities of life . . . in being capable of such dreams! That alone is a divine gift of the gods" (105).

Yet Nora dreams of other things, too—especially of finding herself "the heroine in a hundred princely romances" (9). To a certain extent, this dream also comes true. Practically every man she meets in the novel either attempts to seduce her or proposes marriage; in one astounding passage she recounts the proposals she receives from no fewer than seven suitors (299–300). However, unlike the heroic Widow of Sanyo from *A Japanese Blossom,* who marries and sacrifices her seven husbands for patriotic ends, Nora exploits her singular attractiveness to feed her vanity. Flattered by their attentions and afraid of hurting their feelings, she accepts the proposals of three men—two journalists and an editor. Her primary obsession, however, remains a wealthy Richmond socialite, Roger Avery Hamilton, who functions as a combination love object, father figure, mentor, and financial angel.

From the moment she meets him, she falls under the spell of

his "impelling fascination" (75) and is overcome by "an eloquent desire to prove to him that there was a great deal more to
me than he supposed . . . that I was one of the exceptional human beings of the world" (76). Although he is more than twenty
years her senior and a respected public figure, she entertains
the fantasy that he will fall in love with her, a fantasy that he
finds both ridiculous and flattering. He loans her money, sends
her books, encourages her to go to college (with his financial
support). Finding the two-room apartment Nora shares with
her friend Lolly too small and noisy for her writing activities, he
rents a whole suite of rooms for her in the house of a quiet,
respectable woman lawyer. When Nora asks him why he does
these things even as he continues to insist that he does not
"care" for her, he replies, "I believe you are . . . a wonderful
girl, an exceptionally gifted girl, and I want to give you a chance
to prove it" (179).

Nora, however, mistakes his attentions as patron and mentor for those of a lover. As a result, she both desires and resists
them. She initially refuses to even entertain the thought of taking private rooms since it would mean that she would have to
be "kept," in a monetary sense, by Hamilton. He points out to
her "that if I had a pleasant place like that to live in, I'd soon be
writing masterpieces (ah, he knew which way my desires ran!),
and soon I'd not have to work in offices at all" (236). Yet she
continues to refuse. Finally she admits that if he only returned
her affection, she would let him keep her not only financially
but sexually. "I suppose I have no morals," she says; "I'm only
a girl in love with a man; and if—if—he cared for me as I did
for him, I'd be willing to do anything in the world he wished
me to. . . . But if he didn't—if he didn't care for me, don't you
see, I couldn't take *anything* from him. I should feel degraded"
(239).

In hindsight, she realizes that "it was a tangled, passionate
sort of reasoning" (239). Yet it was only a step away from that
"tangled" reasoning to what *really* was unacceptable to Nora:
that she be looked upon as nothing more than a protégée, a

product of Hamilton's beneficence. When Hamilton calls her his "find," his "discovery," and declares he wants to help her so that he can "watch you, and see you develop," she responds cynically that he considers her nothing more than "a sort of curiosity" (241). Though he denies it, she knows that "that was just how he did regard me, and it made me sick at heart. . . . I wanted to love and to be loved, and it was a cold sort of substitute he was offering me—pretty clothes and fine rooms. I could earn all those things myself" (241).

Nora refuses to give up the hope that Hamilton might fall in love with her and even marry her until she finds out, on the eve of their planned elopement, that not only is he married (as she had suspected) but is already involved with another, long-term, mistress. At this her romantic dreams are crushed. Looking at the picture of Hamilton's mistress in the paper, she realizes that "she was all the things that I was not, a statuesque beauty, with a form like Juno and a face like that of a great sleepy ox. . . . Women like her were the kind men loved. . . . Women like me merely teased their fancy and curiosity. We were the small tin toys with which they paused to play" (349). She later apostrophizes, "You saw me only through the cold eyes of a cynic—a connoisseur, who, seeking for something new and rare in woman, had stumbled upon a freak" (352).

But although she is devastated by Hamilton's deception, it is this realistic assessment of herself that enables her finally to wholly embrace her career as a writer. She initially believes that Hamilton "crushed my beautiful faith, my ideals, my dreams, my spirit, the charming visions that had danced like fairies in my brain. . . he had ruthlessly destroyed Me! I was dead" (351). Yet within hours, she becomes "another person" (351) who packs up her manuscripts and boards a train for New York to become a successful writer. This new "Me" shines, "bright, alive," like the star she sees through her train window (356). Though she has been vanquished in the game of love, she maintains that Hamilton's mistress is still "not better than I. Strip her of her glittering clothes, put her in rags over a wash-tub, and she would have been transformed into a common thing. But I? If you put *me* over a wash-tub, I tell you *I* would have woven a romance, aye, from the very suds" (349–350).

The romance plot of *Me* is clearly inseparable from Nora's artistic development. Some readers of the time criticized Eaton for overemphasizing Nora's romantic exploits: in an otherwise positive review fellow woman novelist Elia Peattie remarked that "the number of lovers, would-be seducers, and other masculine choruses are too large and overbalance the sopranos" (8). Eaton perhaps acknowledged this potential criticism of her novel when Nora remarks, "People who have called me clever, talented, etc.—oh, all women writers get accused of such things!—have not really reckoned with a certain weak and silly side of my character" (149). The preponderance of romantic elements in Eaton's story, however, was consistent with the conventions of the working-girl romance, in particular those by Laura Jane Libbey, where "Little Leafy" or "Little Sunshine" encounters one sexual predator after another in the workplace, only to end up in the arms of a true (and wealthy) hero who lifts the heroine out of the workaday world and ensconces her in the respectable and protected capacity of wife and mother.[15]

Eaton's exploitation of romantic conventions and her reliance on the voice of the romantic heroine were also consistent with other novels about women artists published at the time. Nora's obsession with Hamilton and the "choruses" of other male figures who both threaten Nora's artistic ambitions and support them is mirrored in Mary Austin's *A Woman of Genius,* where Olivia Lattimore loses, then wins, then loses her great love, Helmeth Garrett; appreciates but eventually rejects the pedestrian affection of her husband, Tommy; and dallies with several other men from the dramatic profession before striking out solely on her own as a great tragic actress. Likewise, in *The Song of the Lark,* Thea Kronberg finds a rarefied love with Frederick Ottenberg and is even seduced by him, but rejects him both on moral grounds and in the service of her art. Even in Virginia Woolf's *The Voyage Out* (1915), the story of an aspiring pianist is subsumed by that of her romantic interest in an idealistic young novelist. For all of these heroines, love and art are inseparable. In the voice of Olivia Lattimore, Austin writes that for men, "what is called love, is a thing apart from work, a loosening and letting down. But with women love and work are all of one piece, a star that dartles [sic] red and blue as it is turned in the hand" (379).

The artistic and the sexual are certainly a significant component of male "portraits of the artist," where the young man is either inspired by an ideal muse or tempted by the lure of sex in his pursuit of art. *Jude the Obscure* fails in life because he can never bring himself to reject the lusty Arabella and the physical world that she represents; Stephen Dedalus, in contrast, foreshadows his success when he denies sexual desire in the Nighttown chapter of *Ulysses*. Theodore Dreiser, in *The "Genius,"* which was published the same year as *Me,* presented an ambiguous figure: the sex-obsessed artist Eugene Witla derives his artistic inspiration from the parade of women he possesses but fails to raise his inspiration to the level of true art. Yet women represent something different to the male artist than men represent to the artistic woman. Whereas for men, women function as muses, inspirations for art—or simply as corrupting symbols of sensuality—in novels about women artists, as Linda Huf has noted, men "are not muses or models who guide or lift [the female artist] upward and onward. Rather they are despots or dunces who drag her down" (9). They are, for the most part, the representatives of societal mores and patriarchal authority—and thus embody what these women both desire and desperately want to escape. Olivia's husband, Tommy, is pure Higgleston, the small town in "Ohianna" that Olivia escapes in order to realize her dream to be an actress. He fully believes that "human intercourse was organized on the belief that whatever a woman has of intelligence and worth . . . is to be excised as a superfluous growth, a monstrosity" (218).

Eaton's Roger Avery Hamilton is of a more progressive mind, but he is no less concerned about Nora's reputation in society. He constantly questions and criticizes the company she keeps, worries about her poor clothes and the poor impression they make, and insists that Nora attend college, not only to provide her the education she needs "to accomplish the big things" she plans (175) but also because, he tells Nora, "association at my age meant everything" (200). He is cruel to Nora—at one point, calling her an—"ignorant, untrained, undisciplined girl" who is "stubborn, foolish," and "pigheaded" to boot (175)—and manipulative, alternately bribing or threatening her to get her to do what he wants. At points, Nora finds his proscriptions as well as his constant offers to pay for her clothes, her rooms, and her education constricting and ultimately insulting: "No man had a right to impose his will in this way on a girl," Eaton writes. "I was no doll or parasite who needed to be carried by others. No! . . . Only women without resources in themselves, without gifts or brains, were 'kept' by men, either as mistresses or wives or from charity, as Hamilton wished to 'keep' me" (243–244).

In novels by women, the artist must break free of her would-be lovers and mentors—and even her family and community—in order to fully realize her art. Thea Kronberg reflects in *The Song of the Lark,* "Why did these men torment her? . . . All these things and people . . . were lined up against her, they were there to take something from her. Very well; they should never have it. They might trample her to death, but they should never have it" (183). Olivia Lattimore, too, does everything she can to protect her "Gift," her "Shining Destiny." For this she comes under attack: her husband Tommy, her sister Anna, her friend Pauline, and even her lover, Helmeth, find her morally bankrupt because she refuses to sacrifice her art on the altar of marriage and motherhood. Yet, Olivia reflects, "I am a successful actress. Whatever else has happened to me, I am at least a success" (500).

Huf notes that "readers have always excused self-love in the artist—if the artist is male" (3). When the artist is a woman, however, the turn inward is perceived to be selfish and even unnatural, unwomanly—like Mary Wollstonecraft a century earlier, these women who desired lives that transgressed the bounds of the domestic sphere were nothing but "unsex'd women." The nineteenth-century British writer Harriet Martineau described her decision to become a professional writer precisely as one that would "unwoman" her, writing, "I must brace myself to do and suffer like a man. . . . Undertaking a man's duty, I must brave a man's fate."[16] The anxieties suffered by women writers in their inability to separate their professional and private lives were particularly heightened in their autobiographies.[17] Huf argues that until the twentieth century, even wealthy white women writers were hesitant in their own writing to "strike the grandiose pose" of the artist, and were often derided by their male contemporaries and even family members for doing so.[18] In *A Woman of Genius,* Olivia attributes woman's resistance to full disclosure to "the general social conspiracy against her telling the truth about herself" (4): Olivia argues that even autobiography is inadequate to tell the untold story of all women, not just women artists.

Although Eaton is the only one of these novelists to depict a young woman writer, she was certainly not the first to do so. However, *Me* was one of the first to locate the source of the writing impulse to the simple desire to create. In the nineteenth century, women defended their writing on grounds of religious fervor or financial necessity to show a motive for writing that lay outside of arrogant, "mannish," Romantic individualism and exemplified the domestic ideals of moral authority, nurturing, and self-sacrifice. With the advent of the New Woman, the task of proving oneself "a real woman in spite of her genius," as Terry Lovell puts it, became even more difficult, since the old plots of victimization and self-sacrifice exploited in earlier novels only succeeded in "re-naturalizing the qualities of orthodox womanliness" (quoted in Boumelha 174).

The plot that Austin, Cather, and Eaton all turn to in order to prove the womanliness of their female artists is that of romance. By demonstrating their sexual potency alongside their artistic genius, all three writers effectively cloaked the unwomanly, artistic side of their characters—in some cases, so effectively that readers overlooked that side altogether. Even a critic as astute as H. L. Mencken misread the main point of *The Song of the Lark* as "merely one more version . . . of the ancient fable of Cinderella, probably the oldest of the world's love stories."[19] Mary Austin relates that when her publisher's wife convinced her husband to pull the book out of circulation, she did so out of horror, not because Olivia Lattimore chooses a career as actress over that of a wife, but because her sexual conduct is "immoral" (*Horizon* 319–320).

Likewise, what Eaton's reviewers found "vicious" and "distasteful" (Peattie 8) in *Me* was not Nora's presumption in taking the "grandiose pose" of the artist, but Eaton's often blunt descriptions of the sexualized workplace. For example, she wrote: "I've had a fat broker tell me that a girl like me didn't need to work; I've had a pious-looking hypocrite chuck me under the chin, out of sight of his clerks. . . . I've had a man make me a cold business proposition of ten dollars a week for my services as stenographer and type-writer, and ten dollars a week for my services as something else. I've had men brutally touch me, and when I have resented it, I have seen them spit across the room in my direction, and some have cursed me" (124–125). The publicity for *Me* emphasized the potentially scandalous nature of Eaton's novel. One advertisement described it as "a breathless story of love, adventure, and daring. It is worth a dozen sociological volumes as a revelation of what the eager, attractive, romantically innocent girl meets who goes forth into the business world of men." In her introduction to the novel, Eaton's intimate friend Jean Webster also advertised *Me* as "a suggestive sociological study . . . an illuminative picture of what may befall a working-girl who, at the age of seventeen, gaily ventures forth to conquer life with ten dollars in her pocket" (viii).[20]

In Eaton's particular case, the high proportion of romantic incident may have served to de-emphasize—and thereby render less threatening—the claims Eaton makes about the potential for womanly—and ethnic—achievement. In her study of the female portrait of the artist, Huf laments her inability to find a single text depicting a black woman writer, concluding that "if the white heroine sees herself as presumptuous in her aspiration to become an artist, the black heroine must see herself as preposterous" (14). Roger Hamilton may believe that Nora is a "mongrel by blood, but a thoroughbred by instinct" (318), but he also clearly finds her a singular exception to the rule. Certainly, anyone who believed it impossible to attribute qualities of genius to wealthy, white, well-educated women would find it ludicrous for a poor, uneducated, mixed-race woman to claim such status for herself. N. K. Royse, for example, believed that although parental ability was not a prerequisite of genius, one's race was "an indispensable factor—indeed, the most fundamental physical condition of genius" (212). Frances Galton also placed the utmost importance on racial affiliation with genius, restricting his study to men of European descent; in the preface to the 1892 edition, he wrote, "The natural ability of which this book mainly treats, is such as a modern European possesses in a much greater average share than men of lower races" (x).[21]

Contradicting these views, Eaton significantly locates the source of Nora's artistic ability in her foreign mother rather than her artist father. Though she claims that she "would have given anything to look less foreign" and that her "darkness marked and crushed" her (166), her foreign background is what makes Nora exceptional, both as a woman and as an artist. Until she attempts to write about her "mother's land," her writings were nothing but "odds and ends . . . wisps of thoughts, passionate little poems that could not bear analysis." But when she turns her mind to "that quaint, far country," she "wrote easily" (125). Hamilton questions her ability to write these stories when she has never been there, and she explains, "I have an instinctive feeling about that country. A blind man can find his way over paths that he intuitively feels. And so with me. I feel as if I knew everything about that land, and when I sit down to write— why, things just come pouring to me, and I can write—*anything* then" (176). The fact that Eaton even hints that Nora's mixed-race heritage is the source of her artistic ability thus flies in the face of convention.

Eaton's mystical connection to her mother's country parallels that of Thea Kronberg to the Mexican community on the outskirts of Moonstone and later the cliff dwellers in the desert. Her artistic inspiration comes from these "other" cultures rather than that of her Swedish family or of Midwestern Moonstone, both of which she leaves behind. Her first teacher, Wunsch, notes that when Thea read or sang, her voice changed from its halting, quiet, often inarticulate mutter to a "soft, rich, contralto" that "was no longer the voice which spoke the speech of Moonstone" (70). It was, in fact, a voice that had more in common with the Mexicans on the outskirts of town—a quality that Spanish Johnny, Thea's lifelong friend, noticed from the time Thea was a child (206). When Thea is discouraged or frustrated, singing with Spanish Johnny and the other Mexicans recharges her; it makes her feel "as if all these warm-blooded people débouched into her" and that they "seemed to be within her instead of without, as if they had come from her in the first place" (210). Later she comes to feel the same way about the cliff dwellers. She goes there just at the moment when she has lost her vision and is "not getting on at all" in her studies (258). In Panther Canyon, however, she is immersed in the "sensuous" spirit of the place, and has "intuitions about the women who had worn the path. . . . She found herself trying to walk as they must have walked, with a feeling in her feet and knees and loins which she had never known before. . . . She could feel the weight of an Indian baby hanging to her back as she climbed" (271).[22]

Though the cliff dwellers have long been extinct, she feels a direct connection between her art and their own. The potsherds she finds in the canyons are, like her throat, vessels for art;

"what was any art but an effort to make a sheath, a mould in which to imprison for a moment the shining, elusive element which is life itself . . . ?" (273). After her visit there, her art is transformed. Later, after she has become successful, she tells Fred that her approach to her singing comes "out of the rocks, out of the dead people. . . . They taught me the inevitable hardness of human life. No artist gets far who doesn't know that. And you can't know it with your mind. You have to realize it in your body; deep. It's an animal sort of feeling" (398).

Walter Benn Michaels attributes Cather's appropriation of the culture and history of the cliff dwellers to a general "search for a source of and model for American culture," concluding that "the 'utterly exterminated' tribe . . . and the tribe 'without culture' that exterminated them represent, because the one biologically disappeared and the other culturally never existed, the possibility of an identity that, insofar as it is neither simply biological nor simply environmental, can be properly cultural" (35, 38). He goes on to argue that this logic "is repeated but rotated" (71) in texts by ethnic writers such as Anzia Yezierska (*Bread Givers,* 1925) and Oliver La Farge (*Laughing Boy,* 1929), where both writers rewrite "the *critique* of racial identity" offered by racist nativists such as Thomas Dixon and, to a lesser extent, Cather, "as the *commitment* to racial identity" (72, my emphasis). In La Farge's case, he argues that whereas "the Indian who in Cather . . . embodies the nativist American is made instead to embody the nativist ethnic and in both positions resists assimilation" (70).

Michaels implies that this logical "rotation"—the replacement of nativist American by nativist ethnic—is made possible the moment that an ethnic writer takes up his or her pen. Yet if we look at texts that came before those of Yezierska and La Farge, we can see a gradual transition to the "oppositional and antagonistic" way of treating ethnic identity that Michaels describes as emerging complete from the moment an ethnic voice speaks. The Japanese culture that Eaton takes as her source for her cultural identity in her Japanese romances is really no more

"natural" or "unnatural" than Cather's turn toward Mexico or
the Indians. Having never been to China, and having a mother
who was racially Chinese but culturally Westernized, it is not
really surprising that Eaton chose Japan rather than China as
her cultural "source."[23]

Eaton's choice of Japan has been contrasted, of course, with
her sister Edith's decision to make China the source of her cultural heritage; critics argue that Edith was somehow "truer" to
her ethnicity than Winnifred. Yet Edith had to educate herself
about China, just as Winnifred had to learn about Japan. In
"Leaves," she relates that she learned from books she read at
the library, not from stories heard at her mother's knee, that
China "is the oldest civilized nation on the face of the earth"
(116). When she visits Chinatown in San Francisco for the first
time, she finds that the Chinese there "regard me with sus-
picion," because they mistake her for being one of the "un-
scrupulous white people" who have "imposed" on them in the
past and also because she speaks no Chinese. Without speaking their language, she wonders, "How . . . can I expect these
people to accept me as their own countrywoman?" She is cha-
grined but not surprised when "the Americanized Chinamen
actually laugh in my face when I tell them that I am of their
race" (120).

Likewise, in another early autobiographical ethnic novel, the
protagonist of James Weldon Johnson's *Autobiography of an
Ex-Colored Man* (1912) learns about blacks not from direct experience but from reading (417); though an accomplished pianist in the European classical tradition, he is an adult before he
hears ragtime or sees a cakewalk, which he decides are two
things that "demonstrate that [blacks] have originality and artistic conception."[24] His decision to go to the South and collect
musical material, "to live among the people, and drink in my
inspiration firsthand" (471) is a conscious, deliberate one and
one that his white "millionaire friend" and employer does not
understand; he says, "you are by blood, by appearance, by
education, and by tastes a white man. . . . This idea you have of

making a Negro out of yourself is nothing more than a sentiment" (472–473).

Johnson's text makes a particularly interesting comparison
to Eaton's *Me* because his protagonist, like Nora Ascough, is an
aspiring artist and because, like Eaton, he adopts an extremely
ambiguous racial identity. After witnessing a black man burned
at the stake by a white mob, he decides to retreat from his
decision to "make a Negro out of himself"; he decides, "I would
neither disclaim the black race nor claim the white race." He
recognizes that he does so out of "shame, unbearable shame.
Shame at being identified with a people that could with impu-
nity be treated worse than animals" (499). Nevertheless, he
decides that "it was not necessary for me to go about with a
label of inferiority pasted across my forehead" (499).

His decision to become "non-black" turns out to be a good
one in some ways. He achieves the "white man's success," which
he sums up in one word—money (500)—and marries the girl
of his dreams, whom he describes at one point as "the most
dazzlingly white thing I had ever seen" (503). Though he lives
in "constant fear that she would discover in me some short-
coming which she would unconsciously attribute to my blood
rather than to a failing of human nature," his marriage is a
"supremely happy" one (510). Yet he also has regrets. In the
last paragraphs of the novel, he describes himself as "small and
selfish," simply "an ordinarily successful white man who has
made a little money." He contrasts himself with black activists
like Booker T. Washington, who are "making a history and a
race. I, too, might have taken part in a work so glorious" (511).
Instead, all he is left with is his box of "fast yellowing manuscripts, the only tangible remnants of a vanished dream, a dead
ambition, a sacrificed talent," which brings to mind the irre-
pressible thought that, "after all, I have chosen the lesser part . . . I
have sold my birthright for a mess of pottage."

Nora, too, looks back on her success as a writer with ambivalence. When one of her novels is dramatized for a Broadway production,[25] she goes to the theater marquee "to see if I

could call up even one of the fine thrills I had felt in anticipation. Alas! I was aware only of a sad excitement, a sense of disappointment and despair. . . . My success was founded upon a cheap and popular device, and that jumble of sentimental moonshine that they called my play seemed to me the pathetic stamp of my inefficiency." In an almost eerie echo of Johnson's ex-colored man, she, too, declares, "Oh, I had sold my birthright for a mess of potage!" (153–154).[26]

The story of Esau is certainly one that would have resonated with both writers.[27] Esau, son of Isaac and Rebecca, is dark-skinned, emerging from Rebecca's womb "red, hairy all over like a hair-cloak" (Genesis 25:25).[28] His twin brother, Jacob, follows soon after, grabbing his heel. God has foreordained that the twins will live in a state of conflict. He tells Rebecca,

> Two nations in your womb,
> two peoples, going their own ways from birth!
> One shall be stronger than the other;
> the older shall be servant to the younger. (25:23)

Esau and Jacob do go their own ways: Esau becomes a hunter, while Jacob lives "a settled life . . . among the tents" (25:27). One day, Esau returns from a hunt, exhausted, and asks Jacob to give him a bowl of stew he has prepared. Jacob refuses to do so unless Esau promises to give him his birthright in exchange. Esau replies that he is "at death's door; what use is my birthright to me?" (25:32). He agrees to do as Jacob asks, and Jacob gives him the bowl of stew.

The actual transfer of the property entailed in Esau's birthright does not occur until years later. And again, the stew pot plays a major role.[29] The aging Isaac, now blind and feeble, decides to bestow the blessing that would give Esau his inheritance and asks him, in commemoration of the occasion, to hunt a deer and prepare for him a bowl of venison stew. Isaac's wife, Rachel, overhears Isaac and instructs Jacob to give him a bowl of stew she has prepared herself, with the hope that Isaac will mistake Jacob for Esau and give the blessing (and the inheritance) to her favorite. She makes him wear a sheepskin to convey the effect of Esau's hairy skin; although Isaac is initially suspicious of Jacob's offering, he decides, upon feeling Jacob's hide-covered arm, that although "the voice is Jacob's voice, . . . the hands are the hands of Esau" (27:22). He thus places greater value on Jacob's (false) skin than on his (true) voice. He blesses Jacob and makes him the heir of what would become the kingdom of Israel:

> Peoples shall serve you,
> nations bow down to you.
> Be lord over your brothers;
> may your mother's sons bow down to you. (27:29)

Upon learning of Jacob's deceit, the faithful Esau protests. Isaac sadly explains, however, that he cannot revoke the blessing once given. All he can promise Esau is that "the time will come when you grow restive / and break off his yoke from your neck" (27:40).

Like Esau, Nora and the ex-colored man believe they have potential to inherit the kingdom; Nora says that in her dreams, "I moved among the elect of the earth" (4) and lived in a world where, because of her fame, "all my dear people would be lifted up from want" (153). Johnson's protagonist has "wild dreams of bringing glory and honor to the Negro race" and "dwelt in a world of imagination, of dreams and air castles— the kind of atmosphere that sometimes nourishes a genius" (417). Interestingly, however, they conflate Esau's role as the enslaved, faithful son with the trickery of Jacob. Rather than being betrayed by an impostor brother, both Nora and the ex-colored man take on false skins in an effort to demonstrate themselves to be the true heirs to the kingdom and, in doing so, betray themselves. Johnson's protagonist decides to don the skin of a white man and realizes only later that in doing so, he has achieved a white man's mundane success at the cost of "making a history and a race." Eaton's exchange, however, is more ambiguous. Scholars have generally assumed that Eaton "betrayed" her ethnic self to cater to a literary fad. However, evidence from the text more strongly suggests that by emphasizing her Asian skin, she felt that she actually betrayed her artistic, creative voice. Throughout the novel, she sees herself first and foremost as a writer, an artist—perhaps even as a "woman of genius"—and only secondarily as an ethnic minority or a Eurasian. The "cheap and popular device" of her assumed Japanese ethnicity, then, can be read as the price of her artistic inheritance, not the inheritance itself.

The conflation of the roles of Esau and Jacob in both novels indicates the ethnic artists' paradoxical position: their voices would always be inseparable from and of secondary importance to their skins. But whereas Johnson's portrayal of racial limbo is satirical and certainly critical of those who chose to become "ex-colored," Eaton, from all accounts, actually lived in such a state. Though she never denied her Asiatic background, she also believed she was "culturally white"—since she was, in the contemporary sense of the word, white "by appearance, by education, and by tastes."[30] It is possible to criticize Eaton for her misunderstanding of the Esau story, and it may be pitiful that she blames her skin for her artistic failures. To gain a comprehensive understanding of racial formations of the time, however, we must also be willing to accept Eaton on these grounds rather than dismiss her.

This reading of *Me* demonstrates some of the limitations of present-day paradigms for studying ethnic autobiography. Sau-ling Cynthia Wong has argued that scholars' expectations constitute "a series of mutually incompatible demands" ("Autobiography" 38): we look to the autobiographer as an exceptional individual who is nevertheless "representative" of an entire community and culture, "positing a direct pipeline of cultural authenticity between the collectivity and the individual" (42). In doing so, she writes, we deny the autobiographical text "the freedom to create in literature a sui generis [ethnic] reality" (42).

Though Wong is specifically discussing Chinese American autobiography and literature in her analysis, her point can be applied more generally not only to ethnic autobiography but to "American autobiography," "women's autobiography," and so on. By extending the bounds of a writer's community—in Eaton's case, to a community of writers who all struggled with their own sense of "genius" and who attempted to voice that genius in their own individual ways—we can begin to develop a fuller sense of how they really lived and saw the world outside of a limited set of artificially imposed divisions.

FOUR

Claiming the Big Country

THE ALBERTA NOVELS

[A]s a woman, I have no country. As a woman I
want no country. As a woman my country is the
whole world.
  —Virginia Woolf, *Three Guineas*

EATON MARRIED her second husband, Frank Reeve, in 1917 and
suddenly found herself a rancher's wife in Alberta, Canada.
Undaunted by her rustic surroundings, she rhapsodically described her new home as "Sunny Alberta, the Land of Promise"
(*Cattle* 13). Initially, Eaton kept busy with the business of the
ranch. Her daughter, Doris, recalled that "on the ranch my mother
found it more difficult to write. . . . [I]t was Mamma who put
down the pork, made headcheese, canned peas, beans, beets—
she always seemed to be canning something—made the butter,
candled eggs," and "saw to it that the meals at harvest and
threshing time were taken to the men in the fields" (Rooney
46–47). Finally, in 1921, she took a "room of her own" in town,
in nearby Calgary, and wrote the last of her Japanese romances,
Sunny-San, which was published in 1922. Her return to the
Japanese romance form, however, was short lived. She decided
that she was no longer going to write "fairy stories" but rather
"tales of things and people I had known, of a life I had been a
part of." She planned to "start over again, with a new pseud-

onym and a new type of writing. My work had been chiefly noted for its delicate and even poetic quality. . . . But I was not going to write with a delicate pen now. . . . Now I am writing with a man's pen."[1]

In her next novel, she followed through on her promise: *Cattle* (1924) is set on the Alberta plains and written in a spare, naturalistic style. Eaton boasted that her editor found it the "most brutal" manuscript that had ever come across his desk.[2] Ironically, however, this "brutal," manly mode of writing enabled Eaton to create, for the first time, a matriarchal, multicultural society where her characters were able to speak in "full voice." If she had "reproduced Orientalism with a difference" in her Japanese romances (Ferens 1), we could say that in *Cattle* and *His Royal Nibs* (1925), she reproduced difference with a difference: she infused her writing with the voices of women, immigrants, and racial others in a way that distinguished these novels not only from her earlier work but from the work of other prairie writers. This difference often emerged through narrative disruptions and dislocations, demonstrating Eaton's struggle to contain both her "man's pen" and a newfound sense of freedom that she, as a writer, found on the prairie.

Cattle takes place on the Bar Q Ranch, located on the border between the foothills to the Rockies and the eastern plains of Alberta on the highway between Calgary and Banff.[3] The young, innocent Nettie Day is hired and then raped by "Bull" Langdon, owner of the Bar Q, and is left to care for her illegitimate child with the help of a motley cast of characters: a misanthropic, androgynous woman rancher named Angella Loring; Angus McDermott, the gruff but kindhearted country doctor; and the "half-breed" Jake, a product of one of Bull's earlier conquests. In its style, plot, and characterization, *Cattle* is similar to works by other Canadian "prairie realists" such as Laura Salverson (*The Viking Heart*, 1922 and *When the Sparrows Fall*, 1925), Frederick Grove (*The Settlers of the Marsh*, 1925), R.J.C. Stead (*Grain*, 1926), and Arthur Stringer (*The Prairie* trilogy, 1922) as well as those by American writers such as Willa Cather (*O! Pioneers*,

1913 and *My Ántonia,* 1918), Martha Ostenso (*Wild Geese,* 1922), and Ole Rølvaag (*Giants in the Earth,* 1927).

All of these works, to a greater or lesser degree, attempted to balance the Edenic promise of the western landscape with the antipastoral realities of industrial development and the grinding daily regimen that confronted ranchers and farmers in this new land.[4] They were also similar in their incorporation of women in the male myth of the frontier. Rather than simply painting "portraits of women worn out by the land," prairie writers from the 1910s and 1920s—in particular, Cather, Stringer, Salverson, and Eaton—portrayed women as symbols of "endurance and strength" (Quantic 9). Hardworking, resilient and, in some ways, tougher than their male counterparts, Stringer's Chaddie McKail, Cather's Alexandra Bergson and Ántonia Shimerda, and Eaton's Nettie Day and Angella Loring carve out nurturing homes and successful farms on the prairie.

These women succeeded in spite of the misogyny that ran rampant on the plains. *Cattle*'s Bull Langdon, for example, exhibits the conventional attitude toward women:

> To him cattle and men were much alike. Most men, he asserted, were "scrub" stock, and would come tamely and submissively before the branding iron. Very few were spirited and thoroughbred, and for these the Squeezegate had been invented, in which all who were not "broke," emerged crippled or were killed. . . .
>
> If the Bull looked upon men in the same way as on cattle, he had still less respect for the female of the human species. With few exceptions, he would snarl, . . . women were all scrub stock, easy stuff. . . . A man had but to reach out and help himself to whichever one he wanted. (4)

His wife, "an innocent, harmless creature, soft and devoted," the embodiment of Christian resignation, wastes away in her marriage to Bull, who looks with "indifference and callousness" upon his wife's suffering (5–6). As Mrs. Langdon lies on her deathbed, Bull reaches out and "helps himself" to their hired girl, Nettie Day:

Slowly the Bull's great arms reached down from behind and enfolded her. . . .

She twisted about in his arms, only to bring her face directly against his own. She was held in a vise, in the arms of the huge cattleman. His hoarse whispers were muttered against her mouth, her cheek, her neck.

He chuckled and gloated as she fought for her freedom, dumbly, for her thoughts flew up to the woman upstairs. Above all things, Mrs. Langdon must be spared a knowledge of that which was happening to Nettie.

"Ain't no use to struggle! Ain't no use to cry," he chortled. "I got you tight, and there ain't no one to hear. I been thinkin' of you day and night, gell, for months now, and I been countin' off the minutes for this."

She cried in a strangled voice:

"She's upstairs! She'll hear you! Oh, she's coming down. Oh, don't you hear her? Oh, for the love of God! let me go."

The man heard nothing but his clamoring desires.

"Gimme your lips!" said the Bull huskily. (147)

Although other prairie novels touched on the atmosphere of sexual danger that surrounded hired girls, few did so in quite such graphic detail. In *My Ántonia,* for example, Cather alludes to the sad fate of the "Three Marys" and the "Swedish girls" and implies that the same fate awaits Ántonia when she is hired out to Wick Cutter and his wife; however, when events reach the critical point she has her narrator, Jim Burden, lie in wait in Ántonia's bed to confront the lascivious Cutter in Ántonia's stead. The very displacement of Ántonia from the scene of her intended rape lessens the impact of the episode; it is Jim, rather than Ántonia, who feels "something hairy and cologne-scented" next to his face (158). Jim's narcissistic anger at Ántonia—"She had let me in for all this disgustingness," he maintains (159)—only further distances the incident from Ántonia's very real fear.

Nettie's rape is only one of many "brutal" aspects of *Cattle.* However, these incidents are sometimes so grotesque, so overwrought, that they become almost ridiculous. Eaton's inappropriate shifts in tone reflect a discomfort with the new authorial voice she adopted. This uneasiness is further reflected in the abrupt shifts in point of view that occur throughout the novel. Though the novel is told primarily in the omniscient third person, immediately after Nettie's rape, Eaton abruptly shifts to the first person for one chapter, to the voice of the woman rancher Angella Loring. Here we learn why Angella has come to Alberta, why she has decided to homestead alone, why she has become a recluse. Although this characterization is necessary for developing the themes of female solidarity and independence that are essential to the novel, there is no reason why the third-person omniscient narrator of the rest of the novel could not have revealed it—as the rest of the characterizations are revealed.

At the same time, however, this abrupt insertion is significant. Angella is a kind of impostor on the prairie, and her intrusion into the narrative emphasizes her exclusion from prairie society. In her journal, Angella writes, "I hate men and despise women. . . . I wear men's clothing because they are comfortable and because I want to forget that I am a woman. . . . I broke my own land. I've put in my own crop. I hayed and chored, fenced and drudged, both in house and upon the land. I made most of my own furniture and I practically rebuilt the inside of this old shack" (82–83). Angella takes on a man's role—and even dresses like a man—in the same way that Eaton, in this genre, writes "with a man's pen" and speaks in a male voice. Angella is disillusioned with men and with civilized society: "I do not like Americans. They are noisy, insincere, and a boasting, bragging lot. As far as that goes, I like the English less. The Scotch are hard to tolerate, and as for the Irish, the devil made them in his own likeness. If it comes down to that, I don't know a single nationality that I can respect, and I have lived all over the world" (84). Middle-aged, disgusted by the superficialities of class ("I have no sense of caste whatsoever," she proclaims) and gender roles, Angella has retreated to Alberta to fulfill her "land of promise."

Here she has learned not only to work the land but to use her voice. When she arrived in Alberta, she was ill with tuberculosis—a civilized disease. But now, she writes, "if anyone doubts that my lungs are sound now they should hear me let out a war whoop that would compare well with old Chief Pie Belly's. Pie Belly is a Stoney Indian and I have learned some things of that Indian. . . . [T]here's sport in letting the full volume and force of one's lungs pour out across the utter silence of the prairie. If my voice carries to my neighbors—the nearest is five miles off—no doubt they take me for a coyote" (85). Like Thea Kronberg, who goes to Mexican town to escape the constricting provinciality of Moonstone, Angella wishes to distance herself from cultivated, Western society—in particular, the English nobility from whom she is descended. "The last generation of the Lorings were a soft-handed, dependent race," she writes. "I come of an older, primitive breed, I am a reversion to type, for I love to labor with my hands" (87). Angella, like Eaton herself, consistently denies her past and the influence of inheritance; she "reverts" to an earlier, agrarian type that had been distilled into the English aristocracy and, in doing so, recovers her full voice.

Yet Eaton is unable to contain the full strength of Angella's voice; Angella's diary is a glaring intrusion in the narrative. Other voices also demand acknowledgment in the novel. One of them is that of Jake, the Métis son of Bull Langdon and a local "squaw." Unlike Angella, Jake distinguishes himself by his weakness rather than his strength. In addition to being half-blooded, Jake is half-witted, due to a blow to the head he received at the hands of his father when he confronted him with his parentage. He is an epileptic and also has "a pronounced impediment in his speech" that at times renders him "almost unintelligible" (70). Eaton describes him in a half-pitying, half-disgusted way, as a "breed," a "poor idiot" with a "wild, witless face," homeless and dirty, subject to passionate, even savage, emotions (usually fear) and "slavish devotion" to those who show him even a modicum of kindness.

In her basic characterization of Jake, Eaton makes use of all of the prevailing stereotypes of the "half-breed." Stringer, for example, describes a female Métis servant in *The Prairie Child* (1922) as "the meekest-looking Redskin ever togged out in the cap and apron of domestic servitude" (23); his heroine, Chaddie McKail, refers to her as "Iroquois Annie, that sullen-eyed breed servant of ours." She "will never have any medals pinned on her pinny for neatness," Chaddie says; she burns everything she cooks and fails to understand basic concepts of cleanliness and general housekeeping. Chaddie would "love to ship her" but concludes, "heaven only knows where we'd find any one to take her place" (13).[5] Like "Iroquois Annie," Jake is incompetent. Despite his various deficiencies, he is used throughout the novel as a messenger and witness, and he is singularly ineffective in this role. Although he observes nearly every significant scene in the novel, he has trouble telling anyone what has happened. In fact, the more important the message, the less likely Jake is to make himself understood. His messages cause confusion; they often do not even reach their destination. He is waylaid by bad weather, suffers epileptic attacks, and several times is intercepted by Bull Langdon himself. Amazingly, he never actually succeeds in communicating a single message in the entire novel.

In terms of his role as a character in the novel's narrative structure, he is also unsuccessful. His appearances in the text are abrupt and out of place—and often unnecessary. He surfaces in Angella's narrative just as she is describing, in highly sentimental terms, the "exquisitely madonna-like and lovely" Nettie and her love for the good Cyril Stanley. He "sidles" up to Angella, surprising her, then "jabbered and gibbered" about Nettie's rape, which Eaton has already narrated in the chapter preceding Angella's diary. Angella can "hardly make head or tail of" what Jake is saying, even though she has just had a premonition that something has befallen Nettie on the ranch and also understands that Jake "wanted to tell me something about the Bar Q" (93). Angella alone is absolutely unafraid of the Bull: "*I* have his 'number,'" she boasts (88). However, be-cause she is unable to understand Jake's plea for help, she is unable to come to Nettie's aid. Jake's appearance in Angella's narration may highlight the pathos of Nettie's situation, but even more it calls attention to Jake's inability to communicate.

Later, after Nettie and Angella have taken up homesteading together, they discover that Bull has set his cattle loose on their land, destroying their entire crop. Everything the two women have worked for is ruined. They look over the scene of devas-tation, "overwhelmed by the magnitude of the disaster that had befallen them. Not a word was said, but Angella, as if grown suddenly old, turned blindly to the house, while Nettie threw herself down desperately upon the ground and burst into bitter tears" (227). As Nettie lies in the field in a "stupor of grief," she feels something "pulling at her sleeve, and looking up, she saw the half-breed Jake. He was kneeling beside her, holding out a little bunch of buttercups." Nettie, trying to "smile through her tears," asks wonderingly (as does the reader), "Where'd you come from?" Almost unbelievably, a comic scene follows. Jake, after being told what has happened, acts out the ways in which he might avenge them. "Me—Jake Langdon—me take a peech fork, beeg long likea this, and me jab him in the eye of the Bull, yes? That's kill him," he suggests. Or, he continues, "Get a long big nail—like this big—hammer him into ear. That same way many Indian do." By the time the scene closes, Nettie's tears (and ours) have turned into chuckles; she tells him, "I'll not cry any more. You pick me some more buttercups, Jake . . . *I'm* all right" (228–229).

Eaton's sudden insertion of Jake's deformed, ugly appear-ance in romantic scenes deflates any sense of romance; it also injects comedy into tragic scenes. And unlike Angella, whose voice is confined to one anomalous chapter, he intrudes over and over again. In many ways, Jake is the sort of inverse of Angella Loring. Whereas she is a recluse, he is ever-present and desperately seeks out human contact. She is articulate; he "jab-bers and gibbers." She can sing out, in full voice, across the plains; his speech is impeded and deformed. He is a sort of narrative alter ego for Eaton—if she would *like* to be Angella Loring, she may perhaps really *be* more like Jake Langdon—earnest but flawed. Eaton's sympathy for the "half-breed" prevents her from portraying him in purely conventional terms, yet she is also unable to break free from the racist implications of those conventions. An alien, broken, incomprehensible voice, Jake, like her earlier Japanese "half-caste" heroines, is able to communicate only incompletely and imperfectly across racial divides. In *A Japanese Nightingale,* for example, Eaton describes the hauntingly beautiful song of her heroine, Yuki, as "unfinished, giving to Occidental ears a sense of incompleteness" (9), which both mystifies and seduces her white listeners. Likewise, Jake's voice, if not beautiful, is a haunting, unfinished presence that points to a world outside the narrative, a world that Eaton herself may not have known how to depict even as she lived within it.

Both Angella and Jake are examples of what Patricia Wald has described as "uncanny" presences in literary narratives, voices that disrupt a seemingly closed, codified story. In her analysis of American literature from the mid-nineteenth and early twentieth centuries, she describes how writers such as Frederick Douglass, Herman Melville, and Gertrude Stein struggled to incorporate their idiosyncratic experiences into "national narratives of identity," which could be ideological narratives such as the Declaration of Independence's "We the People" and Manifest Destiny or narrative genres such as autobiography or history. She writes, "National narratives of identity seek to harness the anxiety of questions of personhood, but what they leave out resurfaces when the experiences of individuals conspicuously fail to conform to the definition of personhood offered in the narrative" (10). Thus texts such as Douglass's *Narrative* and Stein's *The Making of Americans* are characterized by formal and narrative disruptions, elements that do not fit their prescribed forms. As a result, Wald continues, "They must therefore be reabsorbed by the official stories they challenge. Yet the extra work required by that reabsorption threatens to expose the discontinuity it is supposed to obscure" (10).[6]

In Eaton's case, both Angella and Jake disrupt the narrative of agrarian expansion and settlement that had become an "official story" in both the United States and Canada (albeit in slightly different forms) by the 1920s. This story, which manifested itself in different forms ranging from Frederick Jackson Turner's "frontier thesis" of 1893 to popular dime novels, characterized the essence of these two nations as benevolently expansive, vitally male, and indisputably white; as Wald wrote of the rhetoric of Manifest Destiny, "A white male body becomes the emblem— the governing body—of the nation, and expansion becomes an expression of its very essence, its white masculinity" (116).[7] In *Cattle,* this national essence is embodied by the domineering Bull Langdon, whose fruitful herds (of both the bovine and human variety) spread, seemingly unstoppably, over the Alberta plains. Yet even though she implied that she would tell Bull's story by taking up a "man's pen," Eaton's narrative turns him into an antihero who is vanquished by the seemingly weak, largely silenced, but ultimately indomitable women and non-whites who halt Bull's advance through the plains.

The narrative disruption that leads directly to Bull's demise is Eaton's most unexpected. It comes at the hands of the ranch's Chinese cook, Chum Lee, who appears only a few times in the novel and never speaks. Eaton describes him as "a thin and musty smelling Chinaman . . . a shrinking, silent figure" (52). His cooking is inedible, and he is lazy, becoming "frenziedly busy" only if Bull is present in the cook car. As in her depiction of Jake, Eaton's characterization of Chum Lee takes advantage of stereotypical representations of the "Chinaman": his "musty" odor, his cowardice, his weakness, his inscrutability. His only narrative function is to provide local color—and of a type that today's readers would consider highly offensive—until the very end of the novel, when he is one of the last people left on the plague-struck Bar Q Ranch. At this point, Eaton devotes several paragraphs to his departure. Eaton writes, "Chum Lee had no desire to die in the white man's land; he wanted to repose in peace under the sacred soil of his ancestors. He would have run away from the camp, but the barren country, with its vast blanket of snow, gave no hope of any refuge." Finally, however, he leaves, "slipping in between the articles of clothing bottles and pipes and boxes filled with redolent odors. He muttered and chattered frantically to himself as he packed, and his hands shook as if with ague. He tied and knotted a stout rope about the bag and, trembling and shivering, put on his old sheepskin coat, muskrat cap and fur mittens. Hoisting the bag upon his back, Chum Lee hastened on panic-winged feet away from the camp" (277).

As Chum Lee departs the ranch, he does something truly inscrutable: he sets free the Bar Q cattle, who have been penned up without food for days during the height of the plague. This herd includes Bull Langdon's prized but vicious bull, Prince Perfection, "whose sires had come from the most famous herds in England and the States, and whose mothers were pure Canadian stock" (96–97), and who Bull believes is "the most perfect Hereford specimen in the world" (101). Chum Lee's decision to free the cattle comes as "a sudden resolution"; as he loosens the gates he thinks, "He would perform a last act of charity and win the favor of the gods" (278–279). Indeed, two chapters later, Prince Perfection confronts and kills "the Bull" just as he is about to take possession of Nettie Day once and for all. Eaton writes: "he drove his horns clear through the cowman's ribs. . . . [S]uddenly Bull Langdon was tossed into the air to fall to earth like a stone. Again and again the savage bull gored and tossed him until he was rent into pieces" (291). After this act of bombastic, if poetic, justice, the story ends happily, with Nettie and her prince, Cyril Stanley, realizing their humble dream of working a farm on the prairie.

Cattle is clearly Eaton's most "serious" piece of literature. As we have seen, however, it also evinces Eaton's difficulty controlling the "man's pen" she took up. Women's voices, indigenous gibberish, and alien "acts of charity" continually disrupt the narrative and, in doing so, reveal both the anxieties that frontier narratives sought to contain and Eaton's own anxieties regarding her chosen literary form. Willa Cather encountered similar problems in her prairie fiction, particularly in *My Ántonia*. The significance of the novel's episodic structure and narrative intrusions have been debated by Cather scholars since its publication in 1918. Lionel Trilling believed the novel indicated Cather's minor talent; later, feminist scholars in particular defended it as a demonstration of Cather's love of "artistic contrast" (Grumbach xxv) and the "liberating possibilities of formal innovation" (Ammons 131).[8] Whether they indicate novelistic experimentation or literary deficiency, however, both novels clearly demonstrate the tensions that resided in the genre of prairie fiction: tensions between different characters, different groups, different voices.

In *My Ántonia,* Jim's story is punctuated by the stories of others—of Peter and Pavel, Mr. Shimerda, the pianist Black D'Arnault, Lena Lingard, and Ántonia herself. However, all of these stories remain securely anchored within Jim Burden's perspective. The song of Old Hata, the tragedy of the Russian wedding, the story of "the Swedish girls" and Wick Cutter: these episodes are all filtered through Jim's narration and told, via indirect discourse, in his voice, despite the fact that he claims to his editor that he is unable to give the stories a comprehensible form (2). What is even more perplexing about Cather's decision to place her narrative consciousness in the persona of Jim Burden is the fact that her title character is a born storyteller. Although she initially cannot speak English, she has "opinions about everything" and could soon "make them known" (22); she translates many of the stories that Jim later relates.[9] Jim admits, "We all liked Tony's stories. Her voice had a peculiarly engaging quality; it was deep, a little husky, and one always heard the breath vibrating behind it. Everything she said seemed to come right out of her heart" (113). Yet though that "heart" is what Jim, sometimes desperately, claims access to, it is clear that for the most part it remains inaccessible. Jim cannot understand why Ántonia prefers to work "like a man" on the farm and only reluctantly confronts the reasons why she runs off with Frank Donovan and eventually ends up with the ineffectual Cuzak surrounded by children.

Jim, despite his sympathy for Ántonia, is unable to reconcile the brute realities of Ántonia's life or the lives of the other "country girls" with his idealistic conception of them. The ever-pragmatic Frances Harling tells him, "You always put a kind of glamour over them. The trouble with you, Jim, is that you're romantic" (146). To keep Ántonia contained within his romantic vision, feminist scholars have noted, he tells her story; he makes her "his" Ántonia by representing her. Failing to control or make sense of her, "his sole method of coercion is through his control of her representation" (Irving 97). However, it is unclear whether or not Jim's motivation to write Ántonia's story, or at least his version of her story, reflected Cather's own attitudes toward "country girls."

Jim's self-mockery as well as statements made by characters such as Frances Harling, support Kathleen Costello-Sullivan's view that Cather represents "the creation of an America on [Ántonia's] own terms, independent of the gendered norms that Jim Burden sought so desperately to enforce or of the hegemonic influence of a dominant, uniform American culture" (16). However, the layers of narrative consciousness that separate both Cather and the reader from Ántonia indicate Cather's ambivalence toward her subject. Not only does she describe Ántonia through the male perspective of Jim Burden, she filters Jim's narrative through an unnamed (but presumably female) editor who also had known her. Over the years, this editor "had lost sight of her altogether," remembering her only as a dim representation of "the country, the conditions, the whole adventure of our childhood" (2). For both the editor and for Jim, Ántonia is a nostalgic figure, "like the founders of early races" (227), a symbol of "the precious, the incommunicable past" (238). Like the dead Indian women Thea Kronberg communes with in *The Song of the Lark,* Ántonia's value to Jim is less personal than symbolic; she is less important to him as an individual than as an exemplar of America's immigrant heritage—a heritage that has faded (if regrettably) from the modern American present into the mists of history.[10]

Ántonia's immigrant background marks her as both "alien" and quintessentially American, and it is important for her symbolic function in Jim's (and Cather's) mind that she remain both of those things. Thus it is appropriate, oddly enough, that after her ill-fated venture in town life—"You ought never to have gone to town," Jim tells her (221)—Ántonia marries one of her "own kind" and returns to the farming life she has always known best. When Jim visits her after an absence of twenty years, he is relieved to find that she has returned to her Bohemian roots, growing Bohemian crops, preparing Bohemian foods, and speaking Bohemian at home to the exclusion of English. Her life with Cuzak affirms to Jim that she hasn't changed, that even after more than two decades, she "ain't never forgot my own country" (151). "In the course of twenty crowded years one parts with many illusions," Jim writes; "I did not wish to lose the early ones. Some memories are realities, and are better than anything that can ever happen to one again" (211).

The final scenes of Ántonia on the Cuzak farm, surrounded by other Bohemians, living a Bohemian life in America, thus preserve Jim's fantasy of a multicultural America grounded in an agrarian, immigrant past. At the same time, the farm's isolation from American "society" and "civilization" and Ántonia's marriage to a fellow Bohemian prevent the multicultural commingling that would have occurred if Jim had gotten "mixed up" with her, as he had earlier wished to do and against which Ántonia had warned him (143). Though the country girls were "real women" (144), they were nevertheless "almost a race apart" (127), and Ántonia understands early on, even if Jim doesn't, that Jim's destiny, unlike her own, was to go "away to school and make something" of himself (143).

As Guy Reynolds persuasively argues, Jim's final visit to the Cuzak farm represents "the recovery of the ideals of an earlier age, suggesting that just below the surface of American life persists a still recoverable, pristine, frontier life; but it also covertly admits failure. The Americanisation of the new world is successful, but only within a radically atomised society—as if in the very act of becoming American the immigrant also became what Melville called an 'isolato'" (98). In subsequent novels, Cather would even more strongly entrench ethnic and racial others in a nostalgic, premodern vision of national identity. In *The Professor's House* (1925), not only the Indians but a modern interpreter and descendant of the Indians, the appropriately named Tom Outland, exist only as memories, and three of her last four novels (*Death Comes for the Archbishop,* 1927; *Shadows on the Rock,* 1931; and *Sapphira and the Slave Girl,* 1940) are set in earlier centuries, times, as Father Latour puts it in *Death Comes for the Archbishop,* when "the Mexicans were always Mexicans, the Indians were always Indians" (286).[11]

Cattle was certainly not devoid of such sentiments. Although Eaton presents the possibility of cross-race and cross-ethnic mixture as well as depicting a vision of self-sufficient female companionship on the Angella-Nettie homestead, by the end of the novel, the various characters are sorted out by nationality and group, and the more anomalous characters drop out of the narrative altogether. The misanthropic Englishwoman, Angella, reconciles herself to marriage with the equally irascible but ultimately kindhearted Scotsman, Dr. McDermott; Nettie and Cyril, likewise descended from English and Scottish immigrants, also marry; Jake, "horribly bruised and deathly pale" after a final beating at the hands of Bull Langdon (268), is left to his own devices several chapters before the end of the novel; and Chum Lee presumably returns, "on panic-winged feet," to the "fair vision of his home and the young wife he had left in China" (277). *Cattle,* like Chum Lee, only temporarily sojourns in the "Land of Promise" that lay outside the customary bounds of race, nation, and class.

Wald notes that national narratives of expansion embodied certain irreconcilable contradictions: in her analysis of a statement made by an early advocate of Manifest Destiny (which she pinpoints as one of the quintessential narratives of American identity), she notes that the unstoppable spread of democratic ideals ironically necessitated the disfranchisement of indigenous populations, and that the "union of any people in 'one social family' had to contend with the hint of miscegenation intrinsic to that metaphor" (114–115). The conflicts we see presented and then reconciled in both *Cattle* and *My Ántonia* also appeared in works by writers who more explicitly asserted their own ethnic voices in the form of prairie fiction. The novels by Laura Salverson (of Icelandic descent), Frederick Grove (a German immigrant), and Martha Ostenso (originally from Norway) reflected the desire to maintain national distinctions within immigrant populations by promoting each writer's particular subcommunity at the expense of the others. In Salverson's *When the Sparrows Fall* (1925), for example, it is clear that despite her Icelandic heroine's declaration that Icelanders and Norwegians are "next of kin so far as race was concerned," she (and Salverson) still distinguishes between them. She is openly critical of the Lutheranism practiced by her Norwegian friends and intimates that it is a natural Norwegian tendency toward sensuality and materialism that eventually corrupts them.

Although a number of critics have described prairie fiction as a distinctly pro-immigrant genre, most of these writers (and their readers) supported only certain kinds of immigrants. In both the United States and Canada, policy makers who had initially encouraged immigration became concerned about the influx of "undesirables" from eastern and southern Europe and from China and Japan,[12] and even those who were immigrants themselves encouraged the enactment of nativist legislation targeted at immigrants from particular countries. As Terence Craig puts it, "the ethnic background and loyalties of Canadian novels [of this period] can too often be predicted on the bases of their authors' biographies. . . . For an author to rise above a personal ethnic affiliation and become sufficiently free and detached to evaluate all groups and group loyalties . . . is a rare achievement in Canadian literature" (23). By and large, settlers from different ethnic groups are depicted as distinct communities, and contact between them is portrayed as a source of conflict. None of these works—and *Cattle* is no exception—provides any evidence that their writers particularly supported the amalgamation of the different "races" on the prairie. Frederick Grove, for example, held unusually liberal views regarding cultural mixture on the Canadian frontier but still believed that communities should be segregated into different racial "federations"— one area for white races, another for blacks, Asians and other "nations," as he put it, "which are too different to admit of even the dream of assimilation" ("Assimilation" 79).

Yet Eaton, in her own idiosyncratic way, suggested the possibility of a cross-cultural and cross-racial society in her next and final novel, *His Royal Nibs* (1925). The O Bar O is a veritable mélange of ethnic and racial types who exist in an almost utopian harmony. Although it takes an almost identical setting and contains similar characters, including another Chinese ranch cook named Chum Lee, Eaton has shifted both the focus and the tone of this novel. Dropping her "man's pen" or, rather, softening its edges, Eaton returned to the form of romantic comedy, which had proved so successful in the past. Demonstrating her comfort with this form, the fractured narrative consciousness of *Cattle* has become centered on her romantic protagonists: Hilda McPherson, the headstrong daughter of the owner of the O Bar O, and "Cheerio," the mysterious English stranger who arrives on the ranch one day seeking employment.

The novel's comedic shift is apparent in the roles played by other characters. P. D. McPherson, Hilda's father, is no Bull Langdon. Although he, too, rules his ranch "with an iron hand," he is neither menacing nor brutish; he takes an intellectual rather than baldly expansionist interest in his land. A "former professor," he applies the evolutionary theories of Darwin and Spencer to produce strains of cattle and grains that are the envy of the entire countryside. The sexually threatening aspect of Bull Langdon has been shifted to a minor character, the ranch hand

Holy Smoke, who has designs on Hilda but is rather easily disposed of. And in contrast to *Cattle*'s Chum Lee, who is described as a "a shrinking, silent figure, who banged down the chow before the men, and paid no heed to protest or squabble" (52), the O Bar O's Chum Lee is immense and content, with "a vast smile of benignant humour" (23) directed toward all the residents of the ranch. He keeps things running smoothly, making the bunkhouses neat and orderly with "assiduous care" (92), providing nourishing, delicious food in the bunkhouse (43), and even keeping the "official" clock for the ranch (107).[13]

The most significant difference, however, is in the character of Hilda McPherson. In contrast to Nettie Day, with her "milk-white" skin, "dead-gold hair," and blue eyes, "a young Juno" (16) of "that blonde type seen often in the northern lands" (20),[14] Hilda is crowned with "chocolate-coloured hair" and "darker eyes," with skin of a "curiously dusky red that seemed burned by the sun into her cheeks" (67). She can "ride the range and wield the lariat with the best of the cowpunchers"; she can "brand, vaccinate, dehorn, and wean cattle . . . she rode a horse as if she were part of the animal itself" (37). Although the book's jacket pictures her as being of distinctly European descent (figure 9), her characterization in the text, like that of Eaton's alter ego Nora Ascough in *Me,* remains somewhat ambiguous. The darkness of her eyes and her skin's "dusky" hue are noted practically every time she appears, and at one point, she refers to her brother contemptuously as a "mutt," implying a mixed-race parentage. Is it Hilda's pure compassion or her "dusky" skin, that is responsible for her sympathetic, almost maternal treatment of the Indians living outside her ranch? Are Hilda and Sandy, like their father's cattle, experiments in cross-breeding? The fact that no Mrs. McPherson is even mentioned in the text leaves these questions tantalizingly unresolved.

P. D.'s espousal of Spencerian evolutionary theories suggests at least the beginnings of an answer. It was Spencer, not Darwin, who coined the phrase "the survival of the fittest"; and it was Spencer's application of Darwinian theories of biological

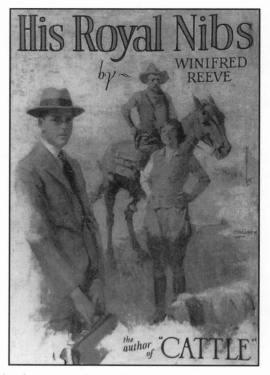

9. *Dust jacket for* His Royal Nibs *(1925). (From the collection of Diana Birchall.)*

evolution to the social sphere that bolstered the eugenicist movement of the late nineteenth and early twentieth centuries. Eugenics, of course, was most often advocated as a method for maintaining racial (white) purity, and Spencer certainly believed that "European races" were further evolved and racially superior to "savage peoples" (Kennedy 37). However, he also believed that evolution occurred through a process of "heterogeneity," the mixing of people, which Eaton, in her own self-aggrandizing way, may have interpreted as racial mixing: she had herself and her siblings to show that mixed-race couplings could produce exceptional people.[15] Eaton's insistence on depicting Hilda as dark-haired, dark-eyed, and dark-skinned is a contrast to her tendency to draw her heroines, even her Japanese half-castes, as fair-skinned, blue-eyed, and light-haired (Sunny-San, her last Japanese heroine, is a full-out blonde); in fact, the only other character she depicts in these terms is her autobiographical alter ego, Nora Ascough, who had "black and shining eyes, . . . black and shining hair," and cheeks "as red as a Canadian apple" (*Me* 6).

Hilda is depicted as a product of P. D. McPherson's progressive philosophies in other ways. To McPherson, European nobility are nothing but "bloody parasites . . . living for generations off the blood and sweat and toil of the poor, blind underdogs" (55). His children, in contrast, are the vanguards of a new "race of supermen and women" (34), educated in a "School of Nature" of his own creation (and modified from an educational model advocated by Spencer)[16] and guided solely by the most advanced scientific principles. "School such as the world knew it," he decides, "was antiquated in its methods and wholly unnecessary and wrong. . . . To teach the young the secrets and mysteries of nature—that alone was needed" to fulfill his Nietzschean vision (33–34). Hilda and her younger brother, Sandy, study natural science and biology to the complete exclusion of literature and poetry, for their father, Hilda relates, "doesn't believe in stories or fiction and books like that. He says it's all made-up stuff and what we want to read—to study, he says—is Truth" (108).

With nothing but the "book of nature" at their disposal, these young progenitors of McPherson's "race of supermen and women" grow up "like young wild things, loose on a great, free range" (35). Although they know little of history or literature, the two children "knew all of the theories concerned in the formation of this earth of ours, and the living things upon it. . . . They had a plausible and a comprehensible explanation for such phenomena as the milky way, the comets, the northern lights, the asteroids and other denizens of the miraculous Alberta sky above them. . . . Insects, ants, butterflies, bees, were known by their scientific names" (36). Nevertheless, the two children rebel against this austere intellectual diet, turning to the ranch hands' bunkhouse for dime novels and story papers. At one point, Sandy says, "Hmph! . . . Yes, Mister Darwin and Mister Huxley and a lot of for'n stuff. . . . Just s'f any boy wanted to read that sort of bunk. It's a doggone shame. If it wasn't for the bunkhouse Hilda and I never would've had no ejucation at all" (108).

If Sandy craves the "blood-and-thunder" tales and adventure stories he gleans from the bunkhouse, Hilda yearns for knowledge about European aristocrats and high society (55). Her ignorance of society is one of the greatest stumbling blocks in her romance with the aristocratic Cheerio. She initially despises him because she "intuitively recognized the fact that this stranger on the ranch belonged to that 'upper world' of which she knew vaguely through the medium of newspapers and tawdry literature emanating from the bunkhouse" (55). As with Sandy, Hilda's lack of a traditional education manifests itself in her speech: a combination of ranch slang, Indian yells, and strings of "cusses"— most of them learned from their unconventional father. "Isn't Dad a perfect peach when he starts swearing?" Hilda says. "I'll bet there's not another man in the entire country can cuss as my dad can. Most of 'em run off just the ordinary common old damns, but Dad—why *Dad* can—can—literally coin cuss words. I'd rather hear my Dad cuss than—than—hear a prima donna sing. Why, do you know, the very first word that either Sandy or I learned to speak was 'damn'!" (232).

For Cheerio, however, Hilda's voice is captivating for the very qualities that embarrass her. Eaton writes, "it was her voice, with its shrill edge of impudent young mirth that sent the colour to the pinched cheeks of the new hand" (23–24). Hilda's rough speech and wild ways are a kind of antidote for the civilized Englishman, who comes, like Angella Loring, from the landed gentry. Like Angella, too, he seeks to rid himself of a past and a society that has done nothing but constrain him; in his own way, he, too has had a limited education that manifests itself in his inability to communicate. His sophisticated English idioms—

"old man," "I say," and the expression that becomes his nick-
name, "Cheerio"—are ridiculed by Hilda and the others on the
ranch. His demeanor is made even more ridiculous, and almost
effeminate, by a stutter that overtakes him at the most inoppor-
tune times. Eaton writes that "when unduly moved, and at psychological moments, when the tongue's office was the most
desired of adjuncts, it generally failed him" (25). When he sees
his first Alberta sunset at the O Bar O, for example, he exclaims, "what a tophole view! Never saw anything to beat it.
Give you my word, it b-b-beats S-switzerland. . . . A chap cannot
look across at a view like that and not feel jolly well uplifted!"
    The ranch hands respond to this "stream of eloquence . . .
anent the beauties of nature" with a "gale of unbridled laughter"; one hand swoons away in another's arms (22). Slowly,
however, they come to accept him as their equal and, in many
ways, their superior. He is widely recognized as the best rider
on the ranch, and even the hard-nosed foreman "had discovered that despite his stammering tongue and singular ways, this
lean and slight young Englishman could 'stand the gaff' of
twenty-four hours at a stretch in the saddle, nor 'batted an eye-
lash' after a forty mile trip and back to Broken Nose Lake, after
a 'bunch' of yearling steers, without a moment off his horse, or
a speck of grub til late at night" (53). The men even begin to
appreciate his "singular ways"—the "pink pie-jammies" he wears
to bed, the "poetry he insisted upon inditing to the moon and
the star-spotted skies . . . the wild flowers he carried into the
bunkhouse and cherished." Eaton writes that "these and other
'soft' actions, which had at first brought upon him the amused
contempt of the men, slowly won at last their rough respect
and approval" (53–54).
    Hilda, however, remains obdurate in her dislike of the man.
Unschooled in his ways, as he is unschooled in hers, the two
characters miscommunicate their ideas and sentiments in one
scene after another. At one point, Cheerio decides to give Hilda
a book from his small library, which he has chosen "carefully,
with a thought rather for what might appeal especially to a girl

of Hilda's type than his own preferences." However, due to his nervousness, he is unable to abandon a formal, stilted mode of presentation: "M-m-m-miss Hilda," he stammers, "I r-r-recommend this f-for b-b-both pleasure and information. It's p-p-part of one's education to read Dumas." Hilda's response is quick and violent. Eaton writes, "Education! The word was inflammatory. It was an affront to her pride. He was rubbing in the fact of her appalling ignorance. . . . While the astonished Cheerio still extended the book—a silent peace offering—Hilda's dark head tossed up, in that characteristic motion, while her foot stamped the ground." Despite herself, she refuses the book, declaring, "I don't care for that kind of rot, thank you. My dad's right. It's better to be real people in the world rather than fake folk in a book" (91). Cheerio, "not versed in the ways of a woman," continually wonders, "What was there about him that should arouse her especial scorn and contempt? Why should her eyes harden and her whole personality seem to stiffen at his approach? . . . He could find no answer to his questions" (62–63). As for Hilda, her "untutored heart" is overcome by "she knew not what. Why was it, she asked herself passionately, that she was unable to speak to this man as to other men?" (73).

As the novel unfolds, however, the two slowly come to understand and trust each other; Hilda recognizes that the "strange new emotion" that comes over her in Cheerio's presence is not hatred but love, and Cheerio begins to gain "a better knowledge and understanding of Hilda. Her odd moods, her chilling, almost hostile attitude and speech no longer distressed him" (113). They reach a mutual understanding of their love for one another when Hilda is threatened by the ranch hand Holy Smoke. As she escapes from his clutches, she runs "like the wind straight along the trail to O Bar O, shouting in her clear, carrying young voice, the Indian cry: 'Hi, yi, yi, yi, yi, yi, yi, yi, yi! Eee-yaw-aw-aw-aw-aw-aw!" Like Angella Loring before her, she has learned from the Indians how to broadcast her voice across the plains. And it is Cheerio who raises an "answering shout" and comes to her aid. "Oh, how that voice, with its unmistakable note of deep anxiety on her behalf, made Hilda's heart leap," Eaton writes (269–270). As the novel comes to a close, we see how the lovers come to hear the voice behind the language, the meaning behind the words, the feelings behind speech. In response to Hilda's promise that she is "never going to say another unkind thing" to Cheerio, he responds, "Whatever you say will sound just right to me—dearest old girl." His words have the subsequent effect on Hilda: "It occurred to Hilda that he possessed a most wonderful and extensive vocabulary. She had never heard such terms before, and when she had read them Hilda had felt embarrassed, and in her rough way had thought: 'Oh, slush!' But," when they come out of Cheerio's mouth, "somehow the words had an almost lyrical sound" (315).

At peace with the understanding that comes despite their respective differences in culture, upbringing, and perspective of the world, Cheerio finally reveals his true identity to Hilda. Although quintessentially conventional as far as the romance formula is concerned, it is a startling one given Eaton's consistent reticence regarding her own identity. Hilda finally asks for Cheerio's "real name," to which Cheerio matter-of-factly responds: he is "Edward Eaton Charlesmore of Macclesfield and Coventry"—the first and only time that Eaton has ever used her own name in any of her works and a clear reference to her father, Edward Eaton, who was in fact born and raised in Macclesfield. This unprecedented revelation, of course, would have gone unnoticed by anyone in Eaton's contemporary audience, but even as a kind of private literary joke it implies a level of narrative comfort absent from Eaton's other texts. Only here, perhaps, in this unlikely tale of romance on the Alberta plains, did Eaton ever find a voice that was truly her own. It was not a voice completely removed from the racialist thinking evinced by her peers and contemporaries; Cheerio's horse, for example, is oddly named Jim Crow, and the Métis Indians, while characterized more sympathetically here than in *Cattle,* are still described as a "passing race" (244). Yet the ethnically ambiguous "child of nature," Hilda McPherson, enabled Eaton to speak in ways that had been impossible in her other works.

The plains, as we see in the work of all of these writers, were a sort of "interior frontier"; Cather's Jim Burden describes it in this way: "There seemed to be nothing to see; no fences, no creeks or trees, no hills or fields. If there was a road, I could not make it out in the faint starlight. There was nothing but land: not a country at all, but the material out of which countries are made. . . . I had the feeling that the world was left behind, that we had got over the edge of it, and were outside man's jurisdiction. . . . I felt erased, blotted out" (7–8). It is fittingly ironic that Eaton pursued her most complex and nuanced vision of ethnicity and the relationships between ethnicity, speech, literary conventions, and writing in a genre and setting that appeared least fruitful for such inquiry. Perhaps it took an unpromising yet unknown location to provide Eaton the space to explore these ideas. Unlike the cherry-blossomed Japan of her early romances, or the bustling city of Chicago that provided the backdrop to *Me,* Alberta was a land both culturally and physically boundless and allowed for a certain deviation from both form and content. Eaton wrote, "in a country like Alberta . . . we do not scrutinize too closely the history of the past of the stranger in our midst. Alberta is, in a way, a land of sanctuary, and upon its rough bosom the derelicts of the world, the fugitive, the hunted, the sick and the dying have sought asylum and cure" (*Cattle* 34–35). In this place, Eaton found room to sound out a new, if largely imaginary, multiethnic frontier.

FIVE

Sound Effects

VOICING FILM

*Watching Ann Darrow's screen test on Carl
Denham's ship, on the way to Skull Island*
CHARLIE THE COOK *(to sailor)*: You think
mebbe he like-a take-a my picture, huh?
SAILOR: Them cameras cost money—
shouldn't think he'd risk it!
—*King Kong* (1933)

WINNIFRED EATON flirted with writing for the burgeoning film industry as early as 1915. She entered a writing partnership with the flamboyant Captain Peacock, director of the popular *Perils of Pauline* serials, but emerged from the failed experiment ashamed of the work she produced, declaring with disgust that if the project had succeeded it may have destroyed her "prestige as an author of any worthwhile standing."[1] But by 1917, following her divorce from her first husband, Bertrand Babcock, she declared her intention to "get into 'harness' again."[2] Over the next few years she sold film rights of *A Japanese Nightingale* to Pathé, which produced the film version of the novel in 1918, wrote the adaptation for the film *False Kisses* (1921, Universal), and sold the rights to *Cattle* to Elmer Clifton, a film director and producer who had worked with D. W. Griffith on *Birth of a Nation* (1915), among other projects. In 1924, after the failure of Frank Reeve's cattle-ranching venture, Eaton gave herself up entirely to the film industry, taking a position as scenario editor at Universal Pictures. Over the next six years, she wrote dozens, if not hundreds, of scenarios, treatments, continuities, and adaptations and received on-screen writing credit for five films.[3]

At Universal, where Eaton spent the bulk of her film writing career, Eaton witnessed firsthand the effect of sound technology on filmmaking. With the phenomenal success of Al Jolson's *The Jazz Singer* (1927), studios scrambled to incorporate synchronized sound and especially spoken dialogue into their productions. And despite the enormous expense required for studios and movie houses to change over their equipment, within only two years nearly all films produced in the United States were "talkies." Many stars were unable to make the transition from silent to sound film. Many writers also experienced difficulties. A scene from *Singin' in the Rain* (1952), a film intimately concerned with the silent-sound shift, illustrates the shift required by writers. During a screening for the fictional *The Dancing Cavalier* (which would later change to *The Singing Cavalier*), the audience laughs uproariously when they hear Lina Lamont (Jean Hagen) and Don Lockwood (Gene Kelly) and the rest of the actors actually speaking the lines that had been written for them in all of their previously successful (but silent) pictures:

> LAMONT *(anguished)*: No! No! No!
>
> VILLAIN *(amorously)*: Yes! Yes! Yes!
>
> LAMONT: No! No! No!
>
> VILLAIN: Yes! Yes! Yes!
>
> [After the screening]
>
> AUDIENCE MEMBER: Whoever wrote that dialogue ought to be shot.

Eaton, whose works had always relied heavily on dialogue, appeared to have no difficulty making the switch to sound. In fact, based on the number of credits she received during this period, Eaton appeared to flourish under the sound system. Aside from her early credit for *False Kisses* in 1921, all of the credits she received came from sound films. Perhaps her sudden success resulted from the fact that for the first time in her career, Eaton's writing produced real voices, voices that were spoken by actual people and heard by a mass audience.

However, Eaton was unable to fully realize the potential of sound. Her attempts to create the kinds of voices that she had featured so prominently in her fiction—in particular, the voices of strong women, mixed-race characters, and racial and ethnic minorities—remained unheard on film due to a number of interrelated factors: the intensively collaborative nature of the film writing process, the studios' concern with mass marketability, and the increasingly restrictive regulation of film content that came with the advent of sound. Comparisons between Eaton's scripts and their final filmed versions reveal how Eaton's treatment of potentially threatening themes such as female power, class struggle, and miscegenation were gradually recuperated into already established film formulas that reified male dominance, class hierarchies, and racial purity.[4]

Eaton, in her fifties when she signed on with Universal, jumped into her new profession with characteristic energy. She wrote to her husband, who remained in Calgary, "Oh just think Frank I've signed the most wonderful contract. . . . I've a great staff under me—it's a very important position. I will be in New York for six months. Then go on to the coast. I get $200 a week for the first six months. Then $250—then $300 and up to $400— a 3 year contract. I get $3000 to $5000 for every original scenario I write tho' the first few months I will be rushed with the work of the department. Its no lazy job believe me. I got to get out and hustle but I don't mind."[5]

She maintained her enthusiasm for her new job even though she almost immediately encountered conflicts with colleagues who slighted her opinions, overruled her decisions regarding scripts, and gave primary writing credit to others.[6] Many of these problems resulted from the fact that she was a salaried writer, on contract to one studio. Unlike writers who signed on with a studio on a project-by-project basis, she received a steady weekly wage. However, as a studio employee, she was freely assigned to other people's projects, switched from project to project, worked with various other staff writers and, as a result, like most other Hollywood staff writers, remained uncredited for most of her work.[7]

In their analysis of film writing, literary critics have generally assumed that writing for the movie industry is essentially the same as writing for a publisher. The writer's work may be affected to some degree by market constraints but still "belongs" to the writer and can be read and analyzed within the context of his or her oeuvre. As the very idea of the "dream factory" implies, however, filmmaking is a corporate, rather than individual, enterprise: ownership of a film belongs not to a writer or a director (as critics of the auteurist mode of film criticism have demonstrated) but to a studio concerned more with market factors than with artistic vision. Janet Staiger writes that in the studios' "attempts to minimize costs and to provide efficiency, regularity, and uniformity of production," a script was little more than "a blueprint for production, and a structure of divided labor [that] controlled this standardized, mass-production system" (34). As such, film writers were expected to create standardized material that could be mass produced yet was differentiated enough to attract repeat customers. "Varying the epidermis is crucial" in such a system, Staiger writes (36). Although differentiating the iterations of an essentially standardized, mass-produced commodity necessitated a certain amount of creativity and ingenuity, many of the writers who came to Hollywood—most famously, Ernest Hemingway and F. Scott Fitzgerald—found it merely stifling.

Eaton, however, was intimately familiar with this kind of literary production. Her magazine stories and Japanese novels "varied the epidermis" both in the metaphoric sense Staiger uses and in a very literal way. They contained enough new material to surprise readers of her earlier work yet were firmly entrenched within generic conventions that enabled old and new readers to anticipate (and desire) the predetermined resolution of the plot. Eaton's experience in manipulating literary genres came in handy at Universal, which at this time was a second-tier studio cranking out dozens of "B" features every year. They employed Eaton on many different kinds of projects, including society melodramas, "fallen woman" pictures, Westerns, and films featuring exotic locales. Of the films for which she received credit, *The Mississippi Gambler* (1929), *Undertow* (1930, an adaptation of her earlier silent script *False Kisses*), and *Young Desire* (1930) were melodramas; *Shanghai Lady* (1929) concerned an American prostitute in China, and *East Is West* (1930), adapted from Samuel Shipman's popular 1921 play, centered on a romance between a Chinese ex-slave and a young man from a wealthy New York family.

Rather than focus on any of these films, however, this chapter focuses on one of her uncredited projects: *Barbary Coast* (1935, MGM). My reasons for selecting this film are partly based on the wealth of documentary evidence regarding its development from script to screen. Extant in the Winnifred Eaton Reeve Fonds and in other archives are different versions of scripts and correspondence from Eaton, the studios, and censorship boards and a filmed version that is readily available today.[8] This project also highlights issues regarding class, gender, and race and clearly shows how Eaton attempted to influence their representation on screen.[9] Finally, it also suggests the role played by sound itself in shaping filmic representations of women and members of different ethnic and racial groups.

Barbary Coast was intended as a vehicle for Universal star Mary Nolan, for whom Eaton had also written *Shanghai Lady* (1929). Eaton worked on two scripts for this project: a fifteen-page treatment written with another writer only listed as "Sumner," and a fuller sixty-four-page treatment written with Charles Logue. The story concerns district attorney Roger Storm's efforts to wipe out the "Barbary Coast," San Francisco's red-light district. In the process, he falls in love with Lily, the daughter of a Barbary Coast saloonkeeper and eventually is forced to choose between his moral vision and his love. The story of the rebellious young woman and the righteous man who wishes to reform her appeared in a number of films from the period, including Mae West's *She Done Him Wrong* (1930) and *Rain* (1932), starring Joan Crawford. In this iteration of the story, Lily is characterized as an irreverent, fun-loving young woman who passionately defends the Barbary and has little patience for sanctimonious moralizing.[10] Storm, meanwhile, believes that Lily must be corrupt because she has grown up surrounded by drunks, prostitutes, and other underworld types, and assumes that she is the mistress, rather than the daughter, of the saloonkeeper Dan Mooney. Eventually, Storm sees the errors of his ways. He discovers that he has misjudged both Lily and the citizens of the Barbary and is forced to admit that his reformist zeal has done little more than destroy peoples' lives.

The contrast between the world of the Barbary and respectable society is drawn out clearly at the beginning of Eaton and Logue's treatment. The scene opens on a "great mass meeting" where "all classes of people are represented." Storm gets on stage and gives what is described as an "eloquent" and "inflammatory" speech. He begins:

> ROGER: When there is a cancerous growth, the surgeon cuts to the root—*(applause)*—and that, my friends, is what we, of the City of San Francisco must do. Barbary Coast is a cancerous growth—*(cheers and wild clapping)* I know that I need not ask for your aid and cooperation. I know that I will have behind me in my righteous campaign the whole of the City of San Francisco *(deafening applause)*—and with such help—and with the help of God Almighty— Ladies and Gentlemen, I will go farther than my first promise. I will pledge you my word that within a month from this date Barbary Coast will cease to exist. (2)

However, his statements, and the enthusiastic applause and cheering they are meant to elicit, are countered with the rumble of the "underworld types" from the Barbary. Their hissing and booing gradually drown out the applause from the "Ladies and Gentlemen," and over it, Dan Mooney, Lily's father, "bellows his defiance": "What do yez know of the Barbary coast, ye white handed, white collared dude?" (2). Storm and Mooney confront each other, Storm accusing Mooney of being "the keeper of one of the worst brothels in the Barbary Coast," Mooney countering, "Tis a dacent place and my liquor and my women are cleaner than the likes of you" (28). The "righteous" speech of Storm and the reformers is contrasted throughout the script with the rough dialect of Mooney and the other Barbary Coasters.

Lily, who boasts that she is "Barbary born and Barbary bred" (31) is fully conversant in this gutter-speak; at the same time, however, she also speaks Storm's language, having been educated (in respectable fashion, as her father would have it) at a convent school in San Francisco. Storm is unable to believe that a girl who "looks like an angelic child" could really be the "bad girl" that she says she is (15). To demonstrate that she really does "belong" to the Barbary (21), she takes Storm with her to her father's saloon. Eaton and Logue write:

> We dissolve into a Barbary Coast street. Lily and Roger come into the scene from the upper city. . . . As she goes down the street, she is greeted by the denizens of the Barbary—Chinamen, sailors, dopes, prostitutes. "Hello Lil!" "Heh, Lil—you back?" "Where're you goin' to hang out?" "Say, Big Dan'll have a fit when he sees you." etc., etc. To all the greetings, Lily, now in her element, returns gay greetings. "Hello Em."—"Ho! Dutchy."— "Hello Tottie"—"how's business?" "Hello Dandy—"—etc. As she goes along, her face is alive with wicked satisfaction in the thought that she is properly shocking Roger Storm. His step becomes slower and heavier. More and more he realizes that this girl *is* actually one of the outcasts of the Barbary. (22–23)

For Lily, these voices signify her community—and even family. For Storm, however, they are nothing more than a cacophony of threatening, corrupt, alien voices: "outcasts" that he wishes to remove from society.

These were exactly the kinds of voices that many others

wished to minimize in sound film. Although concern with film content was as old as film itself, with the addition of sound, moral and religious groups became increasingly strident in their demands for films that would "emphasize that the church, the government, and the family were the cornerstones of an orderly society; that success and happiness resulted from respecting and working within this system" (Black 39). In 1929, the year in which Eaton worked on the *Barbary Coast* script, nearly a hundred bills were being debated at the state and national levels concerning content regulation and film censorship. Earlier on, the film industry had responded to concerns by monitoring its own output in a haphazard, inconsistent way. However, the threat of nationally legislated guidelines for film content (or even worse, a crazy quilt of state censorship statutes) led the industry's trade organization, the Motion Pictures Producers and Distributors Association (MPPDA), to encourage all studios to follow the same guidelines regarding film content. Their content regulation group, the Studio Relations Committee, more commonly known as the Hays Office (named after its head, Will B. Hays), issued a production code in 1930 that encouraged studios to avoid any sympathetic representations of "crime, wrong-doing, evil, or sin"—whether by creating sympathetic characters engaged in criminal or sinful practices or even depicting activities such as drinking, gambling, and lewd dancing. Any implication of extramarital sex, homosexuality, abortion, or miscegenation was to be avoided at all costs.[11]

These guidelines were only reluctantly accepted by the studios, and it was not until after 1934, when the Hays Office was transformed into the Production Code Administration (PCA), that the code achieved widespread control over the film industry. Universal Pictures, however, demonstrated an early commitment to the new rules. Concurrently with *Barbary Coast*, Eaton worked on the adaptation of Edna Ferber's novel *Show Boat,* which featured a subplot concerning a relationship between a light-skinned black woman and a white man. Because it violated the taboo on miscegenation, this subplot was removed entirely. One Catholic group duly praised this revision because it indicated the studio's "willingness to cooperate with the public groups toward the ideal of better pictures" (Cripps, *Slow Fade to Black* 292–293). Eaton's and Logue's sympathetic depiction of the San Francisco underworld would certainly sound alarm bells in this environment, especially since Lily, product of the underworld, remains defiantly proud of her father's profession and her own upbringing, while Storm, the charismatic and seemingly unstoppable reformer, is the one to undergo a conversion to Lily's way of thinking.

Eaton may have been at least partly sensitive to these concerns as the script was being developed. In the earlier outline version, Storm is a priest rather than a district attorney (critical representations of priests were to be absolutely avoided under the new code), and Lily engages in questionable behavior, including drinking, doing the "hoochy-koochy" on a table, and smoking a cigar. In the revised version she does not drink or smoke, expresses disgust at the more dissipated patrons of her father's saloon, and does not shimmy on tables; her dialogue, too, is less vulgar. Whereas she calls Storm a "God Damned dirty psalm-singing, sneaking, prayer-babbling coot" in the outline, in the fuller treatment Lily uses epithets no more damning than "pious prig" and "hypocrite."

However, the revision created its own problems. One major change between the early outline and the revised treatment is the transformation of a secondary character, a prostitute named Magda. In the first version, she is Dan Mooney's mistress, a "passionate cheap girl" who comes after Lily hissing and scratching in jealousy when she misinterprets Lily's daughterly affection as flirtation (5). In the treatment, she is not Dan's mistress nor is she passionate or violent. A "dark, painted girl, . . . appallingly thin" (27), this Madga is weak from tuberculosis and an object of Lily's pity. Although Lily disapproves of Magda's drinking and her dancing (it is Magda, this time, who performs the hoochy-koochy on a table), she takes an almost maternal interest in her that comes to drive the plot of the story. The most directly objectionable aspects of the outline—Lily's immoral behavior—have been displaced onto the character of Magda. However, the sympathetic relationship between them creates, in turn, a sympathy for the "oldest profession" that would not have been allowable on film.

Eaton clearly modeled the female friendship between Lily and Magda on the relationship between Angella Loring and Nettie Day that she depicted in *Cattle*. Lily's solicitude toward the sick, fallen girl, like that of Angella toward Nettie, demonstrates a softer side to her openly defiant, antagonistic character. Near the end of the script, Lily is warned to leave the Barbary as the raid gets under way but stays behind at the saloon to care for Magda, who is now deathly ill. At this point, Eaton and Logue insert the following exchange:

> MAGDA: You're awful good to me, Lil. . . . *(Wistfully)* Most girls like you wouldn't touch a girl like me.
> LILY: I'd like to know why not. Guess you're as good as I am.
> MAGDA: Oh no I'm not—Lil. You oughtn't to be here. You're a good girl and you know what we all are down here. (38)

Lily remains steadfast to Magda even as she mistakenly is rounded up during the raid and taken to the wharf to be deported with Magda and the other prostitutes. Through a series of crosscuts, we discover that Storm has ordered the prostitutes to be taken away to "China, Australia, New Zealand and South America . . . all over the world" (60) because, as the police chief says, "Three quarters of the women ain't Americans anyway" (37). When Lily discovers what fate has in store for her, she initially protests. "They can't—they can't send us away! We've got rights! I'm an American!" (50) she cries. But her protests are meaningless, and she finally resigns herself to going, even after Storm manages to obtain a release for her. Instead, she gives the release to Magda. The script reads:

> GUARD: An order for Lily Mooney to be released.
> *(Lily looks at the order then her glance wavers back toward Magda. . . . Lily smiles radiantly.)*
> LILY: She's all ready—and say, mister—be gentle with her, will you? *(She shoves some money into his hand—)* She's a sick girl.
> *(She comes back to Magda and, kneeling beside her, whispers.)*
> LILY: Magda—they're goin' to take you away.
> *(Magda starts up.)*
> MAGDA: Where—what do you mean, Lil!?
> LILY: Don't ask any questions—just go. I guess one of Big Dan's friends has pulled some wires to get you free.

In both this script and in *Cattle,* Eaton presents female solidarity as an antidote to the cruelty of men. However, by defending the victims of sexual predators and the exploitative sex trade—unwed mothers and prostitutes—Eaton fell on the wrong side of the studios' attempts at self-regulation. Several years earlier, a treatment of *Cattle* that Eaton submitted to Paramount was rejected for precisely that reason; she was told, "We do not like to put on the screen—and our exhibitors like it less than we do—a heroine who has been betrayed and whom we watch looking after her illegitimate child."[12]

Another element of Eaton's Alberta novels surfaces in this script: the character of Chum Lee. A kind of combination between the Chum Lees of *Cattle* and *His Royal Nibs,* the "Chinaman" in Eaton and Logue's script is merely given one "shrill line" in the outline, but a significant speaking part in the treatment. Like his fictional predecessors, he is described in stereotypical terms, "squeeling" [sic] at Storm when ordered by Lily to attack him (45), "scuttling" from one place to another (41), speaking in "ching-chong-Chinaman" dialect. However, he is also given a role in this script that would have been distinctly unusual for the period. He is the one who finally makes

Lily realize that the saloon is about to be raided, accompanies Lily and Magda to the wharf—even remembering to bring along coats and blankets for them—and is the one responsible for rectifying the misunderstanding between Lily and Storm. He confirms to Roger that Lily is indeed a "vellee good girl" and, in the last scene, gains him a final audience with Lily, where the two finally declare their love for each other.

By emphasizing female and cross-racial solidarity in their script, Eaton and Logue reinforce the idea that the underworld is peopled with outcasts rather than criminals, creating sympathy for the kind of society that reform-minded citizens wished to vilify. "Oh, what did we ever do to you that you should persecute us like this?" Lily asks Storm as the saloon is being raided (46). The nature of the misunderstanding between Lily and Storm implicitly criticizes the conventional relationship between class and virtue: those who mistake Lily for one of her father's "women"—"gutter stuff," as Lily's landlady would have it (18)—are forced to admit, by the end of the script, that Lily is as virtuous as any reformer type (and less hypocritical, to boot).

This treatment was approved by the head of the scenario department, screenwriting veteran C. Gardner Sullivan, and a continuity was written by another writer (probably Edward T. Lowe, with whom she adapted *Undertow*) in November 1929.[13] This script, unfortunately, has not been located, but it clearly changed the story Eaton and Logue presented in their treatment. Eaton expressed her dismay with the new script in a memo to Sullivan:

> After reading the continuity of BARBARY COAST I am so depressed I am going to beg you to have some other writer do the continuity of CARNIVAL [which would be released as *Young Desire*]. The original story of BARBARY had flame in it—it was real and the characters were vivid and natural. . . . In my opinion we had a novelty. . . . The story that has been substituted is mechanical and wooden. . . . I am awfully sorry about this, I really feel sick about it but it seemed to me to be nothing short

> of movie vandalism. Our script had already been OKd by you
> and it was a cinch for a continuity writer to work from. . . . [T]he
> fact is, I feel as if I don't want my name on this.[14]

Despite Eaton's protestations, the studio went ahead and submitted the continuity to the Hays Office, which found it highly problematic, though for reasons that differed from Eaton's. The reader assigned to the script wrote, "I think the general theme of the story will be objected to and undoubtedly will be rejected by all of the Canadian provinces as well as by several of our own censors." Jason Joy, who would later succeed Hays as the head of the PCA, also had serious reservations with the story. He wrote in a telegram that he would be "wiring [C. Gardner] Sullivan that I'd like to talk with him. . . . You might tell him [that the] same things [worry me] in [the] script that caused worry when first discussed with me."[15] These "things" in the script, clearly, were the depictions of corrupt (or fallible) city officials and reformers and sympathetic representations of prostitutes, saloonkeepers, and other underworld types.

The film was never produced by Universal. Clearly, after getting such discouraging responses from the Hays Office, the studio decided to look elsewhere for Mary Nolan's next script. However, several years later, Samuel Goldwyn decided to produce a movie with the same title. Based on the information in the PCA file on this production, Goldwyn's studio, MGM, probably purchased the Universal script with the idea that it would be worked over to meet the more stringent standards of Joseph Breen, Joy's successor at the PCA. Over the next few years, at least fifteen writers took a shot at the script.[16] Ben Hecht and Charles MacArthur eventually received credit for the version that was produced in 1935—but, as Gregory Black relates, even they received "a flat rejection" from Breen when they submitted their first draft in August 1934. Breen wrote, "The whole flavor of the story is one of sordidness, and low-tone morality" (219). Over the course of the next few months, Hecht and MacArthur revised the script, in a process that so demoralized

Goldwyn that in January 1935 he announced that he was going to "shelve the picture because he thought it could not pass censors."[17] Black describes the process thus:

> Breen reviewed drafts of the script, which were increasingly devoid of "illicit" sex but continued to strike the censor as "too rough and brutal." Slowly the script changed from a story of an area of San Francisco where men came to find pleasure in drink, prostitutes, and gambling to a typical Hollywood love story that featured a young couple . . . who fall in love amid unlikely surroundings. . . . Breen was delighted with the new direction of the script. He told Hays that it was "definitely not the story which worried us all many months back." It is now a love story, he told Hays, "between a fine, clean girl" and a sentimental young man. While the Barbary Coast serves as a background for the story, there "is no sex, no unpleasant details of prostitution," and, more important, there is "full, and completely compensating, value in the picture." (219)

Hecht apparently "disliked the film and was disgusted by the whole process of sanitizing the Barbary Coast." One can only assume that this writer, who had earlier envisioned *Scarface* (1932) as a movie that attacked the hypocrisy of a society that would condemn gangsterism by day and "party with mobsters" by night (Black 125),[18] would find the process frustrating. But the film was finally produced, and its release proved to be rather anticlimactic: practically nobody was offended.

Although Eaton and Logue thought they had created a "fine, clean girl" in the character of Lily Mooney, the version of her that appeared on film was far finer and far cleaner. Born and bred far away from the Barbary and now named Mary Rutledge (played by Miriam Hopkins), she is a New York society girl who comes to San Francisco during the gold rush to marry a rich San Francisco saloon owner named "Dan Morgan," the obvious stand-in for Lily's father, Dan Mooney. Morgan, however, is killed off before the movie even begins, and Mary decides that she will transform herself into a different kind of gold digger—a woman who will regain the money she would have married into by swindling her fiancé's killer, Louis Chamalis (played by Edward G. Robinson), who has taken over the saloon. Through a series of circumstances, she ends up working a roulette table at the saloon and is courted by Chamalis himself. But she falls in love with a gallant, soft-spoken prospector named Jim Carmichael (Joel McCrea) and eventually gains his affections. She realizes that a "good girl like her" does not belong in a place like the Barbary and returns with Jim (also a New Yorker, it turns out) to polite New York society.

Aside from the film's setting, the story is so different from Eaton and Logue's treatment that it is difficult to believe that the two had anything to do with each other. The procession of writers, editors, scenarists, Hays Office readers, and studio heads gradually transformed a story about a powerful young woman defending her community and a young reformer's realization of the limits of progressive ideology into a romantic melodrama. Changes to a number of characters and scenes that remain in the film indicate the ways in which the script was revised to distance the film's heroine and hero from any taint of moral (or social) contamination and to realign audience sympathies with the conventional side of justice. From the outset, the complicated structure of alliances and antagonisms in Eaton and Logue's treatment—between Lily and Storm, Lily and Magda, Lily and her father, and so on—are remapped onto a conventional love triangle: between Mary, the heroine, Chamalis, the villain, and Jim Carmichael, the love interest. Chamalis, unlike Lily's father Big Dan Mooney in the treatment, is a criminal through and through; he orders people killed without batting an eye, swindles his customers and deals mercilessly with them afterwards, and makes threatening advances toward Mary. Jim has none of Storm's zeal but all of his charisma and Mary, though savvy and independent, remains far removed from the more sordid elements of the Barbary.

Mary's difference from the other inhabitants of the Barbary

10. *The "Latin" prostitute briefly provides local color amid the noise of the Bella Donna (left) before Mary "The Swan" Rutledge (Miriam Hopkins) installs herself at the roulette table, an alluring (but unattainable) vision in white (right).* (Barbary Coast *[1935].)*

Coast is marked from the beginning of the film by her white-ness. As her ship arrives, a crowd gathers at the wharf, buzzing about the fact that there's a "white woman aboard"; after a glimpse of her, one of the onlookers exclaims, "she's whiter than a hen's egg!" She gets off the ship, where she is surrounded by sex-starved prospectors who offer her all their gold in return for her hand in marriage. Mary's entrance into the Barbary is completely the opposite of Lily's, where the Barbary denizens greet her as one of their own. Mary, instead, descends on them like a goddess. This reception continues as Mary is escorted to the Bella Donna Saloon. As she approaches, we cut to a scene of the interior, which is filled with the usual crowd of drunken prospectors and businessmen and several conspicuously Latinesque prostitutes plying their wares. At Mary's entrance, all conversation stops. "White woman!" whispers one aston-ished man; his announcement is echoed by the other patrons and eventually draws the attention of Chamalis. He buys her a drink and offers her a job as "The Swan," the queen of the roulette table. She, it is implied, will provide the draw for prospectors who might otherwise rather hang on to their gold (figure 10).

Unlike Lily, who can speak gutter-speak with the best of them, Mary is distinguished by her refined speech and delicate ways. She cannot help but be disgusted by Chamalis's vulgar display of wealth and the general sordidness of Barbary life. But she finds a kindred spirit in Carmichael, who reads poetry in his spare time and can write, so he says, "like Shelley when I have a mind to." But when he discovers her working the roulette table at the Bella Donna (a place he is not given to frequenting, naturally), he is shocked. Like Storm, he can't believe his eyes. "What's *she* doing in a place like this?" he wonders aloud. Like Storm, too, he decides his eyes cannot be deceiving him and rejects her but is eventually reconciled to her when he finds that she has remained (essentially) virtuous.

They decide to escape together on a ship that is bound for New York that evening. But Chamalis is on to Mary's plan, and one of his henchmen manages to shoot Jim in the leg as the two lovers are rowing out to the steamer. Mary manages to get Jim onto the pier, where they are quickly found by Chamalis. Mary makes Chamalis an offer: if he lets Jim get onto the ship, she will stay behind and love Chamalis, she says, "the way you have always wanted me to." He agrees, and she takes Jim to the ship, where he is so delirious with pain that she is able to make him believe that they have succeeded in escaping and are on their way back to New York together. When she returns to Chamalis, however, she finds that he has decided to let her go; he says, "I don't want you if you have to make a promise in order to be able to love me." At that moment, a vigilante mob that has been searching for Chamalis spills onto the scene and takes him away to his just deserts; Chamalis gives up without a struggle, leaving Mary and Jim completely free to escape together. In this scene, Jim usurps Magda's role as the object of the heroine's sacrifice, eradicating the potentially threatening possibility that female friendship could transcend romantic (het-

*11. In his only "speaking" scene, Ah Wing (Wong Chung) is carried before Louis Chamalis screaming (left), and attempts to defend himself in Chinese before his queue is unceremoniously hacked off by one of Chamalis's henchmen (right). (*Barbary Coast *[1935].)*

erosexual) love. Characterizing Jim and Mary simply as lovers escaping the clutches of an evil villain, rather than associating the heroine with a boatload of foreign prostitutes, provides a much "cleaner" ending to the film in more ways than one. Magda, who plays such an important part of Eaton and Logue's treatment, has all but disappeared from the "cleaner" script: the only part of her character that remains is the Latina prostitute in the initial shot of the Bella Donna Saloon, who speak no lines and does not even face the camera.

And Chum Lee? As with Magda, only a vestige of him remains. Now named Ah Wing, he is, stereotypically enough, a laundryman who witnesses a murder committed by one of Chamalis's henchmen. When he tries to report the crime, Chamalis has him brought into the saloon and cuts off his queue, to much laughter and ridicule (figure 11). Later, another one of Chamalis's men shoots him in the back as he runs screaming unintelligibly down the street. His function in the film is merely to underscore the cruelty of Chamalis and his minions, in a way that only reinforces the belief that "Chinamen" are effeminate, inscrutable, and weak. The only acknowledgment of his earlier importance in the script is the fact that the actor who played him (Wong Chung), unlike most Asians who appeared in films from the period, is listed in the opening credits, even though his lines consist only of ching-chong gibberish and the stereotypical, unintelligible, shriek of the dying Oriental.[19]

The speaking role that Eaton and Logue wrote for Chum Lee reverted to the conventional role that Chinese actors (and ethnic actors in general) played in silent films and in early sound films that incorporated sound effects (as opposed to synchronized dialogue) in their soundtracks. Like Anna May Wong's "Chinese Girl" in *Old San Francisco* (1927), whose dying scream accompanies the crashing and rumbling of the 1906 San Francisco earthquake that ends the movie, Ah Wing survives as nothing more than local color and a sound effect. Of course, Eaton and Logue's depiction of ethnic and racial minorities was not particularly sensitive by today's standards. Magda, whose ethnic background remains vaguely Greek or Italian, never departs from the stereotypical slang of the streetwalker, and what little she says is constantly interrupted by coughing fits and consumptive wheezing—her speaking costs her dearly. And we have seen the sophistication of Chum Lee's lines. But in the film, even these compromised vocalizations are absent. We are left with a film whose primary cast has been homogenized and "elevated," and whose plot has been reduced from a mild attack on progressivist ideals to an even milder, sanitized romance.

Ironically, the sound technology that enabled ethnic actors to speak on screen became a reason to completely remove them altogether. Because of the exorbitant costs required to edit sound film and the American film industry's dependence on foreign markets, studios were encouraged to avoid offending international audiences in their representations of ethnic and national groups. Joseph Breen's secretary, Olga Martin, revealed in 1937 that despite the prevalence of sex and crime in code violations, it was "the film involving a foreign villain, or the political activities of foreign nations" that were "the bane of the industry" (221). She continued, "Since at least 40 per cent of the profit to be made from pictures comes from the exhibition of American films in foreign markets, the importance of observing their regulations is obvious" (225).[20] Moreover, perhaps inspired by the effectiveness with which religious and moral groups shaped film content, ethnic and immigrant groups within the United States grew more vocal about the representation of ethnic types on screen. Vasey notes that "the Italians and the Irish were particularly well placed to protest to Hollywood because of their large and vocal constituencies within the United States, who channeled complaints through the Italian embassy and the Catholic Church" and that "the Greek community was also influential, partly because Greek organizations were quick to contact Hays if they felt that they had been slighted in the movies, and partly because a large number of exhibitors were of Greek origin" (144).

However, the studios' method of accommodating these responses was negative and reductive rather than proactive or productive. Rather than emphasize positive representations of nonwhites and non-Americans, they simply avoided them altogether—or stuck with the kinds of typed representation, like that of "John Chinaman" or the shuffling Uncle Tom popularized in vaudeville, that had become so conventional that it would escape serious consideration. Ironically, nonwhite actors also may have played a role in their silencing on screen (or their disappearance from it altogether). During the silent era, film historian Kevin Brownlow notes, Chinese actors often refused to play scenes that depicted them in opium dens or engaged in white slavery (333); one can only imagine that they would also be reluctant to speak in the kinds of dialect that bore little resemblance to the English they actually spoke.[21]

The problems faced by Asian actors were much like those faced by their African American counterparts. With the arrival of sound, they were given roles that reached back into a vaudeville past rather than giving them a new place in the audible

Hollywood future.[22] As we can see, this "silencing effect" took place with writers as well. The collaborative nature of filmmaking and the value placed on celluloid rather than paper materials in film history may have rendered silent the contributions of nonwhites who never reached the director's chair or spoke on screen.[23] As we have seen, the work they did, like Eaton's contributions to the script of *Barbary Coast,* may simply remain as barely audible echoes that must be painstakingly retrieved. Future histories will have to delve into the studio records to find people like Eaton, who attempted to find a voice within the confines of the "dream factory."

Epilogue

In 1932, Eaton returned to Calgary and lived the rest of her life as a society matron and supporter of the arts. She continued to try to sell story ideas to the movies but never was successful. By the time she died nearly twenty-five years later, in 1954, her works were no longer in print, and few outside of Calgary knew who she was, or who she had once been. She was even forgotten by her own family members. Diana Birchall, daughter of Eaton's son Paul, remembers meeting her grandmother only once. After the psychological breakdown of Birchall's mother, caused in large part by Paul's alcoholism, Birchall was raised in New York City by her Jewish maternal relatives, who were estranged from the Eaton side of the family. She recalls that when she was three years old, a "jolly, laughing lady" came to visit, all the way from Calgary.

> "This is your grandmother, too," the grown-ups said in a bright artificial tone. "Isn't that funny? This lady is your grandma—just like Grandma is!"
>
> "No," I responded, at once. She wasn't. My Grandma was my whole world, the one who loved me, cuddled me, comforted me, took care of me. There couldn't be another one.
>
> "Yes, she's your grandma, too—your other grandma."

Impossible. Uncertainly, I toddled over to the warm, familiar presence. "You're my *good* grandma," I declared.

There was much laughter, and the lady whom everybody now agreed was the Bad Grandma, laughed the loudest of all. . . .

The other grownups apologized profusely. "She doesn't mean it—she doesn't know what she's saying. Denny, you shouldn't say she's bad, she's just as good as—"

The Bad Grandma smiled on. (iii)

As Diana grew older, she nevertheless heard unbelievable stories about her "Bad Grandma": she had supposedly been a writer of best-selling romance novels, had been both rich and famous, was at least part Chinese. Her mother's family dismissed these stories, simply noting that "she was quite a character (this was said with a rolling of eyes)," and "a famous liar" (384). Though she had proof of her grandmother's writing—her Aunt Doris, Eaton's daughter, gave her a copy of *Cattle* when she was a girl—when Birchall tried to read it, she "gave up in boredom. It was about cattle, all right" (384). The dust gathering on the tops of the other books that Birchall found in the library were simply further proof that her grandmother was "a dead issue" (xvi).

It was only years later, after the death of her Aunt Doris in the mid-1970s, that Birchall discovered, on visiting her cousin Tim Rooney, Doris's son, in Calgary, that "the vague stories I'd heard about my grandmother were, in fact, nothing but the truth." She *had* been a famous author, and she really *was* half Chinese. Looking for the first time at a photo of her great-grandmother, Grace Trefusis, Birchall was struck that this "Chinese lady" had "quite a strong family resemblance to no other family member than myself. . . . It seemed improbable, fantastic, sitting in Calgary among my very Canadian cousins, that we could have Chinese ancestors" (388–389). She had always thought of herself as simply half Jewish—Jewish on her mother's side, and Christian on her father's—and had dismissed the stories of her grandmother's Chinese heritage as just one more wild fabrication.

Tim Rooney, in contrast, remembers his grandmother far differently. Whereas Birchall grew up in New York City, Tim grew up in Calgary and even lived with Eaton for a number of years. He grew up in a city that viewed Eaton as an important civic figure—the theater building at the University of Calgary was named after her in 1978—and whose memory of her was kept alive by occasional articles published in the local newspaper and regional magazines. He knew that his grandmother had done exceptional things and took measures to have her papers donated to the University of Calgary library. "I knew the academic world would get around to Winnie one day," he told Birchall (xvi).

Within thirty years of her death, scholars did indeed "get around to Winnie." But the task of recovering Eaton's voice— the selective amplification of echoes that had quickly become buried, as in her screenplays, under layers of other voices— emphasizes both how easily voices are forgotten and how important it is to keep listening for them. Two events from a more recent past bring into sharp focus the fragile relationship between voices, communities, and history. In August 2000, a Hungarian POW from World War II was discovered in a Russian psychiatric hospital, where he had been deposited by Russian soldiers in 1947—seven years before Eaton's death. Because he could not speak Russian, and because no one in the hospital spoke or even recognized Hungarian, his speech was deemed mere gibberish, the words of a madman, until a Slovak doctor visiting the hospital happened to hear him speak, and recognized his utterances as Hungarian. The tragedy of Andras Tamas, however, was even greater than the fifty-three years he had awaited liberation. As an erstwhile prisoner, he had lived in a state of linguistic, and thereby social, isolation for so long that he himself had forgotten where he had come from and who he was. Only after returning to the region where he had grown up did he begin to remember details of his past. In the meantime,

Hungarian officials discovered that Tamas was the last POW taken during World War II, suddenly making this old, forgotten man a distinguished war hero.[1]

The story of Andras Tamas filled the newspapers and the airwaves along with stories about other forgotten voices, though the silencing and subsequent rediscovery of these voices could not have been more different. During the 2000 Republican National Convention in early August, Latino, black, and Asian speakers paraded across the stage during the four days of the party convention, attesting to the proimmigrant vision supposedly embodied by Bush's "compassionate conservatism." Spanish words and speeches filled the air of the First Union Center in Philadelphia, culminating in the appearance of George P. Bush, son of Florida governor Jeb Bush and his Mexican-born wife Columba. "P," as he is known, gave a bilingual speech from the convention stage, followed by his uncle, George W. Bush, who also peppered his acceptance speech with the Spanish phrases he had practiced on the stump throughout his campaign. With his nomination, Bush declared, the Republican Party had become a party of "idealism and inclusion."

The aura of inclusivity at the 2000 Republican convention belied widespread Republican efforts to render immigrant and minority populations silent by supporting legislation that would bar bilingual education from public schools, restrict immigrant rights, and end affirmative action; in fact, affirmative action has been cut back most in Texas and Florida, the states governed by George W. and his brother Jeb. It also belied the less-than-inclusive attitudes of the Bush family; in 1988, grandfather and Vice President George Bush pointed out "P" and his siblings to the Reagans as "the little brown ones."[2] Latino convention delegates evinced pride that their voices were finally being heard; indeed, this was the first time that a convention speech was given entirely in Spanish, by California delegate Abel Maldonado. But outside the convention, critics attacked what they saw as transparent and not particularly compassionate political interest: George W. Bush's personal and even familial ties to Latinos provided an opportunity to tap into the growing Latino population and their votes, which could counterbalance his opponent Al Gore's appeal with African American voters.

The capacity to speak—and to be understood—is at the core of both of these events. They are also at the core of each of the case studies presented here. Like Andras Tamas, Eaton was often considered unintelligible, both by the society in which she lived and by present-day readers. Because she was not considered part of the community, she was easily disregarded and forgotten. The dialect used in the Japanese romances, *The Diary of Delia,* the prairie novels, and *Barbary Coast* is unnatural speech, alien speech. Yet she remained an alien even when she spoke in standard English. In "A Neighbor's Garden, My Own, and a Dream One," she presented the perspective of the suburban housewife she actually was—but this text, perhaps more than all the others, strikes present-day readers as impossible to reconcile with our understanding of race relations in the early twentieth century. The idea that a mixed-race woman could support a family solely on the proceeds from her writing and purchase a house and land in the suburban community of Westchester, New York, is irreconcilable with the narrative of rampant racism and nativism that dominates our history books.

At least in the Japanese romances, she appeared in an "Asian" guise. And unsurprisingly, these are the texts that have received nearly all critical attention. Like the minority Republicans at the GOP convention, she is only heard when she speaks about her identity as a minority and addresses minority issues. California delegate Abel Maldonado recounted, in Spanish, the only story that the non-Spanish-speaking delegates would understand: his family's struggle to come to America, their hunger for American education and American prosperity, their pursuit of the American dream. If he had spoken about privatizing Social Security, tax legislation, or campaign finance reform, he suddenly would no longer be speaking as a Mexican American but as an American—and the point of placing him at the podium would have been completely lost.

Ironically, the only way to demonstrate the inclusiveness of the party was by emphasizing difference. Scholars of ethnic literature have been faced with the same dilemma. Yet in order to demonstrate the diversity that has always been a part of American literature—as the case of Eaton clearly shows—we must find ways of discussing the contributions of ethnic writers in ways that move beyond the narratives of exclusion and oppression that have obscured their participation in the first place. We must allow them what Angella Loring described in *Cattle* as "full voice"; by hearing what these voices actually say, rather than interpreting them according to what we think they ought to be saying, we can truly begin to realize a complete, and inclusive, vision of our community.

Eaton hardly ever discussed her ethnicity and appeared to have had experienced little if any discrimination during her lifetime. She demonstrated little interest in aligning herself with either Chinese American or Japanese American communities. And she appeared to have little trouble crossing racial, class, or geographic boundaries. Eaton is so different from our present-day understanding of the ethnic writer that it may be difficult for some people to believe that she existed at all. How was it possible for a woman of Eaton's background to publish so much and so successfully? How was it possible for her to have traveled from Montreal to Jamaica to Chicago to New York to Calgary to Hollywood and back again? How was it possible for her to have been accepted in New York literary society—to have been the intimate friend of Mark Twain's niece, to have attended William Dean Howells's seventy-fifth birthday party, to have associated professionally and socially with Edith Wharton, Frances Marion, and Anita Loos? How was it possible for her to be in such interesting places at such interesting times—to have been writing short stories at the height of mass-market magazine publishing; to have been in western Canada just when writing by Canadians was being conceived as a national literature; to have been working in Hollywood at exactly the moment that studios were switching from silent to sound film?

Eaton, in many ways, is a classic example of "the exception that proves the rule." Each of her works challenges currently accepted ideas about early-twentieth-century American literature and culture. Most significantly, Eaton demonstrates that Progressive Era literature was not wholly dominated by gentleman authors. Howells and James clearly coexisted—and rather peacefully—with writers like Eaton. Nearly as important, Eaton challenges the commonly held perception that no minority writers before Toni Morrison and Maxine Hong Kingston were financially or professionally successful. Her manuscripts were readily accepted by the American literary establishment, and she fully participated in American literary culture as a professional author.

Writing in popular forms provided Eaton access to a large readership and enabled her to frame her voice in comprehensible and believable ways. At the same time, the very frameworks that enabled her to speak also constrained the ways in which she spoke.[3] Yuki could not wholly reject her role as the "tragic geisha" that had become so firmly entrenched in the American consciousness by John Luther Long's *Madame Butterfly*. Delia could not abandon her role as a maligned and misunderstood domestic servant. Chum Lee would never transcend his role as the ranch cook. In all these cases, the characters Eaton developed could not escape their predefined roles within their respective genres without exiting the genre altogether. If the genre gave them a chance to speak, the lines they spoke may not have been the ones they would have chosen if they had used, as *Cattle*'s Angella Loring did, their "full voice."

When she spoke as an author, Eaton was likewise both enabled and constrained. As Onoto Watanna, she was able to speak as an exotic personality, celebrity author, and native informant, which ironically precluded her from revealing (or enabled her to hide) her background as a poor, uneducated, half-Chinese girl from Montreal. As Nora Ascough, Eaton was able to portray herself as that uneducated, working-class girl but in turn could speak only obliquely about issues of nationality or race, which were incongruent with the working-girl novel and the artist's Bildungsroman. In newspaper and magazine interviews and first-person accounts such as "A Neighbor's Garden, My Own, and a Dream One," she presented herself alternately as a flighty girl-author, a member of the urbane New York literati, booster of Japan, scrappy Hollywood screenwriter, and arbiter of Canadian culture. In personal correspondence, she also revealed herself as a devoted yet sometimes rebellious wife and worried mother—but never once makes any mention of her ethnicity or her adopted authorial personae. The sheer volume of writings she left behind, rather than illuminating her "true" or "authentic" identity, rather than enabling us to recover *her* voice, merely demonstrate the impossibility of such an endeavor—once again demonstrating, as Barthes put it, the "death of the author" as a unified subject.

Eaton shows us that although the voice may have in it "the thing that makes all interpretation," that "thing" is no easy one to define. Yet the contradictory and contingent nature of voice suggests ways in which we might broaden and deepen our understanding of both American and ethnic literature. Although we now recognize the "amazing diversity of Asian American national origins" and the "wide variety of subject positions" represented in Asian American literature (Kim, "Preface" xiii), we could do more to interrogate the forms and conditions that both enable and limit those subject positions and to examine how voices are shaped by a diverse range of material and cultural factors. Without forgetting how voices are suppressed under mainstream culture and often shout against it, we also need to consider how they emerge within it. In her essay "Black Matters," Toni Morrison encourages us to begin examining how "knowledge is transformed from invasion and conquest to revelation and choice." In her passion for words, stories, and voices, Eaton epitomizes that transformation.

Notes

INTRODUCTION

1. S. E. Solberg and Amy Ling were the first scholars to "recover" the work of the Eaton sisters.

2. Thus far, *Miss Numè of Japan* (1899), *The Heart of Hyacinth* (1903), *Me: A Book of Remembrance* (1915), and *A Japanese Nightingale* (1901) have been reissued. Diana Birchall, Eaton's granddaughter, has written an eminently readable biography, and Dominika Ferens's *Edith and Winnifred Eaton* is the first book-length work on both sisters. These and other critical works are listed in the bibliography.

3. For an especially strong statement along these lines, see White-Parks, 33–34.

4. This attitude toward Winnifred's writing mirrors the way popular fiction by women, until recently, has been treated generally. As Jane Tompkins put it in 1985, "the *popularity* of novels by women has been held against them almost as much as their preoccupation with 'trivial' feminine concerns" (xiv).

5. For more about the varying critical responses to Edith and Winnifred, see Lape (188–189) and Ferens (3–4).

6. Winnifred's name is likewise submerged in the titles of the first two pieces written on the Eaton sisters. S. E. Solberg dropped Winnifred's name from the title of his paper, "The Eaton Sisters: Sui Sin Far and Onoto Watanna" (presented at the Pacific Northwest Asian American Writer's Conference, Seattle, Washington, 1976) when he published it in *MELUS* in 1981, despite the fact that the article discusses both. And Amy Ling made clear in the title of her first article on the Eaton sisters that her primary focus was on "Edith Eaton: Pioneer Chinamerican Writer and Feminist," even though she, too, discussed both sisters in her article.

7. The lack of scholarly interest in Winnifred is reflected in her absence from literature anthologies that include the work of Edith. Aside from *The Big Aiiieeeee!,* Edith's work also appears in the *Growing Up Asian American* (1993) and the most recent edition of *The Heath Anthology of American Literature.* Winnifred, however, has received only glancing attention from anthologists. The one recent anthology that includes her work is Blackwell Publishing's *Nineteenth-Century Women Writers,* ed. Karen Kilcup (1997), an odd place for her since she published the vast majority of her writings (including the story in the anthology) in the twentieth century.

8. See Scott for a discussion of "Oriental" music from the late nineteenth to mid-twentieth centuries.

9. I am counting Kingston's *The Woman Warrior* and *China Men* as novels along with *Tripmaster Monkey,* even though they were originally published as nonfiction.

10. The trope of the trickster was first applied to Eaton by Ling and was adopted by a number of other scholars in the late 1980s and early 1990s.

11. In particular, see Ferens, Hattori, Botshon, Oishi, and Najmi.

12. Ferens presents cogent analyses of two of Eaton's "non-Asian" short texts: "Eyes That Saw Not," a story written with her first husband, Bertrand Babcock, and "A Neighbor's Garden, My Own, and a Dream One" (1908), which I discuss in chapter 2. She also provides a short summary of Eaton's other texts. However, the overwhelming bulk of her analysis remains focused on the Japanese romances and *Marion.*

13. See Anzaldúa, Gates, and Chin.

14. Although the cultural nationalist strain of ethnic studies exemplified by Chin and others has been criticized most vociferously by feminist scholars like Anzaldúa, feminists also adhere to the idea of voice as identity.

15. Also see Saldívar.

16. Gavin Jones describes one sketch where an Irish American actor portrayed a Chinese and spoke in a mixture of English, German, and Chinese dialect in lines such as "Velly good, py gollies" and "One piecee beer mit pretzels" (173).

17. Clifford describes this "predicament" of "ethnographic modernity"; particularly relevant to this study are his readings of William Carlos Williams's poem "Elsie" (1–7), and chapter 3, "On Ethnographic Self-Fashioning: Conrad and Malinowski" (92–113).

18. Jones, 9–11; also see the distinction Spivak makes between "speaking about" and "speaking for" in "Can the Subaltern Speak?"

19. Michael Denning uses similar terms to describe the social function of another popular genre: dime novels. He writes that the genre was "a contested terrain, a field of cultural conflict where signs with wide appeal and resonance take on contradictory disguises and are spoken in contrary

accents" (3). Butler's analysis of resignification and ritual recitation in *Excitable Speech: A Politics of the Performative* is also relevant.

20. In this study, "voice" and "genre" are closely intertwined and sometimes mutually constitutive. Eaton was a writer of popular fiction; the voices of her characters were both defined by their genres and made recognizable because of them. Recently, writer Dagoberto Gilb described ethnic literature itself as a genre; he resists defining himself as a Chicano writer because "you're taken *only* as that. You're like a genre. There's mysteries, and there's romance and there's Chicano. That's a little offensive. And I try to transcend that" ("The Realities of Dagoberto Gilb: The Award-winning Writer Chooses to Transcend the Narrow Limitations of Genre," *Austin American-Statesman,* March 6, 2001, E2).

21. David Palumbo-Liu describes this phenomenon as the "fetishization of the present" (58).

22. Although I have teased out Ling's use of vocal tropes, voice per se is not one of his paramount concerns. The ubiquitous (and heretofore uninterrogated) use of "voice" in ethnic literary scholarship is worth noting, however.

23. Also see the introductions to Butler's *Excitable Speech* and *Bodies That Matter* for helpful (if complicated) analyses of the relationship between performative speech acts, agency, subject formation, and political action.

CHAPTER 1. HIDING BEHIND SHOJI

1. *Miss Numè of Japan* was reissued by the Johns Hopkins University Press in 1999, with an introduction by Eve Oishi.

2. In *Romance and the "Yellow Peril,"* Gina Marchetti catalogs the various film versions, which include *Madame Butterfly,* starring Mary Pickford (1915), *Toll of the Sea,* starring Anna May Wong (1922), and *His Birthright,* starring Sessue Hayakawa (1918).

3. See chapter 3 for a discussion of this novel.

4. "The Half-Caste," *Conkey's Home Journal,* [1898–1900?]. Enclosed in a scrapbook containing notes and clippings about Eaton's early work, preceding *A Japanese Nightingale.* Item in Winnifred Eaton Reeve Fonds, University of Calgary (hereafter cited as WER Fonds).

5. Various essays in Meech and Weisberg address the influence of Japanese arts on American painting, architecture, and home furnishings. Also see the volume edited by Holly Edwards, *Noble Dreams, Wicked Pleasures: Orientalism in America, 1870–1930* (Princeton University Press, 2000).

6. October 14, 1904. Photocopy in WER Fonds clipping file 132.

7. "Natural Fighters, She Says of Japs,"*Evening Telegram* (New York), February 12, 1904, photocopy in WER Fonds file 132; "Now Chicago Boasts

of Having a Japanese Woman Writer Who Is Destined to Make a Hit,"*Detroit Free Press,* [1898?], n.p., from scrapbook held in WER Fonds.

8. *Bookman,* [1899?]; *Union and Advertiser* (Rochester, New York), May 6, 1899. Photocopies in WER Fonds clipping file 132.

9. *Post-Intelligencer,* (Seattle), July 10, 1904. Photocopy in WER Fonds clipping file 132.

10. [1899?]. Photocopy in WER Fonds clipping file 132. My emphasis.

11. "Editor's Study,"*Harper's Monthly* 75 (September 1887): 339.

12. Sinclair Lewis, speech given on accepting the Nobel Prize for Literature, 1930.

13. Twenty years after the publication of *Madame Butterfly,* Long wrote a sequel to the story whose manuscript is held in the John Luther Long Papers at the Harry Ransom Humanities Research Center at the University of Texas–Austin. The sequel makes clear that Cho-Cho-San survives her attempted *seppuku,* although it has permanently maimed her. Whether he intended the ending of his original story to end this way is unknown; textual evidence is ambiguous.

14. See Ferens (169).

15. Based on the Harper & Bros sales records, a conservative estimate of Eaton's income from her novels alone, for the period 1899–1914, averages out to three thousand to four thousand dollars per year—a substantial income, especially if one considers that this figure does not include the significant income she would have received for serializations of her novels or for the numerous short stories and articles she published during this period.

16. "Onoto Watanna," supplement to *Harper's Weekly,* December 5, 1003, 1959; "Natural Fighters, She Says of Japs"; [*Conkey's Home Journal?*], n.d. Advance notice of contents of August issue of *Conkey's Home Journal.* Photocopy of clipping in WER Fonds file 132.

17. Review of *The Daughters of Nijo, Indianapolis Reader,* July 1904. Photocopy of clipping in WER Fonds file 132.

18. "You Can't Run Away from Yourself," undated MS, WER Fonds, 1. Thanks to Dominika Ferens for sharing this quotation with me.

19. Story idea for "The Pink Geisha," n.d.; R. W. Gilder to John Luther Long, March 30, 1898. Both items: John Luther Long Archives, 8.6 Correspondence: Literary—General 1893–1922 and n.d., held at the Harry Ransom Humanities Research Center, University of Texas–Austin.

20. My interpretation of "materiality" obviously departs from that presented by Lisa Lowe. However, Lowe's analysis of the material factors imposed on Asians and Asian Americans is relevant in a broad sense.

CHAPTER 2. NOT QUITE AT HOME

1. See Rafael (661, n. 2) for a listing of recent work on American and European imperialism and domesticity. Also see Kaplan, "Manifest Domesticity" for an assessment of mid-nineteenth-century domesticity in light of the American ideology of manifest destiny.

2. I take my definition of the "New Woman" largely from Carroll Smith-Rosenberg (173–177).

3. See Sutherland (169–175) for descriptions of various attempts made to reform domestic service.

4. Noting that American women writing about their experiences in the Philippines also placed domestic affairs in the foreground, Rafael argues that in doing so they were attempting to domesticate American imperialism, thus reifying the policy of "benevolent assimilation" advocated by McKinley (641).

5. *New York Times,* January 12, 1907.

6. Also see Mathews (92).

7. "A Servant Girl's Letter."

8. Salmon's likening of the "class" to "caste line" obviously resonates strongly with the contemporary debate between Booker T. Washington and W.E.B. Du Bois about social equality and the "color line."

9. Eaton's identification with "Norah" continued in her decision to name her alter ego in *Me* Nora Ascough.

10. For an interesting description of suburban women and their sociopolitical leanings, see Sies (193–210).

CHAPTER 3: ME: A BOOK OF REMEMBRANCE

1. Diana Birchall's biography, unsurprisingly, provides the most complete and accurate factual account of her life; Dominika Ferens compares the numerous versions of her biography that appeared in magazines and popular magazines in "Strategies of Authentication," chapter 4 of *Edith and Winnifred Eaton* (113–150).

2. This biography, as earlier chapters have already elaborated, characterized Onoto Watanna as the daughter of an English merchant (descended from English nobility) and the daughter of a samurai warrior; she was purportedly born in Nagasaki but had spent most of her life in the United States. For criticism attributing Eaton's reticence to reveal her true ethnic identity to her need to preserve her audience's belief in her pseudonymous persona, see Ling, "Revelation and Mask"; also see Matsukawa.

3. Ironically, White-Parks relies heavily on *Marion* to flesh out Edith Eaton's childhood period in her literary biography, *Sui Sin Far/Edith Maude Eaton.*

4. There are really too many sources corroborating this statement to

list here. For two particularly salient recent examples, see LeSeur (1) and Feng (20, 32, 42).

5. Sau-ling Cynthia Wong applies this quote from James Olney's essay "Autobiography and the Cultural Moment" to Asian American autobiography; Olney himself was describing African American literature in this statement. I feel it can also apply to "women's literature" as it has come to be known since the feminist movement of the 1970s.

6. Nearly every nonfictional work by Frank Chin written over the past twenty-five years has been a polemic against Asian American autobiography, especially as written by women. For example, see "This Is Not an Autobiography," *Genre* 18:2 (1985): 109–130; "The Most Popular Book in China," *Quilt* 4 (1984): 6–12, a parody of Kingston's *The Woman Warrior*; and "Come All Ye Asian American Writers of the Real and the Fake" (Chan et al. 1–93).

7. Ferens, for example, hardly even refers to the novel in her discussion of Eaton's "authorial identity."

8. "Is Onoto Watanna the Author of the Anonymous Novel *Me*?"

9. See Hapke for a survey of authors and texts.

10. I mention these works for their temporal proximity and their serendipitous titles; among others from the same period are James Weldon Johnson's *Autobiography of an Ex-Colored Man* (1912; this text will be discussed at the end of the chapter), Mary Johnson's *Hagar* (1912), and Virginia Woolf's *The Voyage Out* (1915). A more general study could also include earlier *Kunstlerromane* such as Dickens's *David Copperfield* (1850), Fanny Fern's *Ruth Hall* (1855), Louisa May Alcott's *Little Women* (1869), Elizabeth Stuart Phelps's *St. Elmo* (1867) and *The Story of Avis* (1877), Sarah Grand's *The Beth Book* (1897) and Kate Chopin's *The Awakening* (1899) among many, many others. For a general study of the *Kunstlerroman* (which analyzes only male authors) see Maurice Beebe's *Ivory Towers and Sacred Founts: The Artist as Hero in Fiction from Goethe to Joyce* (New York: New York University Press, 1964). For a lively survey of *Kunstlerromane* written by American women, see Huf. Also see Boumelha; and Terri Doughty's "Sarah Grand's *The Beth Book*: The New Woman and the Ideology of the Romance Ending," in *Anxious Power: Reading, Writing, and Ambivalence in Narrative by Women,* ed. Carol J. Singley and Susan Elizabeth Sweeney (Albany: SUNY Press, 1993).

11. Clemence Dane [Winifred Ashton], *The Women's Side* (1926), quoted in Boumelha (168).

12. For example, Royse's *Study of Genius* (1890) is, in many ways, a response to two magazine articles (one by James Sully that appeared in *Nineteenth Century* in early 1887 and another by Dr. William G. Stevenson that appeared in the March 1887 issue of *Popular Science Monthly*). All of

these works engaged the same debates over insanity/degeneration theories expounded by Lombroso and Hirsch. See Royse (40–51).

13. According to Eugene Taylor's reconstruction of James's 1896 Lowell Lectures on "Exceptional Mental States," James, unlike the writers mentioned here, did not find genius "morbid," "degenerative," or a form of insanity. He ascribed these opinions to an overly narrow view of mental health. Instead, he says, "The real lesson of the genius books is that we should welcome sensibilities, impulses, and obsessions if we have them, so long as by their means the field of our experience grows deeper and we contribute the better to the race's stores; that we should broaden our notion of health instead of narrowing it; that we should regard no single element of weakness as fatal—in short, that we should—*not be afraid of life*. Rather, all these geniuses and their mental peculiarities are organs by which mankind works out the experience which is its destiny" (164).

14. Huf was speaking specifically of the black woman writer, but her statement clearly applies to the absence of works by any writers concerning a woman writer of color. Since Huf's study, scholars have discovered other depictions of women writers of color, although none of these women achieve the kind of literary success that Nora/Eaton does. Ammons, for example, discusses Frances Harper's *Iola Leroy* (1892) and Edith Eaton's "Mrs. Spring Fragrance" (1912), both of whose characters engage in written expression but are neither professional writers nor artists in the conventional sense.

15. See Hapke for an assessment of Laura Jane Libbey's work.

16. *Autobiography* (1877): 2:110, quoted in Corbett (92).

17. For more about this aspect of women's writing, see Mary Kelley's groundbreaking study, *Private Woman/Public Stage: Literary Domesticity in Nineteenth-Century America* (New York: Oxford University Press, 1984). More recently, Corbett helpfully characterizes the "private/public" split and its manifestation in British women's autobiography (especially in chapters 2 and 3).

18. Huf (chapter 1). Also see Fraiman for the British context; and Smith for a general study of the autobiographical impulse in women's writing.

19. *Smart Set,* January 1916; reprinted in *Willa Cather and Her Critics* (Ithaca: Cornell University Press, 7).

20. Webster, incidentally, was the author of the best-selling novel *Daddy-Long-Legs* (1912) and the niece of Mark Twain.

21. Royse notes that all geniuses have been produced by the "Caucasian and Mongoloid races" for reasons that are "so obvious that we hardly need pause to indicate it" (215); unfortunately, he does not mention any "Mongoloid geniuses" in his book.

22. Ammons (128–129) emphasizes the womblike, erotic, feminized nature of Panther Canyon in her reading of the novel.

23. Ferens treats the ethnographic influences on both Winnifred and Edith at length.

24. He names four; the other two are the Uncle Remus stories and the Fisk Jubilee Singers.

25. Eaton was alluding to *A Japanese Nightingale,* which was adapted for the Broadway stage in 1903. See the introduction to *Madame Butterfly and A Japanese Nightingale,* ed. Maureen Honey and Jean Lee Cole (New Brunswick, N.J.: Rutgers University Press, 2002) for more on the production.

26. Misspelling of "pottage" in the original; I assume Eaton's lapse into French was wholly unintentional and hesitate to ascribe any more importance to it than simply to point it out.

27. The figure also resonated with writers of racist persuasions: the subtitle of Madison Grant and Charles Stewart Davison's compilation of nativist essays, *The Alien in Our Midst* (1930), is "Selling Our Birthright for a Mess of Pottage."

28. All citations from *The New English Bible* (Cambridge: Cambridge University Press, 1961).

29. In all likelihood, the stories of Jacob and Esau told in Genesis 25 and 27 are retellings of the same ur-story.

30. Both the certificate from her second marriage and her death certificate listed her race as "white."

CHAPTER 4. CLAIMING THE BIG COUNTRY

1. "You Can't Run Away from Yourself."

2. Interview with Elizabeth Bailey Price, n.d., WER Fonds file 132.

3. The location and description of the Bar Q is reminiscent of the Reeves' ranch, Bow View; see Di Biase (5) for a photograph of the Bow View ranch house.

4. See Harrison, 34–35, 100–124; Melnyk, 90–93; Quantic, xix, 30–32, 126–127.

5. The incompetent Métis servant, in many ways, was the western Canadian counterpart to the incompetent, demoralized "Bridget" who appeared in American domestic fiction and likewise depended on racial prejudice to produce comic effects. See chapter 2 for a discussion of the Irish servant in Eaton's texts.

6. Tompkins and Denning more explicitly relate generic disruptions to ideological debate, Tompkins in sensational fiction and westerns and Denning with respect to dime novels and working-class fiction.

7. Also see Kolodny, *The Lay of the Land,* and Tompkins, *West of Everything,* for discussions of the male ethos of the prairie.

8. In his 1958 essay on *My Ántonia,* John Miller suggests a compromise between these two views. He notes that the novel is "deficient in structure" and that it "is episodic, lacks focus, and abounds in irrelevancies" (51–52), yet he defends the novel by attributing its structure to the cyclical passage of time rather than to a conventional Aristotelian plot.

9. According to a 1916 letter to Dorothy Canfield Fisher, Cather's use of indirect discourse resulted from difficulties she encountered in rendering translations of German immigrant speech in *The Song of the Lark*; according to Guy Reynolds's paraphrase of the letter (the estate does not allow publication of Cather's letters), she decided that her original idea of "using single and double quotation marks to indicate the translated nature of the language" resulted in "unwieldy" prose (2).

10. In 1923, Cather would characterize the era of Nebraskan history that she depicted in her prairie novels as having come to a close. See "Nebraska: The End of the First Cycle," *Nation* 117 (1923): 236–238.

11. Walter Benn Michaels argues that in both *The Professor's House* and *Death Comes for the Archbishop,* Cather's nostalgia for an Indian or Mexican past is enabled precisely because these populations were unable to assimilate to Western culture (35–38, 78–82).

12. For a discussion of Canadian immigration patterns and their similarities to and differences from immigration into the United States, see *The Vertical Mosaic,* by John Porter (1970) and *The Anatomy of Racism: Canadian Dimensions,* by David Hughes and Evelyn Kallen (1976).

13. Many of these characteristics, of course, are equally stereotypical. However, Eaton's depiction stops short of the kowtowing, Confucius-quoting, nauseatingly obsequious "Chinaman" who appeared in other novels and films of the period. One might compare Chum Lee to a "Chinese houseboy" depicted in R.J.C. Stead's 1918 novel, *The Cowpuncher:* "a Chinese boy (all male Chinese are boys) entered, bowing in that deference which is so potent to separate the white man from his silver. The white man glories in being salaamed, especially by an Oriental, who can grovel with a touch of art. And the Oriental has not been slow to capitalize on his master's vanity" (169).

14. Eaton's description of Nettie Day as a "young Juno" recalls the description of Nora Ascough's romantic rival in *Me;* Eaton also described her roommate Anna as an "oxlike" "young Juno" in another autobiographical piece, "New York Days," [1920s?], WER Fonds.

15. Eaton's familiarity with Spencerian thought and eugenics theory in general is indicated by her allusions to Spencer, Darwin, and Huxley not only here but in *Me, Marion,* and several of her Japanese romances. She was also an intimate friend of Samuel Clemens's niece, Jean Webster, a strong advocate for eugenics.

16. Spencer's first published work, *Education: Intellectual, Moral, Physical* (1861) was one of his most popular and was widely read throughout the nineteenth century. See Kennedy (13–14) for more on Spencer's ideas about education.

CHAPTER 5. SOUND EFFECTS

1. Diary in the collection of Diana Birchall. She continued, "I knew the story was no good . . . but none the less . . . I failed. I never failed before! I wish I were dead—." (Thanks to Diana for sharing a transcript of this diary with me.)

2. Letter from Eaton to Frank Reeve, WER Fonds 1.2.

3. The terminology applied to different forms of film writing was varied and variously applied and differed for silent and sound films. The writing process that Eaton followed at Universal was basically as follows: an *outline* would describe the main characters, setting, and plot, essentially a summary of the film. It often contained lines of dialogue or titles but was primarily written in expository style. Once the outline was approved by the head of the scenario department (the department responsible for the bulk of the screenwriting), a *treatment* would be written that would more explicitly describe the action of the movie, dividing the story into sequences and scenes but still containing expository text mixed with stage directions and dialogue. The *continuity* followed the treatment, and was what we would now call a screenplay, with all dialogue and stage directions in place and descriptions of all of the actors and sets required for the production. *Adaptations*, as the name implies, referred to treatments or continuities that were based on preexisting stories, novels, or plays. During the silent era, dialogue was written into the scripts, even though they would not be heard on screen. The dialogue provided direction for the actors and was often incorporated into titles. The bulk of the titles, however, were written after filming was completed.

4. The WER Fonds contain a large amount of material from Eaton's days at Universal, including scripts from the 1929 version of *Show Boat* (3.23), the 1925 version of *Phantom of the Opera* (3.25), *What Men Want* (8.74), *Carnival* (9.88, released as *Young Desire*), *The Love Thief* (10.95), *Shanghai Lady* (11.103), as well as many, many others that were never produced. It also contains screen adaptations for *Me* (3.22), *Cattle* (6.50, retitled *Wild Seed!* and written by Helen Clifton), and *Sunny-San* (9.81).

5. WER Fonds 1.2. This chapter differs from the others in the wealth of archival materials available for this period in Eaton's career. Very little of Eaton's correspondence before 1920 is extant.

6. In December 1925, for example, she protested when Universal gave Mrs. C. C. Wilkening and Coningsby Dawson credit for a script called

Ninety North, about Robert Peary's trek to the North Pole. Eaton claimed that *she* was in fact the primary collaborator and was eventually reinstated (the film, as far as I know, was never produced). Mrs. Wilkening, however, issued the following warning: "If, however, she [Eaton] undertakes to write any original scenario employing any of my materials, which she sells as her own, she must expect me to take action." C. C. Wilkening to Eaton, April 24, 1926. WER Fonds 1.6. Eaton had evidently known Wilkening from her 1915 attempt to write for film serials. Her name is mentioned in the 1915 diary quoted above in the context of being a fellow screenwriter; however, Eaton did not mention anything specific regarding this earlier contact.

7. Eaton to Selig, October 8, 1934. In late 1926 or early 1927—fairly early on during her Hollywood stint—Eaton left Universal briefly to work at Metro-Goldwyn-Mayer and sent a memo to Harry Rapf and David O. Selznick listing 114 different stories that were "original with me" and probably written while she was at Universal. "It may be you will find some among them that may appeal to you for Metro Pictures," she wrote (interoffice memo from Reeve to Rapf and Selznick, January 20, 1927). See filmography for a list of Eaton's film work.

8. Films from the silent and early sound periods are often difficult to locate, particularly if they were "B" pictures, as many of Eaton's projects were, or if they received limited distribution, as was with the so-called "race pictures" made by nonwhite (primarily African American) filmmakers such as Oscar Micheaux. As a result, it has proved difficult to trace the participation of lesser-known film workers and minorities working in film. In their book on Micheaux's silent films, Pearl Bowser and Louise Spence report that they were able to locate viewable copies of only three of Micheaux's twenty-five known silent films (xxi). *Barbary Coast* is readily available on videotape, unlike most of Eaton's films, which are viewable only at university libraries and film archives when they can be located at all. I was able to view a number of films at UCLA (with the much-appreciated help of Dominika Ferens) and at the Library of Congress. Unfortunately, many of these copies were struck from the silent version of the films, making them less suitable for the concerns of this chapter. (During the early sound years, both silent and sound versions of films were released to accommodate theaters that had not yet switched to sound.)

9. Some films that appeared closely affiliated with Eaton's earlier work were not actually guided by her ideas in the same ways as *Barbary Coast.* For example, *East Is West* deals explicitly with miscegenation and features a Chinese heroine (played by Mexican American actress Lupé Velez). However, Eaton's adaptation (coauthored with Tom Reed) differed very little from Shipman's original play, providing little opportunity to analyze

Eaton's role in the production of the film's meaning. (Incidentally, *East Is West* had already been made into a successful 1922 film, with a scenario written by Eaton's friend Frances Marion.)

10. Because I focus on the treatment in my analysis, I have used the character names and descriptions from that script. The changes made from outline to treatment, and even within the texts themselves, were numerous. Lily's name changes from Susy Rooney to Lily Mooney and also appears as Lily Brandon; her father's name changes from Dan Rooney to Dan Mooney and also appears as Bull Brandon (recalling the Bull Langdon of *Cattle*). Roger Storm is also known as Dan Avery and changes occupations from urban priest to district attorney.

11. For more on the production code, see Black and Vasey, among many others.

12. WER Fonds 1.5.10.

13. The WER Fonds contain a description of characters and sets for a continuity of *Barbary Coast* dated November 15, 1929 and signed by Edward T. Lowe, followed by the first two pages of what I assume is the missing continuity script.

14. Eaton to C. Gardner Sullivan, November 26, 1929. WER Fonds 1.6.

15. Unidentified reader's report, December 21, 1929; telegram from Joy to John P. Hutchings, December 17, 1929; both items in the PCA file for *Barbary Coast* (1935), at the Academy of Motion Picture Arts and Sciences (AMPAS). Thanks to Scott Curtis at AMPAS for locating and transcribing this information for me. I have not been able to ascertain Hutchings's role in the project.

16. In addition to Hecht and MacArthur, these writers included William DuBois, Frances Marion, Louis Witzenkorn, Marcus Goodrich, Joel Sayre, Willard Mack, Hugh Wiley, Kenyon Nicholson, Dwight Taylor, Leonard Praskins, Courtenay Terret, Nat J. Ferber, and Oliver H. P. Garrett (letter from Scott Curtis to author, 27 March 1998).

17. *American Film Institute Catalog of Motion Pictures Produced in the United States, Feature Films, 1931–1940* (Metuchen, N.J.: Scarecrow Press, 1971–), 117. Black narrates the pre-production content debates for this and many other films.

18. Many of the elements that reinforced Hecht's ideas were duly excised in the version that was eventually released.

19. In *King Kong,* for example, the Chinese cook has more lines than several of the credited cast members but is left off the credits. Needless to say, Asians without lines were almost never acknowledged. The title of *Aiiieeeee! An Anthology of Asian American Writers* (ed. Chin et al., 1974) alludes to the dying scream of the Oriental.

20. Vasey estimates that between the world wars, the major studios

"derived an average of 35% of their gross revenue from the foreign field, a larger proportion of revenues than most other American export industries earned abroad" (7).

21. Michael Rogin discusses the use of blackface minstrelsy in *The Jazz Singer* (1927) as a transformative moment in cinematic race relations and writes that although the popularity of Jolson's movie created roles for blacks in the 1930s, they primarily consisted of "variations on the narrativized minstrel roles of mammy, tom, and coon" (167); Moy describes the roles of the self-sacrificing Asian woman, the "hop-head," and the nefarious Fu Manchu characters as examples of "authenticated stereotypes" (15) that originated in nineteenth-century representations of Asians in literature, journalism, drama, and vaudeville.

22. James Wong Howe, director Howard Hawks's favored cinematographer, is one extremely visible, if also silent, exception, as is James B. Leong (an assistant director on Griffith's *Broken Blossoms,* 1919, and actor in a number of films).

23. Both Sessue Hayakawa and Anna May Wong left Hollywood for Europe because of the scarcity of compelling film roles.

Epilogue

1. All information taken from the August 12, 2000 UPI wire report, "Russia Frees POW after 53 Years."

2. All information on the 2000 Republican National Convention taken from CNN Web site article, "At GOP Convention, Bush Nephew Attracts Younger Voters, Hispanics," by Mike Ferullo, August 4, 2000 (www.cnn. com/2000/ALLPOLITICS/stories/08/03/bush.young/ [consulted October 9, 2000]).

3. Janice Radway, Jane Tompkins, Michael Denning, and Houston Baker, among others, have shown how formula and genre fiction both contain resistance and enable instances of subversion. Thus, according to Radway and Tompkins, writers of romance and of sensational fiction simultaneously uphold patriarchal narrative structures and empower their female readers. Likewise, Baker argues, African American writers of the late nineteenth and early twentieth centuries engaged the tropes of minstrelsy to simultaneously cater to a racist white readership and to undermine racist ideology.

Bibliography

WORKS BY WINNIFRED EATON

The Winnifred Eaton Reeve (WER) Fonds at the University of Calgary contain many unpublished manuscripts, including several autobiographical pieces.

NOVELS

1899   *Miss Numè of Japan.* Chicago: Rand, McNally.
1901   *A Japanese Nightingale.* New York: Harper and Brothers.
1902   *The Wooing of Wistaria.* New York: Macmillan.
1903   *The Heart of Hyacinth.* New York: Harper and Brothers.
1904   *The Daughters of Nijo.* New York: Harper and Brothers.
       The Love of Azalea. New York: Dodd, Mead.
1906   *A Japanese Blossom.* New York: Harper and Brothers.
1907   *The Diary of Delia: Being a Veracious Chronicle of the Kitchen with Some Side-Lights on the Parlour.* New York: Doubleday, Page. (Originally serialized in the *Saturday Evening Post,* 1907.)
1910   *Tama.* New York: Harper and Brothers.
1912   *The Honorable Miss Moonlight.* New York: Harper and Brothers.
1915   *Me: A Book of Remembrance.* New York: Century. (Originally serialized in *Century Magazine,* 1915.)
       Miss Spring Morning. Serialized in *Blue Book Magazine* (January 1915): 666–720.
1916   *Marion: The Story of an Artist's Model.* New York: W. J. Watt. (Originally serialized in *Hearst's Magazine,* 1916).
1920s *Movie Madness.* Serialized in *Screen Secrets* [n.d., 1920s]. WER Fonds, box 15.
1922   *Sunny-San.* New York: George H. Doran.
1924   *Cattle.* New York: W. J. Watt.
1925   *His Royal Nibs.* New York: W. J. Watt.

SHORT STORIES AND MAGAZINE ARTICLES

1897 or 1898   "A Japanese Girl." *Cincinnati Commercial Tribune.*

1898   "A Half-Caste." *Frank Leslie's Popular Monthly* (September): 489–496.

1899   "Where the Young Look Forward to Old Age." *Ladies' Home Journal* (February): 8.

"The Life of a Japanese Girl." *Ladies' Home Companion* (April): 7.

Letter from "Onoto Watanna" to *Book News,* in response to the question, "Why did you write *Miss Numè of Japan?*" (May): 487.

1900   "New Year's Day in Japan." *Frank Leslie's Popular Monthly* (January): 283–286.

1901   "Two Converts." *Harper's Monthly* (September): 585–589.

"Kirishima-san." *Idler* (November): 315–321.

"Margot." *Frank Leslie's Popular Monthly* (December): 202–209.

1902   "Eyes That Saw Not." With Bertrand Babcock. *Harper's Monthly* (June): 30–38.

"A Contract." *Frank Leslie's Popular Monthly* (August): 370–379.

"Japanese Drama and the Actor." *Critic* (September): 231–237.

1903   "*The Darling of the Gods*: A Japanese Play Criticized by a Japanese." *Critic* (January). [Eaton's authorship of this article is not yet confirmed.]

"The Loves of Sakura Jiro and the Three Headed Maid." *Century Magazine* (March): 755–760.

"Miss Lily and Miss Chrysanthemum." *Ladies' Home Journal* (August): 11–12.

1904   "The Marvelous Miniature Trees of Japan." *Woman's Home Companion* (June): 16–17.

"Every-day Life in Japan." *Ladies' Home Journal* (October): 500–503, 527–528.

1906   "The Wrench of Chance." *Harper's Weekly* (October 20): 1494–1496, 1505; (October 27): 1531–1533.

1907   "The Japanese in America." *Eclectic Magazine* (February): 100–104.

1908   "The Manoeuvres of O-yasu-san." *Saturday Evening Post* (January 25): 9–11, 22.

"A Neighbor's Garden, My Own, and a Dream One." *Good Housekeeping* (April): 347–353; (May): 485–490.

"Delia Dissents." *Saturday Evening Post* (August): 22–23.

1909   "A Daughter of Two Lands." *The Red Book Magazine* (November): 33–48.

"An Unexpected Grandchild." *Lippincott's Monthly* (December): 689–696.

1910   "The Marriage of Okiku-San." *The Red Book Magazine* (June): 254–263.

1912   "The Marriage of Jinyo." *The Red Book Magazine* (February): 740–744.

1919   "Lend Me Your Title." *MacLean's Magazine* (February): 13, 14, 72–74; (March): 16, 18–19, 66–69.
"Other People's Troubles: An Antidote to Your Own." *Farm and Ranch Review* [serialized February–August].

1922   "Starving and Writing in New York." *MacLean's Magazine* (October 15): 66–67.

1923   "Elspeth." *Quill* (January): 23–30.
"The Canadian Spirit in Our Literature." *Calgary Daily Herald,* March 24, 1923. Item 132.102 in WER Fonds.

1924   "Royal and Titled Ranchers in Alberta." *Montreal Daily Star,* August 30, 1924.

1928   "Butchering Brains: An Author in Hollywood Is as a Lamb in an Abattoir." *Motion Picture Magazine* 28–29, 110–111.
"Honorable Movie Takee Sojin." *Motion Picture Classics Magazine* (March).

1929   "What Happened to Hayakawa? The Japanese Gentleman Reveals Why He Forsook the American Screen." *Motion Picture Magazine* (January).
"I Could Get Any Woman's Husband!" *Motion Picture Classics Magazine* (March).
"How Frenchmen Make Love." *Motion Picture Magazine* (June).

1933   "Because We Were Lonely." *True Story* (April): 28–30, 92–96.

MISCELLANEOUS WORKS
1914   *A Chinese-Japanese Cookbook.* With Sara Bosse. Chicago, New York: Rand, McNally.

UNDATED WORKS (HELD IN WER FONDS)
"The Bird of Yonejiro."
"Elmer Clifton" (probably printed in a Calgary newspaper, mid–1920s).
"Ido." *Conkey's Home Journal* (August, probably 1898–1902).
"Literature as a Profession." Radio address, CFAC (Canadian radio, 1920s).
"Motor Hoboes" (1920s).
"The Pot of Paint." *Frank Leslie's Popular Monthly Magazine.*

ARTICLES ABOUT WINNIFRED EATON AND CRITICISM OF HER WORKS
Birchall, Diana. *Onoto Watanna: The Story of Winnifred Eaton.* Champaign: University of Illinois Press, 2001.

Botshon, Lisa. "Out of Bounds: The Politics of Romantic Smuggling in *Tama* (1910) and *Sunny-San* (1922)." Paper presented at the Association for Asian American Studies conference, Scottsdale, Ariz., May 25, 2000.

————. "Winifred Eaton: 'A Life of Not Unjoyous Deceit.'" In "Pretending to Be Me: Ethnic Transvestitism and Cross-Writing," edited by Joseph Lockard and Melinda Micco (1995). Manuscript.

Di Biase, Linda Popp. "The Alberta Years of Winnifred Eaton Babcock Reeve." *Alberta History* 39:2 (spring 1991): 1–8.

Doyle, James. "Sui Sin Far and Onoto Watanna: Two Early Chinese-Canadian Authors." *Canadian Literature* 140 (spring 1994): 50–58.

Ferens, Dominika. *Edith and Winnifred Eaton: The Uses of Ethnography in Turn-of-the-Century Asian American Literature*. Urbana: University of Illinois Press, 2002.

Hattori, Tomo. "Model Minority Discourse and Asian American Jouis-Sense." *differences* 11:2 (1999): 228–247.

Lape, Noreen Grover. "Bartered Brides and Compulsory Bachelors on the Asian-American Frontiers: The Marriage Fiction of Sui Sin Far and Onoto Watanna." In "West of the Border: Cultural Liminality in the Literature of the Western American Frontiers," 177–275. Ph.D. diss., Temple University, 1996.

Ling, Amy. *Between Worlds: Women Writers of Chinese Ancestry*. New York: Pergamon Press, 1990.

————. "Chinese American Women Writers: The Tradition behind Maxine Hong Kingston." In *Redefining American Literary History*, edited by A. LaVonne Ruoff and Jerry Ward Jr., 219–236. New York: Modern Literature Association, 1990.

————. "Creating One's Self: The Eaton Sisters." In *Reading the Literatures of Asian America*, edited by Shirley Geok-Lin Lim and Amy Ling, 305–318. Philadelphia: Temple University Press, 1992.

————. "Revelation and Mask: Autobiographies of the Eaton Sisters," *A/B Auto/Biography Studies* 3:2 (summer 1987): 49.

————. "Winnifred Eaton: Ethnic Chameleon and Popular Success." *MELUS* 11:3 (1984): 5–15.

Matsukawa, Yuko. "Cross-Dressing and Cross-Naming: Decoding Onoto Watanna." In *Tricksterism in Turn-of-the-Century U.S. Literature,* edited by Elizabeth Ammons and Annette White-Parks, 106–125. Hanover: University Press of New England, 1994.

Moser, Linda Trinh. Afterword to *Me: A Book of Remembrance,* 357–372. Jackson: University Press of Mississippi, 1998.

————. "Chinese Prostitutes, Japanese Geishas, and Working Women: Images of Race, Class and Gender in the Work of Edith Eaton/Sui Sin Far and Winnifred Eaton/Onoto Watanna." Ph.D. diss., University of California–Davis, 1997.

Najmi, Samina. Introduction to *The Heart of Hyacinth*, v–xlvi. Seattle: University of Washington Press, 2000.

———. "Racio-Cultural Fluidity as Rebellion in Onoto Watanna's *The Heart of Hyacinth*." In "Representations of White Women in Works by Selected African American and Asian American Authors," 126–158. Ph.D. diss., Tufts University, 1997.

Oishi, Eve. Introduction to *Miss Numè of Japan*, xii–xxxi. Baltimore: The Johns Hopkins University Press, 1999.

Rooney, Doris. "Souvenir from the Past." *Field, Horse, and Rodeo* (July 1963): 45–47.

Shea, Pat. "Winnifred Eaton and the Politics of Miscegenation in Popular Fiction," *MELUS* 22:2 (summer 1997).

Solberg, S. E. "Sui Sin Far/Edith Eaton: First Chinese-American Fictionist." *MELUS* 8:1 (spring 1981): 27–39.

Spaulding, Carol Vivian. "Turning Japanese: Ethnic Improvisation in the Work of Winnifred Eaton/Onoto Watanna." In "Blue-Eyed Asians: Eurasianism in the Work of Edith Eaton/Sui Sin Far, Winnifred Eaton/Onoto Watanna, and Diana Chang," 164–248. Ph.D. diss., University of Iowa, 1996.

White-Parks, Annette. *Sui Sin Far/Edith Maude Eaton: A Literary Biography*. Urbana: University of Illinois Press, 1995.

OTHER WORKS CONSULTED

Addams, Jane. *Twenty Years at Hull House*. 1910. Reprint, New York: Signet, 1938.

Alexander, Ruth M. *The Girl Problem: Female Sexual Delinquency in New York, 1900–1930*. Ithaca: Cornell University Press, 1995.

Ammons, Elizabeth. *Conflicting Stories: American Women Writers at the Turn into the Twentieth Century*. New York: Oxford University Press, 1992.

Amott, Teresa L., and Julie A. Matthaei. *Race, Gender, and Work: A Multicultural Economics History of Women in the United States*. Boston: South End Press, 1991.

Anderson, Benedict. *Imagined Communities: Reflections on the Origin and Spread of Nationalism*. Rev. ed. London: Verso, 1991.

Angstman, C. S. "The Story of a Houseworker." *Independent*, July 11, 1907.

Anzaldúa, Gloria. *Borderlands/La Frontera: The New Mestiza*. San Francisco: Aunt Lute Books, 1987.

Austin, Mary. *Earth Horizon*. New York: Literary Guild, 1932.

———. *A Woman of Genius*. 1912. Reprint, New York: Houghton Mifflin, 1917.

Bacon, Alice Mabel. *Japanese Girls and Women*. Rev. ed. Boston: Houghton Mifflin, 1902.

Bailey, L. H. *Manual of Gardening: A Practical Guide to the Making of Home Grounds and the Growing of Flowers, Fruits, and Vegetables for Home Use*. New York: Macmillan, 1911.

Baker, Houston. *Modernism and the Harlem Renaissance*. Chicago: University of Chicago Press, 1987.

Banta, Martha. *Imaging American Women: Idea and Ideals in Cultural History*. New York: Columbia University Press, 1987.

Barbary Coast. Directed by Howard Hawks. Screenplay by Ben Hecht and Charles MacArthur. MGM, 1935.

Beauchamp, Cari. *Without Lying Down: Frances Marion and the Powerful Women of Early Hollywood*. New York: Scribner, 1997.

Bederman, Gail. *Manliness and Civilization: A Cultural History of Gender and Race in the United States, 1880–1917*. Chicago: University of Chicago Press, 1995.

Bennett, Ida. *The Flower Garden: A Handbook of Practical Garden Lore*. New York: McClure, Phillips, 1903.

Bernardi, Daniel, ed. *The Birth of Whiteness: Race and the Emergence of U.S. Cinema*. New Brunswick, N.J.: Rutgers University Press, 1996.

Bernstein, Matthew. Introduction to *Visions of the East: Orientalism in Film,* edited by Matthew Bernstein and Gaylyn Studlar, 1–18. New Brunswick, N.J.: Rutgers University Press, 1997.

The Bitter Tea of General Yen. Directed by Frank Capra. Performances by Barbara Stanwyck, Nils Asther, and Toshia Mori. Columbia, 1932.

Black, Gregory D. *Hollywood Censored: Morality Codes, Catholics, and the Movies*. New York: Cambridge University Press, 1994.

Blodgett, E. D. "Fictions of Ethnicity in Prairie Writing." In *Configuration: Essays in the Canadian Literatures,* 85–111. Downsview, Ont.: ECW Press, 1982.

Bogle, Donald. *Toms, Coons, Mulattoes, Mammies, and Bucks: An Interpretive History of Blacks in American Films*. New York: Viking, 1973.

Bordwell, David, Janet Staiger, and Kristin Thompson. *The Classical Hollywood Cinema*. New York: Columbia University Press, 1985.

Borus, Daniel H. *Writing Realism: Howells, James, and Norris in the Mass Market*. Chapel Hill: University of North Carolina Press, 1989.

Boumelha, Penny. "The Woman of Genius and the Woman of Grub Street: Figures of the Female Writer in British *Fin-de-Siècle* Fiction." *English Literature in Translation* 40:2 (1997): 164–180.

Bourdieu, Pierre. *Distinction: A Social Critique of the Judgment of Taste*. Cambridge: Harvard University Press, 1984.

———. *The Rules of Art: Genesis and Structure of the Literary Field*. Stanford: Stanford University Press, 1996.

Bowser, Pearl, and Louise Spence. *Writing Himself into History: Oscar*

Micheaux, His Silent Films, and His Audiences. New Brunswick, N.J.: Rutgers University Press, 2000.

Brodhead, Richard. *Cultures of Letters: Scenes of Reading and Writing in Nineteenth-Century America.* Chicago: University of Chicago Press, 1993.
———, ed. *The Journals of Charles W. Chesnutt.* Durham: Duke University Press, 1993.

Broken Blossoms. Directed by D. W. Griffith. Assistant director James B. Leong (uncredited). Technical adviser Moon Kwan. Performances by Lillian Gish and Richard Barthelmess. United Artists, 1919.

Brownlow, Kevin. *Behind the Mask of Innocence.* New York: Knopf, 1990.

Butler, Judith. *Bodies That Matter: On the Discursive Limits of "Sex."* New York: Routledge, 1993.
———. *Excitable Speech: A Politics of the Performative.* New York: Routledge, 1997.

Cahan, Abraham. *The Rise of David Levinsky.* 1917. Reprint, New York: Penguin, 1993.

Cather, Willa. *A Lost Lady.* 1923. Reprinted in *Willa Cather, Later Novels,* edited by Sharon O'Brien. New York: Library of America, 1990.
———. *My Ántonia.* 1918. Reprint, Boston: Houghton Mifflin, 1988.
———. *O! Pioneers.* 1913. Reprint, Boston: Houghton Mifflin, 1941.
———. *The Professor's House.* New York: Knopf, 1925.
———. *The Song of the Lark.* 1915. Reprint, New York: Houghton Mifflin, 1988.

Ceplair, Larry. *A Great Lady: A Life of the Sreenwriter Sonya Levien.* Lanham, Md.: Scarecrow Press, 1996.

Chamberlain, Basil Hall. *Letters from Basil Hall Chamberlain to Lafcadio Hearn.* Compiled by Kazuo Koizumi. Tokyo, Hokuseido Press, 1936.
———. *Things Japanese.* 5th ed. London: J. Murray, 1905.

Chan, Jeffery Paul, et al., eds. *The Big Aiiieeeee!: An Anthology of Chinese American and Japanese American Literature.* New York: Meridian, 1991.

Chang. Directed by Merian C. Cooper and Ernest B. Schoedsack. Titles by Achmed Abdullah. Paramount, 1927.

Chesnutt, Charles. *The Conjure Woman and Other Stories.* 1899. Reprint, Ann Arbor: University of Michigan Press, 1969.
———. *The Marrow of Tradition.* Boston: Houghton Mifflin, 1901.

Cheung, King-Kok. *Articulate Silences: Hisaye Yamamoto, Maxine Hong Kingston, Joy Kogawa.* Ithaca: Cornell University Press, 1993.

Chin, Frank. *"The Chickencoop Chinaman" and "The Year of the Dragon": Two Plays.* Seattle: University of Washington Press, 1981.
———. *Donald Duk.* Minneapolis: Coffee House Press, 1988.

Chin, Frank, et al., eds. *Aiiieeeee! An Anthology of Asian-American Writers.* Washington, D.C.: Howard University Press, 1974.

Chisholm, Lawrence. *Fenollosa: The Far East and American Culture.* New Haven: Yale University Press, 1963.

Chopin, Kate. *The Awakening.* 1899. Reprinted in *"The Awakening" and Selected Stories.* New York: Penguin, 1986.

Chu, Patricia P. *Assimilating Asians: Gendered Strategies of Authorship in Asian America.* Chapel Hill: Duke University Press, 2000.

————. "'The Invisible World the Emigrants Built': Cultural Self-Inscription and the Antiromantic Plots of *The Woman Warrior.*" *Diaspora: A Journal of Transnational Studies* 2:1 (spring 1992): 95–115.

Chuman, Frank F. *The Bamboo People: Japanese-Americans, Their History and the Law.* 1976. Reprint, Chicago: Japanese American Research Project, Japanese American Citizens League, 1981.

Clifford, James. *The Predicament of Culture: Twentieth-Century Ethnography, Literature, and Art.* Cambridge: Harvard University Press, 1988.

Cohen, Rose. *Out of the Shadows.* New York: George H. Doran, 1918.

Corbett, Mary Jean. *Representing Femininity: Middle-Class Subjectivity in Victorian and Edwardian Women's Autobiographies.* New York: Oxford University Press, 1992.

Costello-Sullivan, Kathleen. "'In a New Country': Women and Nation in *My Ántonia.*" In *Domestic Goddesses,* edited by Kim Wells, November 28, 2000. *www.womenwriters.net/domesticgoddess/costellowsullivan. html* (consulted March 27, 2001).

Couvares, Francis. "Hollywood, Main Street, and the Church." In *Movie Censorship and American Culture,* edited by Francis Couvares, 129–158. Washington, D.C.: Smithsonian Institute Press, 1996.

Cowan, Ruth Schwartz. *More Work for Mother: The Ironies of Household Technology from the Open Hearth to the Microwave.* New York: Basic Books, 1983.

Craig, Terence. *Racial Attitudes in English-Canadian Fiction, 1905–1980.* Waterloo, Ont.: Wilfred Laurier University Press, 1987.

Crane, Stephen. *Maggie: A Girl of the Streets: A Story of New York.* 1893. Reprint, New York: W. W. Norton, 1979.

Cripps, Thomas. "The Making of *The Birth of a Race*: The Emerging Politics of Identity in Silent Movies." In *The Birth of Whiteness: Race and the Emergence of U.S. Cinema,* edited by Daniel Bernardi, 38–55. New Brunswick, N.J.: Rutgers University Press, 1996.

————. *Slow Fade to Black: The Negro in the American Film, 1900–1942.* New York: Oxford University Press, 1977.

Dardis, Tom. *Some Time in the Sun.* New York: Scribner's, 1976.

Davies, Margery. *Woman's Place Is at the Typewriter: Office Work and Office Workers, 1870–1930.* Philadelphia: Temple University Press, 1982.

Davis, Angela. *Women, Race, and Class.* New York: Random House, 1983.

Dearborn, Mary. *Pocahontas's Daughters: Gender and Ethnicity in American Literature.* New York: Oxford, 1986.

Denning, Michael. *Mechanic Accents: Dime Novels and Working-Class Culture in America.* London: Verso, 1987.

Dick, Bernard F. *City of Dreams: The Making and Remaking of Universal Pictures.* Lexington, Ky.: University Press of Kentucky, 1997.

Dreiser, Theodore. *Jennie Gerhardt.* 1911. Reprint, New York: Penguin, 1992.

———. *Sister Carrie.* 1900. Reprint, New York: Signet, 1961.

DuBois, Ellen Carol, and Vicki L. Ruiz. *Unequal Sisters: A Multicultural Reader in U.S. Women's History.* New York: Routledge, 1990.

DuBois, W.E.B. *The Souls of Black Folk.* 1903. Reprinted in *Three Negro Classics: "Up from Slavery," "The Souls of Black Folk," and "The Autobiography of an Ex-Colored Man."* New York: Avon Books, 1965.

Dudden, Faye. *Serving Women: Household Service in Nineteenth-Century America.* Middletown, Conn.: Wesleyan University Press, 1983.

Dulles, Foster Rhea. *Yankees and Samurai: America's Role in the Emergence of Modern Japan.* New York: Harper and Row, 1965.

East of Borneo. Directed by George Melford. Story by Dale Van Every. Screenplay by Edwin H. Knopf. Continuity by Winnifred Eaton Reeve and Isadore Bernstein (uncredited). Universal, 1931.

Eaton, Edith [Sui Sin Far]. "Leaves from the Mental Portfolio of an Eurasian." 1909. Reprinted in *The Big Aiiieeeee!: An Anthology of Chinese American and Japanese American Literature,* edited by Jeffery Paul Chan et al., 111–123. New York: Penguin, 1991.

Ellis, Lorna. *Appearing to Diminish: Female Development and the British Bildungsroman, 1750–1850.* Lewisburg: Bucknell University Press, 1999.

Ely, Helena Rutherfurd. *A Woman's Hardy Garden.* New York: Macmillan, 1903.

Emerson, John, and Anita Loos. *How to Write Photoplays.* New York: James A. McCann, 1920.

Erb, Cynthia. *Tracking King Kong: A Hollywood Icon in World Culture.* Detroit: Wayne State University Press, 1998.

Evans, Sara M. *Born for Liberty: A History of Women in America.* New York: Free Press, 1989.

Eyman, Scott. *The Speed of Sound: Hollywood and the Talkie Revolution, 1926–1930.* New York: Simon and Schuster, 1997.

Fairbanks, Carol. *Prairie Women: Images in American and Canadian Fiction.* New Haven: Yale University Press, 1986.

Feng, Pin-chia. *The Female Bildungsroman by Toni Morrison and Maxine Hong Kingston: A Postmodern Reading.* New York: Peter Lang, 1998.

Fetterley, Judith. "Willa Cather and the Fiction of Female Development." In *Anxious Power: Reading, Writing, and Ambivalence in Narrative by*

Women, edited by Carol J. Singley and Susan Elizabeth Sweeney, 221–234. Albany: State University of New York Press, 1993.

Fine, Lisa. *The Souls of the Skyscraper: Female Clerical Workers in Chicago, 1870–1930.* Philadelphia: Temple University Press, 1990.

Fine, Richard. *Hollywood and the Profession of Authorship.* Ann Arbor: UMI, 1985.

Fitzgerald, Michael. *Universal Pictures.* New York: Arlington House Publishers, 1977.

Fraiman, Susan. *Unbecoming Women: British Women Writers and the Novel of Development.* New York: Columbia University Press, 1993.

Francke, Lizzie. *Script Girls: Women Screenwriters in Hollywood.* London: BFI, 1994.

Fraser, Mary (Mrs. Hugh). *Letters from Japan: A Record of Modern Life in the Island Empire.* 2 vols. New York: Macmillan, 1899.

Friedman, Lester. *Unspeakable Images: Ethnicity and the American Cinema.* Urbana: University of Illinois Press, 1991.

Gaines, Jane. *Fire and Desire: Mixed-Race Movies in the Silent Era.* Chicago: University of Chicago Press, 2001.

————. "Fire and Desire: Race, Melodrama, and Oscar Micheaux." In *Black American Cinema,* edited by Manthia Diawara, 49–70. New York: Routledge, 1993.

Galton, Francis. *Hereditary Genius: An Inquiry into Its Laws and Consequences.* 1869. Reprint, London: Macmillan, 1914.

Gates, Henry Louis. *The Signifying Monkey: A Theory of African-American Literary Criticism.* New York: Oxford University Press, 1988.

Gilman, Charlotte Perkins. *Herland.* 1912. Reprint, New York: Pantheon Books, 1979.

————. *Women and Economics: A Study of the Economic Relation between Men and Women as a Factor in Social Evolution.* 1898. Reprint, New York: Harper and Row, 1966.

Gledhill, Christine. *Home Is Where the Heart Is: Studies in Melodrama and the Woman's Film.* London: BFI, 1987.

Godman, Inez A. "Ten Weeks in a Kitchen." *Independent,* October 17, 1901, 2459–2464.

Goritzina, Kyra. *Service Entrance: Memoirs of a Park Avenue Cook.* New York: Carrick and Evans, 1939.

Grant, Madison. *The Passing of the Great Race; or, The Racial Basis of European History.* New York: Scribner's, 1916.

Grove, Frederick Philip. "Assimilation." *MacLean's Magazine* (September 1, 1929): 75–79.

————. *Settlers of the Marsh.* 1925. Reprint, Toronto: McClelland and Stewart, 1966.

Grumbach, Doris. Foreword to *My Ántonia,* by Willa Cather. Boston: Houghton Mifflin, 1988.

Gubar, Susan. *Racechanges: White Skin, Black Face in American Culture.* New York: Oxford University Press, 1997.

Hamilton, Ian. *Writers in Hollywood, 1915–1951.* New York: Harper, 1990.

Hapke, Laura. *Tales of the Working Girl: Wage-Earning Women in American Literature, 1890–1925.* New York: Twayne, 1992.

Harrison, Dick. *Unnamed Country: The Struggle for a Canadian Prairie Fiction.* Edmonton: University of Alberta Press, 1977.

Hasanovitz, Elizabeth. *One of Them: Chapters from a Passionate Autobiography.* Boston: Houghton Mifflin, 1918.

Hayden, Dolores. *The Grand Domestic Revolution: A History of Feminist Designs for American Homes, Neighborhoods, and Cities.* Cambridge: MIT Press, 1981.

Hazard, Louise Lockwood. *The Frontier in American Literature.* New York: Thomas Y. Crowell, 1927.

Hearn, Lafcadio. *Exotics and Retrospectives.* Boston: Little, Brown, 1898.

———. *Glimpses of Unfamiliar Japan.* 2 vols. Boston: Houghton Mifflin, 1894.

———. *In Ghostly Japan.* Boston: Little, Brown, 1899.

———. *Japan, an Attempt at Interpretation.* New York: Macmillan, 1904.

———. *A Japanese Miscellany.* Boston: Little, Brown, 1901.

———. *Kokoro: Hints and Echoes of Japanese Inner Life.* Boston: Houghton Mifflin, 1896.

———. *Out of the East: Reveries and Studies of New Japan.* Boston: Houghton Mifflin, 1895.

Hecht, Ben. *A Child of the Century.* New York: Simon and Schuster, 1954.

Henderson, Elliott. "Harper's Bookshelf." *Harper's Advertiser* (December 1901): 66–67.

Heung, Marina. "The Family Romance of Orientalism: From *Madame Butterfly* to *Indochine.*" In *Visions of the East: Orientalism in Film,* edited by Matthew Bernstein and Gaylyn Studlar, 158–183. New Brunswick, N.J.: Rutgers University Press, 1997.

Higashi, Sumiko. *Cecil B. DeMille and American Culture: The Silent Era.* Berkeley: University of California Press, 1994.

———. "Ethnicity, Class, and Gender in Film: DeMille's *The Cheat.*" In *Unspeakable Images: Ethnicity and the American Cinema,* edited by Lester Friedman, 112–139. Urbana: University of Illinois Press, 1991.

Holliday, Wendy. *Hollywood's Modern Women: Screenwriting, Work Culture, and Feminism, 1910–1940.* Ph.D. diss., New York University, 1995.

Howard, Hilda. *The Writing on the Wall.* 1921. Reprint, Toronto: University of Toronto Press, 1974.

Howells, William Dean. "A Psychological Counter-Current in Recent Fiction." *North American Review* (December 1901): 872–888.

Huf, Linda. *A Portrait of the Artist as a Young Woman: The Writer as Heroine in American Literature.* New York: Frederick Ungar, 1983.

Hughes, David, and Evelyn Kallen. *The Anatomy of Racism: Canadian Dimensions.* Montreal: Harvest House, 1976.

Hutchinson, George. *The Harlem Renaissance in Black and White.* Cambridge: Harvard University Press, Belknap Press, 1995.

Hwang, David Henry. *M. Butterfly.* New York: Plume/Penguin, 1986.

Iriye, Akira. *Pacific Estrangement: Japanese and American Expansion, 1897–1911.* Cambridge: Harvard University Press, 1972.

Irving, Katrina. "Displacing Homosexuality: The Use of Ethnicity in Willa Cather's *My Ántonia.*" *Modern Fiction Studies* 36 (spring 1990): 90–102.

"Is Onoto Watanna Author of the Anonymous Novel '*Me*'?" *New York Times Book Review,* October 10, 1915.

James, Henry. *The Bostonians,* edited by R. D. Gooder. New York: Oxford University Press, 1984.

————. "Greville Fane." In *The Complete Tales of Henry James,* edited by Leon Edel, 8:1891–1892. Philadelphia: J. B. Lippincott, 1963.

The Jazz Singer. Directed by Alan Crosland. Performances by Al Jolson, May McEvoy, Warner Oland, and Eugenie Besserer. Warner Brothers, 1927.

Johnson, James Weldon. *The Autobiography of an Ex-Colored Man.* 1912. Reprinted in *Three Negro Classics: "Up from Slavery," "The Souls of Black Folk," and "The Autobiography of an Ex-Colored Man."* New York: Avon Books, 1965.

Jones, Gavin. *Strange Talk: The Politics of Dialect Literature in Gilded Age America.* Berkeley: University of California Press, 1999.

Kaplan, Amy. "'Left Alone with America': The Absence of Empire in the Study of American Culture." In *Cultures of United States Imperialism,* edited by Donald Pease and Amy Kaplan, 3–21. Durham: Duke University Press, 1993.

————. "Manifest Domesticity." *American Literature* 70 (September 1998): 581–606.

————. "Romancing the Empire: The Embodiment of American Masculinity in the Popular Historical Novel of the 1890s." *American Literary History* 2 (winter 1990): 659–690.

————. *The Social Construction of American Realism.* Chicago: University of Chicago Press, 1988.

Katzman, David M. *Seven Days a Week: Women and Domestic Service in Industrializing America.* New York: Oxford University Press, 1978.

Kelley, Mary. *Private Woman/Public Stage: Literary Domesticity in Nineteenth-Century America.* New York: Oxford University Press, 1984.

Kennedy, James G. *Herbert Spencer*. Boston: Twayne, 1978.

Kim, Elaine H. *Asian American Literature: An Introduction to the Writings and Their Social Context*. Philadelphia: Temple University Press, 1982.

——. Preface to *Charlie Chan Is Dead: An Anthology of Contemporary Asian American Fiction*, edited by Jessica Hagedorn, vii–xiv. New York: Penguin, 1993.

Kirihara, Donald. "The Accepted Idea Displaced: Stereotype and Sessue Hayakawa." In *The Birth of Whiteness: Race and the Emergence of U.S. Cinema*, edited by Daniel Bernardi, 81–100. New Brunswick, N.J.: Rutgers University Press, 1996.

Klotman, Phyllis. "The Black Writer in Hollywood, circa 1930: The Case of Wallace Thurman." In *Black American Cinema*, edited by Manthia Diawara, 80–92. New York: Routledge, 1993.

Kolodny, Annette. *The Land before Her: Fantasy and Experience of the American Frontiers, 1630–1860*. Chapel Hill: University of North Carolina Press, 1984.

——. *The Lay of the Land: Metaphor as Experience and History in American Life and Letters*. Chapel Hill: University of North Carolina Press, 1975.

Kornfeld, Eve, and Susan Jackson. "The Female Bildungsroman in Nineteenth-Century America: Parameters of a Vision." *Journal of American Culture* 10 (winter 1987): 69–75.

Koszarski, Richard. *An Evening's Entertainment: The Age of the Silent Feature Picture, 1915–1928*. Vol. 3 of *History of American Cinema*, edited by Charles Harpole. New York: Scribner's, 1990.

Kreisel, Henry. "The Prairie: A State of Mind." In *Trace: Prairie Writers on Writing*, edited by Birk Sproxton, 3–17. Winnipeg: Turnstone, 1986.

Lea, Homer. *The Valor of Ignorance*. New York: Harper, 1909.

Lears, T. J. Jackson. *No Place of Grace: Antimodernism and the Transformation of American Culture, 1880–1920*. New York: Pantheon, 1981.

Lee, Rachel. *The Americas of Asian American Literature: Gendered Fictions of Nation and Transnation*. Princeton: Princeton University Press, 1999.

LeSeur, Geta J. *Ten Is the Age of Darkness: The Black Bildungsroman*. Columbia: University of Missouri Press, 1995.

Levenstein, Harvey A. *Revolution at the Table: The Transformation of the American Diet*. New York: Oxford University Press, 1988.

Li, David Leiwei. *Imagining the Nation: Asian American Literature and Cultural Consent*. Stanford: Stanford University Press, 1998.

Lim, Shirley Geok-lin, and Amy Ling, eds. *Reading the Literatures of Asian America*. Philadelphia: Temple University Press, 1992.

Ling, Jinqi. *Narrating Nationalisms: Ideology and Form in Asian American Literature*. New York: Oxford University Press, 1998.

"The Literary Invasion of Asia." *Publisher's Weekly,* October 7, 1911, 1410.

Little, Frances. *The Lady of the Decoration.* New York: Century, 1906.

Liu, Eric. *Accidental Asian: Notes of a Native Speaker.* New York: Random House, 1998.

Lloyd, David. *Nationalism and Minor Literature: James Clarence Mangan and the Emergence of Irish Cultural Nationalism.* Berkeley: University of California Press, 1987.

Lombroso, Cesare. *The Man of Genius.* New York: Scribner's and Sons, 1891.

Long, John Luther. "Her Dear Barbarian." *Metropolitan* (July 1914): 20–22+.

————. John Luther Long Papers, 1870–1958. Harry Ransom Humanities Research Center, Austin.

————. *"Madame Butterfly." "Purple Eyes." "A Gentleman of Japan and a Lady." "Kito." "Glory."* New York: Century, 1898.

————. *Miss Cherry-Blossom of Tokyo.* Philadelphia: Lippincott, 1895.

————. "The Outrageous Miss Dawn-Dream." In *"Sixty Jane." "The Strike on the Schlafeplatz Railroad." "Our Anchel." "The Lady and Her Soul." "The Beautiful Graveyard." "Lucky Jim." "The Outrageous Miss Dawn-Dream." "The Little House in the Street." "The Atonement."* New York: Century, 1903.

————. "Temple of the Countless Gods." *Century Magazine* 87 (February 1914): 493–502.

————. *The Way of the Gods.* New York: Grosset and Dunlap, 1906.

Loos, Anita. *San Francisco.* 1936. Reprint, edited by Matthew Bruccoli, Carbondale: Southern Illinois University Press, 1976.

Lopez, Ana M. "Are All Latins from Manhattan? Hollywood, Ethnography, and Cultural Colonialism." In *Unspeakable Images: Ethnicity and the American Cinema,* edited by Lester Friedman, 404–424. Urbana: University of Illinois Press, 1991.

Lowe, Lisa. *Immigrant Acts: Asian American Cultural Politics.* Durham: Duke University Press, 1996.

Lyman, Stanford M. *The Asian in North America.* Santa Barbara: ABC-CLIO, 1970.

Ma, Sheng-mei. *Immigrant Subjectivities in Asian American and Asian Diaspora Literatures.* Albany: State University of New York Press, 1998.

Maas, Frederica Sager. *The Shocking Miss Pilgrim.* Louisville: University of Kentucky Press, 1999.

Mailloux, Steven. *Reception Histories: Rhetoric, Pragmatism, and American Cultural Politics.* Ithaca: Cornell University Press, 1998.

————. *Rhetorical Power.* Ithaca: Cornell University Press, 1989.

Malkiel, Theresa. *The Diary of a Shirtwaist Striker.* 1910. Reprint, Ithaca: Cornell University, ILR Press, 1990.

Maltby, Richard. "'Baby Face' or How Joe Breen Made Barbara Stanwyck Atone for Causing the Wall Street Crash." In *The Studio System,* edited by Janet Staiger, 251–278. New Brunswick, N.J.: Rutgers University Press, 1995.

———. "'To Prevent the Prevalent Type of Book': Censorship and Adaptation in Hollywood, 1924–1934." In *Movie Censorship and American Culture,* edited by Francis Couvares, 97–128. Washington, D.C.: Smithsonian Institute Press, 1996.

Marchetti, Gina. *Romance and the "Yellow Peril": Race, Sex, and Discursive Strategies in Hollywood Fiction.* Berkeley: University of California Press, 1993.

———. "Tragic and Transcendent Love in *The Forbidden City*." In *The Birth of Whiteness: Race and the Emergence of U.S. Cinema,* edited by Daniel Bernardi, 257–270. New Brunswick, N.J.: Rutgers University Press, 1996.

Marion, Frances. *Off with Their Heads!* New York: Macmillan, 1972.

Martin, Ann, and Virginia M. Clark, eds. *What Women Wrote: Scenarios, 1912–1929.* Frederick, Md.: University Publications of America, 1987.

Martin, Olga J. *Hollywood's Movie Commandments: A Handbook for Motion Picture Writers and Reviewers.* New York: H. W. Wilson, 1937.

Marx, Leo. *The Machine in the Garden: Technology and the Pastoral Idea in America.* New York: Oxford University Press, 1964.

Matthews, Glenna. *"Just a Housewife": The Rise and Fall of Domesticity in America.* New York: Oxford University Press, 1987.

May, Lary. *Screening Out the Past: The Birth of Mass Culture and the Motion Picture Industry.* New York: Oxford University Press, 1980.

Mayne, Judith. *Directed by Dorothy Arzner.* Bloomington: University of Indiana Press, 1994.

McClatchy, V. S. *Four Anti-Japanese Pamphlets.* 1919. Reprint, New York: Arno Press, 1978.

———. *The Germany of Asia: Japan's Policy in the Far East, Her "Peaceful Penetration" of the United States, How American Commercial and National Interests Are Affected.* Sacramento: Sacramento Bee, 1920.

McClung, Nellie L. *Painted Fires.* Toronto: McClelland and Stewart, 1925.

———. *Purple Springs.* Boston: Houghton Mifflin, 1922.

McCready. Marsha. *The Women Who Write the Movies: From Frances Marion to Nora Ephron.* Secaucus, N.J.: Carol Publications Group, 1994.

McCullough, Kate. *Regions of Identity: The Construction of America in Women's Fiction, 1885–1914.* Stanford: Stanford University Press, 1999.

McGilligan, Pat. *Backstory: Interviews with Screenwriters of Hollywood's Golden Age.* Berkeley: University of California Press, 1986.

Meech, Julia, and Gabriel P. Weisberg, eds. *Japonisme Comes to America:*

The Japanese Impact on the Graphic Arts, 1876–1925. New York: Abrams, 1990.

Melnyk, George. *From Writing-on-Stone to World War II.* Vol. 1 of *The Literary History of Alberta.* Edmonton: University of Alberta Press, 1998.

Meyerowitz, Joanne J. *Women Adrift: Independent Wage Earners in Chicago, 1880–1930.* Chicago: University of Chicago Press, 1988.

Michaels, Walter Benn. *Our America: Nativism, Modernism, and Pluralism.* Chapel Hill: University of North Carolina Press, 1995.

Micheaux, Oscar. *The Homesteader: A Novel.* 1917. Reprint, College Park, Md.: McGrath, 1969.

Miller, John. "*My Ántonia*: A Frontier Drama of Time." *American Quarterly* 10 (winter 1958): 476–484.

Montgomery, L. M. *Anne of Green Gables.* Boston: L.C. Page, 1908.

Morse, Edward Sylvester. *Japanese Homes and Their Surroundings.* 1885. Reprint, New York: Dover Publications, 1961.

Morrison, Toni. "Black Matters." In *Playing in the Dark: Whiteness and the Literary Imagination.* Cambridge: Harvard University Press, 1992.

Mott, Frank Luther. *Golden Multitudes: The Story of Best-Sellers in the United States.* New York: Macmillan, 1947.

Moy, James. *Marginal Sights: Staging the Chinese in America.* Iowa City: University of Iowa Press, 1993.

Musser, Charles. "Ethnicity, Role-playing, and American Film Comedy: From *Chinese Laundry Scene* to *Whoopee* (1894–1930)." In *Unspeakable Images: Ethnicity and the American Cinema,* edited by Lester Friedman, 39–81. Urbana: University of Illinois Press, 1991.

Nelson, John. "Shall We Bar the Yellow Race?" *MacLean's Magazine* (May 15, 1922): 13–14+.

Noguchi, Yone. *The American Diary of a Japanese Girl.* "By Miss Morning-Glory." Philadelphia: Frederick A. Stokes, 1902.

———. *Lafcadio Hearn in Japan.* New York: Mitchell Kennerley, 1911.

———. *The Story of Yone Noguchi: Told by Himself.* Philadelphia: George W. Jacobs, 1915.

Norden, Martin F. "Women in the Early Film Industry." *Wide Angle* 6:3 (1984): 58–67.

Norris, Kathleen. *Mother: A Story.* 1911. Reprint, Garden City, N.Y.: Doubleday, Page, and Co., 1924.

Ohmann, Richard. *Selling Culture: Magazines, Markets, and Class at the Turn of the Century.* New York: Verso, 1996.

Old San Francisco. Directed by Alan Crosland. Performances by Warner Oland, Dolores Costello, Anna May Wong, and Sojin. Warner Brothers, 1927.

Omi, Michael, and Howard Winant. *Racial Formation in the United States:*

From the 1960s to the 1980s. New York: Routledge and Kegan Paul, 1986.

Ostenso, Martha. *Wild Geese.* New York: Grosset and Dunlap, 1925.

Palumbo-Liu, David. "Theory and Subject of Asian American Studies." *Amerasia Journal* 21:1–2 (1995): 55–66.

Pascoe, Peggy. *Relations of Rescue: The Search for Female Moral Authority in the American West, 1874–1939.* New York: Oxford University Press, 1990.

Peattie, Elia. "Books and the People Who Write Them." *Chicago Daily Tribune,* August 21, 1915, 8.

Pitkin, Walter B. and William M. Marston. *The Art of Sound Pictures.* New York: D. Appleton, 1930.

Porter, John. *The Vertical Mosaic.* Toronto: University of Toronto Press, 1970.

Price, Elizabeth Bailey. "Onota [sic] Watanna Has Written a New Book," *Canadian Bookman* (April 1922): 123–125.

Quantic, Diane Dufva. *The Nature of the Place: A Study of Great Plains Fiction.* Lincoln: University of Nebraska Press, 1995.

Radway, Janice. *Reading the Romance: Women, Patriarchy, and Popular Literature.* 1984. Reprint, Chapel Hill: University of North Carolina Press, 1991.

Rafael, Vicente L. "Colonial Domesticity: White Women and United States Rule in the Philippines." *American Literature* 67 (December 1995): 639–666.

Rain. Directed by Lewis Milestone. Performances by Joan Crawford and Walter Huston. Adapted by Maxwell Anderson. Based on story, "Miss Thompson," by W. Somerset Maugham. Feature Productions, 1932.

Ramsaye, Terry. *A Million and One Nights: A History of the Motion Picture.* New York: Simon and Schuster, 1964.

Regester, Charlene. "Black Films, White Censors: Oscar Micheaux Confronts Censorship in New York, Virginia, and Chicago." In *Movie Censorship and American Culture,* edited by Francis Couvares, 159–186. Washington, D.C.: Smithsonian Institute Press, 1996.

Review of *A Japanese Blossom. New York Times,* January 12, 1907.

Reynolds, Guy. *Willa Cather in Context: Progress, Race, Empire.* London: Macmillan, 1996.

Rice, Alice Caldwell Hegan. *Mrs. Wiggs of the Cabbage Patch.* New York: Century, 1901.

Richardson, Dorothy. *The Long Day: The Story of a New York Working Girl as Told by Herself.* New York: Century, 1905.

Ricou, Laurence. *Vertical Man, Horizontal World: Man and Landscape in Canadian Prairie Fiction.* Vancouver: University of British Columbia Press, 1973.

Robeson, Susan L., ed. *Women, America, and Movement: Narratives of Relocation*. Columbia: University of Missouri Press, 1998.

Rogin, Michael. *Blackface, White Noise: Jewish Immigrants in the Melting Pot*. Berkeley: University of California Press, 1993.

Rølvaag, Ole. *Giants in the Earth*. New York: Harper and Bros., 1927.

Romero, Mary. *Maid in the USA*. New York: Routledge, 1992.

Rosenstone, Robert. *A Mirror in the Shrine: American Encounters with Meiji Japan*. Cambridge: Harvard University Press, 1988.

Rosten, Leo C. *Hollywood: The Movie Colony, the Movie Makers*. New York: Harcourt Brace, 1941.

Royse, N. K. *Study of Genius*. Chicago, New York: Rand, McNally, 1890.

Rubio-Goldsmith, Raquel. "Civilization, Barbarism, and Norteñas Gardens." In *Making Worlds: Gender, Metaphor, Materiality*, edited by Susan Hardy Aiken et al., 274–287. Tucson: University of Arizona Press, 1998.

Said, Edward. *Orientalism*. New York: Pantheon, 1978.

Saldívar, José David. *Border Matters: Remapping American Cultural Studies*. Berkeley: University of California Press, 1997.

————. *The Dialectics of Our America: Genealogy, Cultural Critique, and Literary History*. Durham: Duke University Press, 1991.

Salmon, Lucy. *Domestic Service*. 2d ed. New York: Macmillan, 1901.

Salverson, Laura Goodman. *When Sparrows Fall*. Toronto: Thomas Allen, 1925.

San Francisco. Directed by W. S. Van Dyke. Performances by Jeannette MacDonald and Clark Gable. MGM, 1936.

Schatz, Thomas. *The Genius of the System: Hollywood Filmmaking in the Studio Era*. New York: Pantheon, 1988.

Schultheiss, John. "A Study of the 'Eastern' Writer in Hollywood in the 1930s." Ph.D. diss., University of Southern California, 1973.

Scott, Derek B. "Orientalism and Musical Style." *Critical Musicology Journal* (1997). www.leeds.ac.uk/music/Info/CMJ/Articles/ 1997/02/01.htm (consulted February 2001).

Seaton, Beverly. "Gardening Books for the Commuter's Wife, 1900–1937." *Landscape* 28:2 (1985): 41–47.

————. "'Making the Best of Circumstances': The American Woman's Back Yard Garden." In *Making the American Home: Middle-Class Women and Domestic Material Culture, 1840–1940*, edited by Marilyn Ferris Motz and Pat Browne, 90–94. Bowling Green: Bowling Green State University Popular Press, 1988.

"A Servant Girl's Letter." *Independent*, January 2, 1902, 36.

Sessing, Trevor. "How They Kept Canada Almost Lily White." *Saturday Night* 85:9 (1970): 30–32.

Shanghai Express. Directed by Josef von Sternberg. Screenplay by Jules

Furthman. Performances by Marlene Dietrich, Anna May Wong, and Warner Oland. Paramount, 1932.

Shapiro, Laura. *Perfection Salad: Women and Cooking at the Turn of the Century.* New York: Farrar, Straus, and Giroux, 1986.

Shaw, Stephanie. *What a Woman Ought to Be and to Do: Black Professional Women Workers in the Jim Crow Era.* Chicago: University of Chicago Press, 1996.

She Done Him Wrong. Directed by Lowell Sherman. Performances by Mae West and Cary Grant. Paramount, 1933.

Shohat, Ella. "Gender and Culture of Empire: Toward a Feminist Ethnography of the Cinema." In *Visions of the East: Orientalism in Film,* edited by Matthew Bernstein and Gaylyn Studlar, 19–66. New Brunswick, N.J.: Rutgers University Press, 1997.

Sies, Mary Corbin. "The Domestic Mission of the Privileged American Suburban Homemaker, 1877–1917: A Reassessment." In *Making the American Home: Middle-Class Women and Domestic Material Culture, 1840–1940,* edited by Marilyn Ferris Motz and Pat Browne, 193–210. Bowling Green: Bowling Green University Popular Press, 1988.

Sifton, Clifford. "The Immigrants Canada Wants." *MacLean's Magazine* 35:7 (1922): 16.

Singin' in the Rain. Directed by Stanley Donen and Gene Kelly. Performances by Gene Kelly, Debbie Reynolds, and Donald O'Connor. MGM, 1952.

Sklar, Robert. *Movie-Made America: A Cultural History of the Movies.* 2d ed. New York: Vintage, 1994.

Sloan, Kay. *The Loud Silents: Origins of the Social Problem Film.* Urbana: University of Illinois Press, 1988.

Smith, Henry Nash. *Virgin Land: The American West as Symbol and Myth.* Cambridge: Harvard University Press, 1950.

Smith, Sidonie. *A Poetics of Women's Autobiography: Marginality and the Fictions of Self-Representation.* Bloomington: University of Indiana Press, 1987.

Smith-Rosenberg, Carroll. *Disorderly Conduct: Visions of Gender in Victorian America.* New York: Knopf, 1985.

Sollors, Werner. *Beyond Ethnicity: Consent and Descent in American Culture.* New York: Oxford University Press, 1986.

———. *Neither Black nor White yet Both: Thematic Explorations of Interracial Literature.* New York: Oxford University Press, 1997.

Spivak, Gayatri Chakravorty. "Can the Subaltern Speak?" In *The Post-Colonial Studies Reader,* edited by Bill Ashcroft et al., 24–28. London: Routledge, 1995.

———. *In Other Worlds: Essays in Cultural Politics.* New York: Methuen, 1987.

————. *The Postcolonial Critic: Interviews, Strategies, Dialogues.* New York: Routledge, 1990.

Spofford, Harriet Prescott. *The Servant Girl Question.* Boston: Houghton Mifflin, 1881.

Staiger, Janet. "'Tame' Authors and the Corporate Laboratory: Stories, Writers, and Scenarios in Hollywood." *Quarterly Review of Film Studies* (fall 1983): 33–43.

Stead. Robert. *The Cowpuncher.* Toronto: Musson, 1918.

————. *Grain.* Toronto: McClelland and Stewart, 1925.

————. *The Homesteaders.* 1916. Reprint, Toronto: University of Toronto Press, 1973.

Stedman, Edmund Clarence. "Genius." 1886. Reprinted in *Genius and Other Essays.* Port Washington, N.Y.: Kennikat Press, 1966.

Stempel, Tom. *Framework: A History of Screenwriting in the American Film.* New York: Continuum, 1991.

"The Story of an Irish Cook." *Independent,* March 30, 1905, 715–717.

Strasser, Susan. *Never Done: A History of American Housework.* New York: Pantheon, 1982.

Stringer, Arthur. *Prairie Stories. (The Prairie Wife, The Prairie Mother, The Prairie Child)* New York: A. L. Burt, 1922.

"Successful Scenario Writers." *Moving Picture Stories* 6:151 (1915): 28+.

Sundquist, Eric. *To Wake the Nations: Race in the Making of American Literature.* Cambridge: Harvard University Press, Belknap Press, 1993.

Sutherland, Daniel E. *Americans and Their Servants: Domestic Service in the United States from 1880 to 1920.* Baton Rouge: Louisiana State University Press, 1981.

Takaki, Ronald. *Iron Cages: Race and Culture in Nineteenth-Century America.* New York: Knopf, 1979.

————. *Strangers from a Different Shore: A History of Asian Americans.* Boston: Little, Brown, 1989.

Tarbell, Ida. *On the Business of Being a Woman.* New York: Macmillan, 1912.

Taylor, E. "William James on Exceptional Mental States: The 1896 Lowell Lectures." In *Genius and Eminence.* 2d ed., edited by Robert S. Albert. New York: Pergamon, 1992.

Tompkins, Jane. *Sensational Designs: The Cultural Work of American Fiction, 1790–1860.* New York: Oxford University Press, 1985.

Trinh, T. Minh-Ha. *Woman, Native, Other: Writing Postcoloniality and Feminism.* Bloomington: Indiana University Press, 1989.

Urgo, Joseph R. *Willa Cather and the Myth of American Migration.* Urbana: University of Illinois Press, 1995.

Van Vorst, Mrs. John [Marie]. *The Woman Who Toils.* New York: Doubleday, 1903.

Vasey, Ruth. *The World according to Hollywood, 1918–1939.* Madison: University of Wisconsin Press, 1997.

Veblen, Thorstein. *The Theory of the Leisure Class.* 1899. Reprint, New York: Dover, 1994.

Wald, Patricia. *Constituting Americans: Cultural Anxiety and Narrative Form.* Raleigh: Duke University Press, 1995.

Weatherford, Doris. *Foreign and Female: Immigrant Women in America, 1840–1930.* New York: Schocken Books, 1986.

Weber, Ronald. *The Midwestern Ascendancy in American Writing.* Bloomington: Indiana University Press, 1992.

Webster, Jean. *Daddy-Long-Legs.* New York: Century, 1912.

Weisberg, Gabriel P. "Japonisme: The Commercialization of an Opportunity." In *Japonisme Comes to America: The Japanese Impact on American Graphic Arts, 1876–1925,* edited by Julia Meech and Gabriel P. Weisberg, 15–40. New York: Harry Abrams, 1990.

Wharton, Edith. *The House of Mirth.* 1905. Reprint, New York: Norton, 1990.

———. *The Touchstone.* New York: C. Scribner's Sons, 1914.

Wiebe, Robert H. *The Search for Order, 1877–1920.* New York: Hill and Wang, 1967.

Wiggin, Kate Douglas. *Rebecca of Sunnybrook Farm.* Boston: Houghton Mifflin, 1903.

Wilkinson, Endymion. *Japan versus the West: Image and Reality.* London: Penguin, 1990.

Wilson, Edmund. "The Boys in the Back Room." In *Classics and Commercials,* 19–56. New York: Farrar, Straus, and Co., 1950.

Wong, Sau-ling Cynthia. "Autobiography as Chinatown Tour? Maxine Hong Kingston's *The Woman Warrior* and the Chinese American Autobiographical Controversy." In *Maxine Hong Kingston's "The Woman Warrior": A Casebook,* edited by Sau-ling Cynthia Wong, 29–53. New York: Oxford University Press, 1999.

———. *Reading Asian American Literature: From Necessity to Extravagance.* Princeton: Princeton University Press, 1993.

Wright, Mabel Osgood. *The Garden of a Commuter's Wife.* New York: Grosset and Dunlap, 1901.

Wu, Jean Yu-wen Shen, and Min Song, eds. *Asian American Studies: A Reader.* New Brunswick, N.J.: Rutgers University Press, 2000.

Wu, William F. *The Yellow Peril: Chinese Americans in American Fiction, 1850–1940.* Hamden, Conn.: Archon Books, 1982.

Yezierska, Anzia. *The Bread Givers.* 1925. Reprint, New York: Persea Books, 1999.

————. *Children of Loneliness: Stories of Immigrant Life in America.* New York: Funk and Wagnalls, 1923.

————. *Hungry Hearts and Other Stories.* New York: Persea Books, 1985.

Filmography

The sheer volume of film writing and correspondence about Eaton's film writing career in the Winnifred Eaton Reeve (WER) Fonds at the University of Calgary helped ascertain Eaton's role in various films, yet made determining the exact dimensions of that role hopelessly complicated. I checked items held in the WER Fonds against the *American Film Institute Catalog*, the Internet Movie Database (www.imdb.com), the catalog files at the Academy of Motion Picture Arts and Sciences, and other archival collections. Included here is information about all of Eaton's credited projects as well as those uncredited projects in which Eaton played a significant role. I hope that this appendix may inspire future research on Eaton's involvement in the film industry and on the participation of women in film writing during the silent and early sound eras.

EATON'S CREDITED WORKS

1921   *False Kisses* (Universal). Adaptation. Released November. Directed by Paul Scardon. Scenario by Wallace Clifton. Based on the story "Ropes," by Wilbur Daniel Steele (*Harper's Magazine* 142 [January 1921]: 193–208). Melodrama centered around a blind lighthouse keeper, his wife, and his friend; the main theme is jealousy. (See *Undertow* for a later version.)

1929   *The Mississippi Gambler* (Universal). Dialogue, with H. H. Van Loan. Released October, sound and silent. Directed by Reginald Barker. Scenario by Edward T. Lowe Jr. Titles by Dudley Early. Story by Karl Brown and Leonard Fields. Romantic drama in which a gambler swindles a rich old gentleman of his entire fortune; the gentleman's daughter plays the gambler cards for it, is allowed to win, and falls in love with him.

1929   *Shanghai Lady* (Universal). Scenario/dialogue, with Houston Branch. Released November, sound and silent. Directed by John S. Robertson. Based on the play *Drifting*, by John Colton and Daisy H. Andrews (the play opened in New York on December 21, 1910). In this Mary Nolan vehicle, the actress plays a disreputable woman in Shanghai who poses as a respectable lady to win over a white man, who is an escaped convict posing as a respectable man to avoid capture.

1930   *Undertow* (Universal). Adaptation/dialogue, with Edward T. Lowe Jr. Released February, sound and silent. Directed by Harry Pollard (who also directed *Uncle Tom's Cabin*). Based on the short story "Ropes," by Wilbur Daniel Steele (see *False Kisses*). Similar to *False Kisses* but "cleaner."

1930   *Young Desire* (Universal). Adaptation/dialogue, with Matt Taylor. Sound and silent. Based on William Doyle's play *Carnival* (which opened in New York on April 24, 1924). Another Mary Nolan picture; she plays a carnival sideshow dancer who leaves to "become respectable"; meets a nice kid who wants to marry her, but she doesn't want to ruin his life with her past. Finally commits suicide to save his reputation.

1930   *East Is West* (Universal). Listed under Winnifred Eaton. Adaptation, with Tom Reed. Lupe Velez plays Ming Toy, a young woman sold into slavery in China who eventually comes to the U.S. She falls in love with a well-to-do young man, is fought for by Chinatown chop suey magnate Charlie Yong (Edward G. Robinson), and is revealed to be half Spanish—and thus "white" and an appropriate mate for the young hero.

Eaton's Uncredited Works

n.d.   *The Heart Breaker.* A six-part, two-reel series written with Donn Cobb. Script in the WER Fonds 15.137.

1925   *The Phantom of the Opera* (Universal; also 1930 sound version). Correspondence in the WER Fonds contains numerous references to Eaton's involvement in writing the dialogue continuity.

1926   *The Love Thief* (Universal). Credited to John McDermott, for whom Eaton later might have been a ghostwriter (this may also have been one of the ghostwriting project she did for him). Eaton's significant participation in this project is alluded to in a January 1926 letter in the WER Fonds 1.6.19.

1929   *Show Boat* (Universal). Eaton wrote an early continuity or synopsis for this in 1926 (with Eleanor Fried); letters in the business files in the WER Fonds indicate that she was removed from this project and thus did not get credited.

1929   *Prince of Hearts* (Imperial). Story credited to John Reinhardt, who also played a role in the movie. This silent film starred Norman Kerry, who also starred in the 1926 film *The Love Thief* (see above). The information in the *AFI Catalog* is sketchy: "No information about the precise nature of this film has been found." The script in the WER Fonds (10.95), written for Universal, has both titles (*The Love Thief* and *Prince of Hearts*), and Eaton tried to get *Prince of Hearts* rejected by Universal so that she could submit it elsewhere (WER Fonds 1.6.19). It is possible that this script or one based on it became the basis for the Imperial film.

1930   *What Men Want* (Universal). A full continuity exists in the WER Fonds (8.74) as does a letter in which Eaton expresses her distaste for the project (1.6.58). Adaptation and dialogue credited to John B. Clymer and Dorothy Yost. Scenario credited to Warner Fabian. A society drama.

1931   *East of Borneo* (Universal). Story by Dale Van Every. Script by Edwin Knopf. According to the *AFI Catalog,* the film was also known under two other names, *Ourang* and *White Captive.* A continuity for *Ourang* is in the WER Fonds, by Eaton and Isadore Bernstein, based on a story by Fred de Gresac (5.41).

1935   *Barbary Coast* (MGM). Directed by Howard Hawks. Screenplay by Ben Hecht and Charles MacArthur. Eaton and Charles Logue wrote a treatment for this that was the basis of the 1935 production, but their story was radically altered through the course of many revisions (and at least fifteen other writers). (*Barbary Coast* was also reissued, according to the *AFI Catalog,* as *The Port of Wickedness* in 1960.)

Index

About the Author

JEAN Lee Cole is an assistant professor in the Department of English at Loyola College in Maryland. She is the coeditor, with Maureen Honey, of *"Madame Butterfly" by John Luther Long and "A Japanese Nightingale" by Winnifred Eaton: Two Orientalist Texts* (Rutgers University Press, 2002).